Comrades and Vexations

Born and educated in Scotland, Marshall Walker lectured in English and American literature at Glasgow University from 1965 to 1980 after a spell at Rhodes University in South Africa.

From 1981 until 2006 he was Professor of English at the University of Waikato in Hamilton, New Zealand. As Dean of Humanities he initiated and oversaw the establishment of the University's Conservatory of Music.

An occasional broadcaster on music and literature, he introduced, for Radio New Zealand and the Australian Broadcasting Corporation, concerts of the 2005 Sydney Sibelius Festival in which Sibelius's symphonies were performed by the Sydney Symphony Orchestra conducted by Vladimir Ashkenazy.

His books include *Robert Penn Warren: A Vision Earned*, *The Literature of the United States of America*, *Scottish Literature Since 1707* and *Dear Sibelius: Letter from a Junky*. He lives in Hamilton, New Zealand, with his wife, the Brazilian writer, Cláudia Pacce.

By Marshall Walker

Robert Penn Warren: A Vision Earned

The Literature of the United States of America

La letteratura degli Stati Uniti
(with Federico Siniscalco)

Scottish Literature Since 1707

Dear Sibelius: Letter from a Junky

Music for Life: Conversations
(with Tim Dodd)

Comrades
and
Vexations

Some Objects in a Life

Marshall Walker

To Frances
with thanks for the memory
& all good wishes —

Marshall
12/04/13

Kennedy & Boyd

Kennedy & Boyd
an imprint of
Zeticula Ltd
The Roan
Kilkerran
KA19 8LS
Scotland

http://www.kennedyandboyd.co.uk
admin@kennedyandboyd.co.uk

First published in 2013
Text Copyright © Marshall Walker 2013
Cover photograph of Lalomanu, Upolu, Samoa
© Marshall Walker 2013
Cover photograph of Marshall Walker © Cláudia Pacetta-Walker
2013

Photographs © Marshall Walker, except as listed, or in the public
domain.

ISBN 978-1-84921-121-5

For

Anna, Bridget, Elsie,
Jeanne, Maitland, Maria

with love and thanks for the good times

Think you, 'mid all this mighty sum
Of things forever speaking,
That nothing of itself will come,
But we must still be seeking?

William Wordsworth, 'Expostulation and Reply'

We two kept house, the Past and I.

Thomas Hardy, 'The Ghost of the Past'

Acknowledgements

I owe much to many but wish especially to thank Tim Dodd, David Fine, David Foreman, Martin Lodge, Sheila Park, Jan Pilditch, Hugh C. Rae, Alan Riach, Peter and Coral Shaw, Guyon and Sonia Wells, and Michael and Colleen Lascelles. They are all well aware of my indebtedness to them; I hope they may be equally aware of the depth of my gratitude. As always, I owe most to my beloved wife and comrade, Cláudia Pacetta-Walker.

'Wordsworth in Memphis' first appeared in *London Magazine*, Volume 14, Number 6; the second part of 'Edwin Morgan: First Poet' is adapted from 'Edwin Morgan: Futurist' in *London Magazine*, Volume 35, Numbers 7 & 8 and from Chapter 11 of my *Scottish Literature Since 1707* where quotations are by permission of Carcanet Press Ltd., Manchester and Mariscat Press, Edinburgh; a different version of 'Pop Goes the Culture' appeared in *London Magazine*, Volume 34, Numbers 5 & 6; 'New York: Port Authority' first appeared in *Landfall 170*; a modified version of 'A Bit More' was published in *The Flight of the Turtle: New Writing Scotland 29*; a different version of 'The Kailyard and the Kraal' appeared in *The Drouth* for Spring 2005.

MW, Hamilton, New Zealand, September 2012

Contents

Illustrations

Preface

It's a miscellany, a smörgåsbord, even a gallimaufrey. Life in terms of objects. The object can be a person, a book, an island, a letter, a problem or a writer. Some objects are friendly, companionable like the waste-paper basket in 'Lorry Driver', the boy next door in 'ARP', Edwin Morgan, an aunt, Mr Jeremy Fisher, the isle of Lismore and the diary of an eleven-year-old girl who sailed on a clipper ship from London to Brisbane in 1895. Some are vexing in the sense that they have perplexed, occupied mental space one way or another, for a long time, like God, the American South, Captain Ahab, cancer, popular culture and Scottish devolution. So my objects divide into comrades and vexations. You help yourself to a smörgåsbord; I hope this assortment goes beyond mere self-indulgence and that you will be pleased to help yourself to some of the objects on the table.

1. Lorry Driver

The first object is a waste-paper basket. It belonged to the house with the rest of the furnishings. It was in almost all respects an archetypal waste-paper basket made of creaky, woven raffia, its one dubious distinction being its colour. Someone must have thought purple would be a selling point, but it really just made the basket look gloomy. Someone must have carried it proudly home, perhaps from a stall at the week-end market, thinking purple exotic or likely to 'tone in' with a carpet or soft furnishings though there was nothing within hailing distance of purple in the house in our time. We even called it 'the gloomy waste-paper basket' to distinguish it from the ordinary straw-coloured baskets in other rooms. It lived under the wash-hand basin in the upstairs bathroom, so it tended to attract spent toothpaste tubes, empty medicine bottles and used cotton wool rather than mere paper.

The house itself in Whitecraigs on the South Side of Glasgow was quite cheerful except for the dining room which faced darkly north, making it as gloomy as the purple waste-paper basket; but that's where the gramophone lived so it could be a place of magic. The street was Woodvale Avenue, a misnomer as with so many streets, since there was nothing woodsy about it and no hint of a vale. Dead flat, it was, with broad, smooth pavements, ideal for racing pedal cars. I raced Peter, the boy next door. The contest was unequal because he had an enviably sleek, low-slung speedster made of plywood painted an intimidating shade of black and I had a garish red and green lorry, with a payload of sturdy wooden boxes, which was more solidly built but couldn't match Peter's turns of speed. Under our auspices the elderly were an endangered species. My lorry was better at terrorising pedestrians, partly because it was less manoeuvrable than his car, so if I was in line to crash into people it was their responsibility to get out of my way, whereas Peter could nip round one pedestrian, accelerate, dodge another and another and keep zooming down the street leaving dumbstruck gentry in his slipstream. My lorry and I were not so nimble. When he caught me setting off along a busy pavement, scattering perjink, squeaking ladies under implausible hats and indignant gentlemen out for their constitutionals, my father would run after me, blurting apologies: 'Sorry, madam, so sorry, he's just learning. Sorry, sir, I beg your pardon, it's a new toy'. I felt it demeaning to have my brave lorry relegated to the status of plaything and conceived my earliest ambition to become a real lorry driver, king of the highways by volume if not by velocity. I'd stop at transport cafés for gigantic fried breakfasts of eggs, bacon and square slices of spicy sausage. After a pedal car episode it was my father's custom to clip my fingernails. I suppose this was a sort of punishment. He favoured short back and sides for hair and close to the quick for nails. That was masculine. He'd clip a nail and hold up the finger for me to see what a real boy's nails should look like.

The second object is an air-raid siren. It was wartime and when we moved to the house on the South Side in 1940 we had 'evacuated'. We'd left a rented top-floor tenement flat at Anniesland, on the margin of West Glasgow, overlooking a tram terminus with a view of the Old Kilpatrick Hills, because it was on the Luftwaffe's flight path to the River Clyde where there were shipyards to be bombed. A fairly slight error in navigation could drop a bomb on Anniesland so we were safer on the South Side, but the new address seemed to bring the war closer. A Nazi bogey man fell from the sky. After the failure of attempted negotiations via Sweden, Hitler's 'Deputy to the Führer', Rudolf Hess, made his crackpot solo flight from Germany to Scotland in May 1941. His plan was to meet the Duke of Hamilton, who would help him to negotiate a peace treaty between the Third Reich and Britain. First detected north of Newcastle-upon-Tyne, he made for Lindisfarne, then headed inland, flying his Messerschmitt Bf110 below radar sweeps over Kilmarnock and the Fenwick Moor, short distances from Whitecraigs along the road to Ayr where my father and his partner had a branch of their office of Chartered Accountants. Close to the nearby village of Eaglesham Hess parachuted from his plane and was arrested by a farmhand allegedly wielding a pitchfork. From there he was escorted to the Home Guard HQ in Giffnock, where we often went shopping. The War was following us around. News came that my father's partner had been killed at Dunkirk.

On the way home from shopping, my mother stopped and looked up at the sky. I saw nothing, but heard the plane's engines.

'You see that dot in the sky?' said my mother.

'Yes', I said because I knew I was expected to.

'That's a German reconnaissance plane', my mother said.

'What's reconnaissance?'

'Looking around'.

'Can it see us?'

'We'd better take the shopping inside'.

'Do you think it could be another bogey man, like the one in the news on the wireless?'

'I shouldn't think so. Look where you're going'.

The drone of the German plane's engines was scary, but the warning wail of the air-raid siren was the most frightening sound in the world. Especially after dark. The end was coming; we might be going to die tonight. Families would take refuge in their basements if they were big enough. Some residents in our street had erected corrugated-iron Anderson air-raid shelters in their back gardens. The shelters were £5 each from the government if you earned less than £250 a year and £7 if you earned more. Partially buried, most of the shelters were covered with soil and some people planted flowers, even vegetables, on top and in the banked-up earth along the sides. We had only a small basement area where gardening implements were kept, and no shelter of our own. There was no public shelter that I can remember in the vicinity. Our only protection was the South Side location. There were no targets in the area of obvious interest to the Germans but there was always the indiscriminate malevolence of an enemy intent on bringing Britain to its knees. It helped when my psychologically astute mother said, 'Oh, listen, there's our friend again, Softy the Siren'. When the doleful noise sent me burrowing under the bedclothes I'd say out loud, 'There goes old Softy'. But who was I kidding? I was dealing with twin terrors, War and the darkness I was sealed into when my grown-ups said good-night, shut my bedroom door and deserted me for an evening in the sitting room downstairs. Softy wailed, the darkness deepened and I lay folded stiffly into myself, fettered by leaden time and inimical space, the embodiment of abject funk.

Why didn't I get up, and open the door, leaving it comfortingly ajar till morning, with a slant of light enough to cheer me from the skylight in the upstairs hall? The trouble was the window in my room. My parents were fresh-air fiends and insisted I sleep, summer and winter, with an open window. A breeze could close the door noisily, bringing a parent upstairs to find me guilty and shut the door with scolding admonitions. Then inspiration came: the gloomy waste-paper basket. I padded to the bathroom and saw that the basket was serviceably loaded with rubbish weighty enough to keep it stable. It made a perfect wedge to keep my door open and I'd be awake early enough to return it to its place under the wash-hand basin before the rest of the household were up. There was a good chance my wickedness would pass unnoticed by grown-ups because they didn't pass my door on their way to bed and because the basket's gloomy purple made it almost invisible in the dark. Of course someone might notice the basket wasn't in its usual place at night, but this was a risk worth taking. I had triumphed over the master race that was trying to annihilate us; I had beaten the darkness and neutralised the War. I could sleep and dream of steering my mighty lorry along the highway, superior to all roadsters. I'd wave happily to pedestrians, especially the elderly taking their constitutionals, and they'd wave approvingly back at this king of the road. Let's hear it for the gloomy waste-paper basket.

I got away with it for ten nights. Then a bronchial ailment put me to bed. My fevered brow was soothed, medicine administered. I was bidden good-night and my door firmly closed, leaving the world to darkness, to Softy, and the War.

2. ARP

The next object is a tin helmet. The War determined what kind of fun a boy could have. Rich kids with indulgent parents and significant pocket money collected perfect 'Dinky Toy' miniatures of tanks, armoured cars, anti-aircraft guns, planes, destroyers and aircraft carriers. Lilliputian wars accompanied by blood-curdling yells and imitations of explosions were waged in playrooms, lounges or in the street on warm days. Trade wars, too, went on as boys, practising to be business tycoons, swapped, bought and sold their toys. The less affluent made do with what could be produced from tin cans and sticks. A popular creation was a field telephone consisting of two empty Heinz Beans cans joined by a taut string along which messages were shouted from one tin can to the other.

A more elaborate bit of play-acting, which required the participation of grown-ups, was to become an Air Raid Precaution Warden. The Wardens handed out gas masks and supervised public air-raid shelters. Knowing the residents of their designated area enabled them to find and reunite family members who might become separated in the rush to reach the safety of a shelter. There were 1.4 million ARP Wardens, including Peter from next door and me.

Peter and MW as ARP Wardens, September 1941

We reasoned that someone had to be alert to the possibility of dirty German tricks during the day, maybe daytime bombing, or spying, not only at night. After all it was on a sunny afternoon that my mother had spotted a German reconnaissance plane. Our patrols were therefore conducted in daylight. We harassed pedestrians with grave interrogations and stern demands for proof of identity, hoping they wouldn't recognise us as pedal-car terrorists; and we required our fathers, returning from work, to show us their identity papers before being cleared for entry to their homes with permission to sit down to an evening meal.

Wartime fun was serious business.

3. Nipper and the god in the gramophone

In 1921 London-born Francis Barraud told his story about 'His Master's Voice', the painting that made him famous: 'The said painting was originally designed and painted by me some time prior to the year 1899 but in its original form the dog was listening to a phonograph which is a cylinder machine'. He couldn't explain how the idea came to him, he said, 'beyond the fact that it suddenly occurred to me that to have my little dog listening to the Phonograph with an intelligent and rather puzzled expression, and call it "His Master's Voice" would make an excellent subject. We had a phonograph and I often noticed how puzzled he was to make out where the voice came from. It was certainly the happiest thought I ever had'. After completing the painting Barraud showed it to several publishers as he thought there could be a demand for it as a reproduction. No luck. He turned down one publisher's offer of £5; another publisher objected that nobody would know what the dog was doing.

Dissatisfied with the trumpet in the phonograph painting — 'It was black and ugly'— Barraud visited the Gramophone Company to ask them for the loan of a brass horn to paint from. When the manager saw his photograph of the painting he asked if the work

Nipper (after Francis Barraud)

was for sale and if Barraud could replace the picture of the phonograph with a Gramophone made by the Company. Barraud replied that the painting was for sale and agreed to make the alteration if the Company would let him have an instrument to paint from. In September 1899 he accepted the Company's offer of £100, the purchase conditional on his painting out the phonograph and replacing it with the then current model of the Gramophone. A model was sent to his studio in Piccadilly and one of the world's most successful trademarks was born. Nipper made his first appearance in the Gramophone Company's advertising literature in 1900. Nine years later he appeared for the first time on the Company's Black Label records. In 1941 he was waiting for me in the dining room of the house on the South Side, my favourite dog for ever.

Like the gloomy purple waste-paper basket in the upstairs bathroom and all the principal furniture, the gramophone that sat on the dining room carpet belonged to the house. The three ten-inch records I found beside it must have been imported by my parents or my enterprising Aunt Jessie, though she usually preferred piano records by Frederic Lamond and Artur Schnabel which only she was allowed to play. These three discs initiated my musical consciousness eclectically. Nipper presided over Tchaikovsky's Overture to the *Nutcracker Suite* and two numbers from Grieg's *Peer Gynt*, 'Morning' and 'The Death of Åse', which gave me a digest of the cycle of life from the promise of a new day to lights out, birth to death in a masterpiece of compression. The third record was Paul Robeson singing 'Ol' Man River, top of my pops until someone carelessly left it on a chair. My myopia was then so acute that the chair was a blur, the record disappeared into its upholstery, and the next thing I knew when I sat down was the horror of shellac fragments. It took my grown-ups some time to persuade me that I hadn't killed God.

Bit by bit I learned about the godlike *basso profundo* who made the gramophone so alive: his university career as athlete and scholar, his law degree at Columbia University, his successes in plays by Eugene O'Neil, his performance of 'Ol' Man River' in Jerome Kern and Oscar Hammerstein's *Show Boat* and his legendary interpretation of the noble Moor in Shakespeare's *Othello*. Then speaking out against Fascism and racism and, on account of his undisguised admiration for the principles of Communism, his investigation by the House Committee on Un-American Activities and persecution by the American establishment. Excellent credentials for a god, I thought, being too young to appreciate how wrong he was about Stalin. More Paul Robeson records appeared in the dining room, so in the *persona* of the Southern Afro-American of an era now thankfully gone with the wind, I heard him sing 'My Lindy Lou', an unsurpassable love song:

> Lindy, did you hear that mockingbird sing last night?
> Honey, he was singing so sweet in the moonlight.
> Up in that old magnolia tree, bursting his heart with melody,
> Honey, that's the way I love you,
> My Lindy Lou, Lindy Lou,
> I'd lay right down and die, and die,
> If I could sing as sweet as that to you,
> My little Lindy Lou.

And there was 'My Curly-headed baby', the lullaby my mother loved to croon when she thought nobody was listening. Perhaps she sang it to me when I was too wee to remember. Once, just once, she did sing it to me when I was about half-past four. Now, looking back, I suspect it was only once because she felt she might burst with love and embarrass her son. Emotional display wasn't seemly in those days, certainly not in our family. I was speechless when she ended the song in a whisper, but the tears that overcame me when I was out of her earshot were the happiest of my life:

> Oh, my baby, my curly-headed baby,
> We'll sit below the sky and sing a song
> To the moo-oo-oo oo-oon.
> Oh, my baby, my little darkie baby,
> Your daddy's in the cotton field,
> Workin' for the foo-oo-oo oo-ood.
>
> So, la-la la-la la-la lullaby-by,
> Does you want the moon to play with?
> All the stars to run away with?
> They'll come if you don't cry.

So, la-la la-la la-la lullaby-by,
In the mammy's arms be creepin',
An' soon you'll be a-sleepin',
La-la la-la la-la la-la lullaby.

Oh, my baby, my curly-headed baby,
I'll dance you fast asleep and love you so
As I si-ii-ii ii-ing.
Oh, my baby, my little darkie baby,
Jus' tuck your head like little bird
Below its mammy's wi-ii-ii ii-ing.

Then a final repeat of the chorus: 'So, la-la la-la la-la lullaby-by', etc.
But it was the song of the slave in 'Ol' Man River' that prepared my heart and mind for identification with the anti-apartheid struggle in South Africa and the Civil Rights Movement in the USA:

You and me, we sweat and strain,
Body all achin' and racked with pain.
'Tote that barge!' 'Lift that bale!'
You get a little drunk and you land in jail.

I get weary and sick of tryin',
I'm tired of livin' and scared of dyin',
But ol' man river, he just keeps rollin' along.

Martin Luther King and Nelson Mandela had landed in jail more than once. Mandela was still there, on Robben Island. Their bodies must have ached often under the stress imposed on them, but, no matter how weary and scared of dying, they kept going, King right on to the great March on Washington in 1963 and delivery of the 'I have a dream' speech which electrified a quarter of a million people of all ethnicities. Warned that his life would be in danger if he spoke in Memphis, Tennessee, he said, 'I have been to the mountain top...Like anybody I would like to live a long life...But I'm not concerned about that now...I just want to do God's will. And he's allowed me to go up to the mountain. And I've looked over. And I've seen the promised land. I may not get there with you. But I want you to know tonight that we, as a people, will get to the promised land'. The next day he was assassinated, shot on 4th April 1968 at the Lorraine Motel, no doubt to applause from J. Edgar Hoover.

With the capacity for response instilled by Paul Robeson and 'Ol' Man River' via the gramophone in the South Side dining room, I went to Memphis in 1970. A visiting professorship for a year at Memphis State University was an opportunity to see the American South for myself and learn what I could about the region first-hand, an ambition for which Joel Chandler Harris's Uncle Remus and William Faulkner must take partial responsibility. Memphis city and the State of Tennessee were still distressed by racial complexities and Faulkner's Mississippi had a way to go before emerging from the dark ages. It was a tough year and my Scottish liberalism was put to a test beyond both complacency and expectation. Twenty miles from Nashville a roadside placard said, 'Welcome to Klan country'.

4. Wordsworth in Memphis

A Campus Incident in five parts

> She dwelt among the untrodden ways
> Beside the springs of Dove,
> A maid whom there were none to praise
> And very few to love:
>
> A violet by a mossy stone
> Half hidden from the eye!
> — Fair as a star, when only one
> Is shining in the sky.
>
> She lived unknown, and few could know
> When Lucy ceased to be;
> But she is in her grave, and, oh,
> The difference to me!

William Wordsworth

I

THE CLASSROOM, ENGLISH 2102, SECTION 220
Monday, 27 July, 1970: 7.30 p.m.

Professor: The ways are 'untrodden', there are 'none' to praise, 'few' to love. Wordsworth tells us that Lucy lived 'unknown' and adds that 'few could know' when she 'ceased to be'...So here's a poem in which a powerful emotional effect is achieved partly through an extremely imprecise use of language...Is there any further comment?

Mrs Moore: Well, I guess the poem tells about a pretty girl who just meant a whole lot to Wordsworth even if she was kind of ordinary.

Professor: I think we'd all agree to that...Following what we've been saying, this is hardly a revolutionary interpretation.

Mrs Moore: Not *revolutionary*?

Professor: Yes. Not revolutionary in the sense that what you're saying is not strikingly different from what we've all agreed on. You're not altering the present state of the poem by a radically new view of it.

Mrs Moore: O.K.

II

FIRST DEPOSITION: THE POLICEWOMAN
(All Depositions to Mr Jerry Frye, Assistant Director of Security, Memphis State University)

Dear Sir,

Thursday, July 30, 1970 a young male colored entered the classroom with a student and sat down in the back row. He stated he was going to bust this class and show this teacher a thing or two. He opened a brief case and said he was going to play chess and cards in class. The student, Mrs Edie Moore, asked him to not sit beside her because she needed to pass the course and she didn't want Mr Walker to think she was involved.

He stated that 'shit on him, he would give him an A in this course if he knew what was good for him'.

He then moved to the far right of the room, and then to the desk in front of the class. He opened the drawer and took out a map. He sat in the teacher's chair and spread the map on the desk. He then took a poster off the bulletin board and put it on a seat in the front row. He tried to borrow a textbook but the class tried to ignore him.

I went to Mr Walker's office and told him about this young man and what his plans were for the class.

I went back to the classroom and the young man was gone but his briefcase was in his chair.

After class started and Mr Walker was giving his lecture on Wordsworth, this young man entered the class without knocking, nor did he excuse himself. Mr Walker asked him if he was enrolled in this class and asked him his name. He asked Mr Walker for a pen and he said he would write it for him. Mr Walker said that was all right but he would write it himself. This young man asked where the assignment was and Mr Walker told him and explained what author we were studying.

The man wanted to ask a question before Mr Walker could start the lecture. Mr Walker explained that we had the lecture first and then had a question period afterwards. The young man then asked for a pen or a pencil. Mr Walker stated he did not have one.

The young man raised his hand and made large sighing noises constantly. Mr Walker asked him to please remain quiet so he could deliver the lecture. The young man then took out a deck of cards and asked Mr Walker if he cared to play poker.

Mr Walker declined. These petty annoyances kept up and finally Mr Walker told him that if he didn't stop he would have to leave the class. He ignored Mr Walker and continued his sarcasm. After a long period of time, Mr Walker warned him again.

The young man paid no attention and Mr Walker told him to leave. He stated to Mr Walker, 'Are you telling me or asking me?' Mr Walker said, 'I am telling you'. The young man said, 'You will leave before I do'.

I then left the room and went for the Security Police.

After I returned to class, Mr Walker left the room with the guard to discuss the situation in the corridor outside and this young man started to raise the blinds and use curse words. Several of the men asked him to leave so we could have our class. He said, 'fuck you and the class'. I stood up and told the ladies we should go across the hall to the rest room so we wouldn't have to listen to this talk. He said something smart which I didn't understand. The ladies left the room.

Mr Walker showed more patience than could be expected of a man, and tried to get this young man to behave in the face of every insult he could have received as a man and as a teacher.

This young man came to class and stated he intended to bust the class and made everyone miserable also.

This young man is not interested in an education and apparently doesn't want anyone else to get one. Allowing him to remain on campus could only cause trouble for the University.

Respectfully submitted,
(Signed) Eva Gatlin
409-54-4936

III
SECOND DEPOSITION: THE REALTOR

Dear Mr Frye:

I would like to register a formal complaint against a young male Negro who said he was an MSU student, and said his name was George Boylin.

On July 30, a few minutes before our class was to begin, Boylin entered the room and asked a female student if he could borrow her book. She told him to get his own and quit bothering her. He then said out loud and within easy hearing of most students, 'Oh fuck it' and then proceeded to another part of the classroom. He again sat down and pronounced his intention to 'bust' the class.

He then left. Shortly thereafter Mr Walker arrived and class began on an orderly note, Mr Walker giving a lecture on Wordsworth, and the students taking notes.

Approximately 6.15 in the middle of the lecture, Boylin entered the classroom without knocking and proceeded to flop down in a chair directly in front of Mr Walker.

Mr Walker very graciously asked him his name and if he was a student registered for the course. Boylin then became more insolent, and spelled his name about five times, unintelligibly, making sure that no one could understand him.

Mr Walker endured with the patience of a saint, and asked for the spelling again at which point Boylin replied, 'I'll write it for you since you are so damned stupid'.

Boylin meantime had pulled a paper off the bulletin board and was using it for a fan. He began making disconcerting noises by jangling the metal chain around his neck, breathing hard, dropping items on the floor and shuffling cards.

At this point class was totally disrupted, and the only Negro student, Mrs Edith Moore, was so ashamed she left the room almost crying and did not return.

Mr Walker finally told Boylin that he would have to leave if he continued interfering with the class. Boylin became vehement, saying, 'You'll leave before I do'.

Mr Walker announced that all class activities would be suspended until Boylin left. Boylin immediately got up and said, 'Well fuck it' at which point the male class members asked that all women leave the room, and they did so immediately. One of the female students reported the incident to campus security at this time.

Up until this moment no one had retaliated or made any statement to Boylin. After the women left, several of the male class members asked Boylin to leave and as he retorted continually, some of the men told him exactly what they thought of his actions.

At no time was Boylin under any threats of violence from any member of the class, or from the instructor. I might add the following conclusions:

Prior to the beginning of the class Boylin announced his intentions of disrupting the classroom.

He was treated by the instructor and members of the class in the most reasonable manner possible, considering the circumstances.

He infringed upon my rights and the rights of other students by wasting our valuable class time.

He used insolent and obscene language in front of ladies, and was insolent and insulting to the instructor.

Campus security was called, and did an effective job, only after his insults and insolence had reached an uncontrollable point.

I would like to say that it makes me particularly sad to see a foreign instructor subjected to this kind of behaviour, when he has come to our country to educate and instead is attacked from the classroom floor. Boylin made me ashamed of Memphis State University and ashamed of our nation. It is inconceivable to me that such an animal can be bred in our society.

I would like to make it perfectly clear that this statement is voluntary on my part, and I would hope that disciplinary action will be taken, and that if Boylin is in actuality a student, I ask that he be expelled from Memphis State University.

Sincerely,
(Signed) W. Percy Galbreath
409-82-4404

IV

THIRD DEPOSITION: THE PROFESSOR

For the attention of Mr Jerry Frye, Assistant Director of Security:

On Thursday, 30 July 1970, shortly after 6.00 p.m., when I was on the point of going to Room 325, Miss Eva Gatlin, a policewoman and student in my class, called at my office. She told me that she thought I was 'going to have trouble tonight', and explained that a young man had appeared in the classroom and disturbed the students by stating his intention to disrupt the affairs of the class. He had used obscene language, stated that he would force me to 'give' him an A, tried to borrow a copy of the text book and, finding nobody prepared to lend him one, gone away. I thanked Miss Gatlin for her warning, collected my papers and followed her to Room 325 where I resumed my commentary of the previous evening on Wordsworth's Preface to *Lyrical Ballads*.

At approximately 6.20 p.m. the door opened and a young man strolled in with studied casualness, a drinking straw in his mouth and not so much as a nod in my direction. He crossed in front of the lectern and occupied a seat in the centre of the front row. I asked him who he was and he said, 'This is 2102, isn't it?' I asked for his name. His reply was unintelligible and I asked him to spell his name for me. He continued to speak with deliberate indistinctness, but I asked him to spell his name again. He responded aggressively with the question, 'What's your name?' I repeated my question to him and with theatrical overemphasis he supplied: GEORGE BOYLIN. In a very impertinent tone he offered to write it down for me.

I ignored the obvious insolence of his manner, asked him if he had a copy of the text, which by this time he had, and advised him to open his book at the work being studied. He brandished his book and put it away under his chair. Again I ignored the blatant provocation and briefly recapitulated my remarks made to the class before his arrival. From the beginning he continually interrupted me with questions and I requested him to remain silent until I had finished my lecture and to save his questions until afterwards. I advised him to take notes and in a tone of elaborate surprise he asked, 'Do we have to take notes?' I replied, 'You do not have to, but I think you might find it difficult to remember everything of importance if you do not'. He then said, 'I haven't got a pencil. Have you got a pencil?' and interrupted my negative reply with, 'Have you got a pen?' I said I had not, asked him to listen and proceeded to lecture. In spite of my repeated request that he keep questions till later, he continued to interrupt and from his briefcase he noisily produced pieces of a linked metal object, apparently a decorative belt, and a pack of playing cards. He fitted the metal pieces together, draped the result round his neck, jangling it noisily, and turned his attention to the cards.

On a third or fourth request from me that he should not interrupt again, he insisted that the class should be involved in discussion rather than in listening to my remarks. I told him that he must follow my instructions and put away his cards or leave the room. He said, 'Are you asking me or telling me?' and added an invitation to play poker. I replied that I was telling him. He informed me that I could not do this, that I did not know how to teach, and that I would leave before he did. I ordered him to leave and he refused, whereupon I told the class that our activities would be suspended 'until the departure of Mr Boylin'.

Miss Gatlin left the room in search of the University Security Officers. She returned with two officers who questioned me and spoke to Mr Boylin. While I was in the corridor with the officers Mr Boylin raised the two window blinds and appeared to signal to the outside. A number of women students left the room because of his abusive language at this point. Mr Boylin left the room with the officers and I returned to the lectern. Shortly afterwards you arrived with a Security Officer and questioned me about the incident.

(Signed) Marshall Walker
Visiting Professor of English

V

BOYLIN

Monday, 27 July, 1970, 10.00 p.m.

Why do that Edie Moore still ride in the back a the bus? Hateful backass of a bus. Backasses for black asses. So I'll lay me down cross this one's now she's gone. Well, I be dawg, that Memphis State honky was right — she a high-yeller looker but she ain't no revolutionary. She don't got enough soul. Now whitey don't ride 'em we got right of the whole bus, 'cept in the drivin' seat. I done showed one whole busloada niggers last January how it could *all* be black by shovin' that drivin' honky out into the snow. Wouldn't lemme ride for want of twenty-five cents. Man, he was white all right when I rolled him on the ground. Bus was all black when I put that white mother in the snow an' them suckin' pigs in badges gwina come an' take me to town — three times they're takin' me to town for stuff I done — gonna put me way outa sight, blind me with the Mace. I fooled 'em last time. Made 'em turn me loose in that rest room. Even with bars an' on the third floor ain't no pig in Memphis can move fast enough to keep me from reachin' the pipes and turnin' on the steam. Man, I flooded that place. They called me boy while they 'fraid a gettin' they feet wet. They so 'fraid a gettin' they feet wet they let me fly right outa the top a that winda. I gets away 'cos of the spirit in me. The spirit in me that's gonna bring that Wordsworth mother that's standin' in fronta Edie's class way down. 'Cos he done got too high. Edith Moore ain't of the revolutionary spirit. I am.

5. Mr Bill of Yoknapatawpha

If you called in at the Rexall drugstore on the square in Oxford, Mississippi fifty years ago, the pharmacist would show you where Mr Bill used to stand outside on the sidewalk, watching the theatre of the town after he'd bought his pipe tobacco. Across the square the courthouse gleamed whitely in the heat haze, fronted by the Confederate soldier perpetually on guard against trouble from the North. Negro idlers lounged in shop porches. Retailers bore Faulknerian-sounding names: Vadah B. Gower; Toxey T. Fortinberry. Men in white shirts and black brogues, emerging from litigious offices, were hail-fellow-well-met. Immaculate wives with bouffant hair piled high like ziggurats repaired their make-up, sashaying from bloated sedans in sinuous slow motion as if they were doing the air a favour. Mr Bill was contemplating the latter-day Jefferson of his fiction.

'Tell about the South', Shreve McCannon asks Quentin Compson in Faulkner's *Absalom, Absalom!* 'What's it like there? What do they do there? Why do they live there? Why do they live at all?' Quentin is one of four narrators who piece together the story of the rise and fall of Thomas Sutpen to expose the Southern malaise in terms of its origin in slavery and evolution into prolonged, cruel and tragic absurdity. As the story comes to an end in 1910, all that remains of Sutpen's grand design to found a dynasty is his only living descendant, an idiot Negro, howling like a demented chorus in the ashes of a ruined mansion. The novel has shown what the South is like, how it came to be that way and what people do, but the only plausible answer to Shreve's third question is that people live there because they belong. Belonging, they share Sutpen's enslavement to a hierarchy of values that prefers incest to miscegenation and denies blacks human status. Faulkner belonged all his life to the South. His works represent a lifetime spent trying to answer the questions he gave Shreve McCannon.

Before a Faulkner story gets very far the voice has pulled you in. His style is a literary deployment of regional speech. He's an exemplary Southern raconteur sitting on his porch, saying either nothing at all over his bourbon and branch-water or saying everything, in one measured, passionately monotonous and convoluted sentence. *Light in August* is divided into sentences, paragraphs and chapters, but is a single, fluent expression. The voice begins, 'Sitting beside the road, watching the wagon mount the hill toward her, Lena thinks, "I have come from Alabama: a fur piece. All the way from Alabama a-walking"', and the voice doesn't stop, scarcely pauses, until the final return to Lena and her concluding, imperturbable, 'My, my. A body does get around. Here we ain't been coming from Alabama but two months, and now it's already Tennessee'. These are the beginning and ending of the single, manifold image to which Faulkner gives the title *Light in August*. Between them are the stoicisms and grudges, the lethal prejudices, the ruthless Calvinist bigotry, the violence which contrasts with Lena's not entirely ingenuous serenity, the changes of perspective, the flashbacks. Truth is not linear. It's a fabric of cross-references, overlappings, fluidity. As V. K. Ratliff, the itinerant sewing-machine salesman says in *The Town*, 'if it ain't complicated up enough it ain't right'. No reader has understood this better than the poet, Conrad Aiken, who describes Faulkner's style as a way of keeping 'the form – and the idea – fluid and unfinished, still in motion, as it were, and unknown, until the dropping into place of the very last syllable'. Syntactical densities and labyrinthine sentences can make him difficult to read; he often uses too many words — 'profound', 'terrific' and 'savage' work overtime — and he's given to hyperbole. His characters are sometimes endowed with an implausibly receptive sensory apparatus; yet the voice holds you, the story is always surprising and there's surely no region on earth more amply endowed than the American South with what we might lamely call human interest but he would call, so much more precisely, 'the human heart in conflict with itself'.

His writing life began properly in 1926. He had just retired from the job of postmaster to the University of Mississippi with the celebrated observation: 'I won't be at the beck and call of every son-of-a-bitch who happens to have two cents', and was living in New Orleans where he got to know Sherwood Anderson. In 1953 Faulkner wrote an appreciation of Anderson in which he said: 'During those New Orleans days and weeks, I gradually became aware that here was a man who would be in seclusion all forenoon – working. Then in the afternoon he would appear and we could walk about the city, talking. Then in the evening we would meet again, with a bottle now, and now he would really talk; the world in miniscule would be there in whatever shadowy courtyard where glass and bottle clinked and the palms hissed like dry sand in whatever moving air. Then tomorrow forenoon and he would be secluded again – working; whereupon I said to myself, "If this is what it takes to be a novelist, then that's the life for me'". The story goes that when Anderson heard Faulkner had written a book he promised to persuade his publishers to accept it, provided he himself didn't have to read it.

Faulkner Room, University of Mississippi

The book was *Soldier's Pay* and it wasn't a success. Neither was *Mosquitoes*. With his third novel, *Sartoris,* he discovered that his 'own little postage stamp of soil was worth writing about', and embarked on the creation of Yoknapatawpha County, proclaiming himself 'sole owner and proprietor', and basing its county seat, Jefferson, on the Oxford of his upbringing. He was on his way to becoming the grandee of Southern literature. *Sartoris* introduces themes he would develop in a series of works which he called 'the book', perhaps thinking of Balzac's *La Comédie Humaine* or the interconnected novels of Proust. There's the continuation of the past in the present, the isolation of the individual, the moral decay of the old South and the erosion of its traditions by the remorselessly secular values of the modern age. In *Sartoris* modernism is represented by the car Bayard Sartoris drives recklessly along the dusty roads in a frantic effort to exorcise the ghosts of his recently killed twin brother and his long dead great-grandfather by courting what he sees as the redeeming violence of their deaths.

Another facet of modernism, deadlier than the automobile, is the Snopes family. Their chronicle of avarice, perversion and murder occupies Faulkner in the trilogy, *The Hamlet*, *The Town* and *The Mansion* with 'Barn Burning', the first of *Collected Stories*, as preface. The Snopeses are 'a seemingly inexhaustible family which for the last ten years had been moving into town in driblets from a small settlement known as Frenchman's Bend'. *Sartoris* refers to Flem, the first Snopes to move to Jefferson. In the trilogy he cheats and manipulates his neighbours until he controls them all, marries the earth-goddess daughter of his chief victim, swindles a poor farmer with non-existent buried treasure thereby driving him insane, and moves on to Jefferson with his tribe of almost uniformly decadent relatives in tow to corrupt the town. Popeye, the gangster of *Sanctuary*, and the Snopeses are the mechanistic anti-community forces that cause all modern alienations. Three years before the action of *Sartoris* Flem has become vice-president of old Bayard Sartoris's bank. A bookkeeper in the bank is Byron Snopes, characteristically employed writing obscene letters to a well-bred young lady and eventually absconding with money from the bank. And there's Montgomery Ward Snopes who, by keeping a plug of tobacco under his left armpit for several hours to speed up his heartbeat before his army medical, gets himself rejected for military service. Later he leaves for France as a YMCA worker and, while running an Army canteen, imports a French girl to entertain the boys in the backroom, thus proving himself a true Snopes.

Faulkner's humour – in *As I Lay Dying*, or *The Reivers* – is the joint product of his shrewd eye and the folk tradition of the south-west. The laconic repartee of the planing-mill workers in *Light in August* is spiked with idiomatic Southern humour, foil to the sullen Joe Christmas and garrulous, noisy Lucas Burch, alias Joe Brown. The violence is rooted in history. Destruction of the old South released suppressed forces of disorder which were intensified by an army of occupation and the exploitations of the Carpetbaggers, those Northerners who tried to dominate Negro votes in their efforts to gain government positions. An old Southern order of moral values was replaced by cynical materialism; but it's no simple contest between good and evil. The leaders of the old South are associated with principled lives, social decorum and bravery and nearly all the Snopeses are morally derelict; but the aristocratic Southern families are stained by the sin of slavery which had to be expiated by defeat in the Civil War and the ordeal of Reconstruction. Their moral decadence offers no effective resistance to the onslaught of Snopesism and they are culpably backward-looking and ineffectual in matters of racial prejudice and inequality. A subsidiary theme in *Light in August* is the South's preoccupation with the past, exemplified by the Reverend Gail Hightower, an unfrocked minister, who neglects his wife and loses his church because of his fanatical obsession with the memory of his grandfather, killed in the Civil War. Literature, like art, is an inseparable part of history, illuminating it and being illuminated by it. Serious study of Southern history prescribes a trip to Yoknapatawpha County.

Many of Faulkner's fellow-Southerners opposed his attitude to the race problem. In the early 1950s Robert Penn Warren travelled in the South talking about segregation to people in Kentucky, Tennessee, Arkansas, Mississippi and Louisiana. As Warren reports in his book, *Segregation: The Inner Conflict in the South*, he found Faulkner no generally accepted prophet in his own country. In a motel bar Warren joins a conversation about a film being made nearby which is receiving local acclaim for containing no 'criticism'; he asks:

> 'Didn't they make another movie over at Oxford?' [The film of Faulkner's *Intruder in the Dust*].
> The man nods, the woman says yes. I ask what that one had been about. Nobody had seen it, not

the woman neither of the men. 'It was by that fellow Faulkner', the woman says. 'But I never read anything he ever wrote'.

'I never did either', the man behind the desk says, 'but I know what it's like. It's like that fellow Hemingway. I read some of his writings. Gory and on the seedy side of life. I didn't like it'.

'That's exactly right', the woman says, and nods. 'On the seedy side of life. That fellow Faulkner, he's lost a lot of friends in Mississippi. Looking at the seedy side'.

'Does he criticise?' I ask.

She turns away. The man goes through a door behind the desk. A well-dressed young man has long since become engrossed in a magazine.

Yet there is nothing militant in the comment Faulkner made in 1956. Of the Negro's claim to equality he said: 'His equality is inevitable, an irresistible force, but as I see it you've got to take into consideration human nature, which at times has nothing to do with moral truths. Truth says this and the fact says that. A wise person says "Let's use this fact. Let's obliterate this fact first". To oppose a material fact with a moral truth is silly'. Read in historical context this may just pass for practical wisdom; today, with an Afro-American in the White House, it appears temporisingly specious; but Faulkner certainly was an offending liberal to many of his fellow Southerners: in the mid-50s they were calling him 'small-minded Willie, the nigger lover'. He received abusive mail and crank telephone calls. There were stores and gasoline stations around Oxford that refused to serve him. In terms of later 20th century ideas, however, there's nothing of the conventional liberal about the letter he wrote to a University of Alabama student at the time of riots over the admission of a Negro: 'I vote that we ourselves choose to abolish [segregation], if for no other reason than, by voluntarily giving the negro the chance for whatever equality he is capable of, we will stay on top; he will owe us gratitude; where if his equality is forced on us by law, compulsion from the outside, he will be on top from being the victor, the winner against opposition. And no tyrant is more ruthless than he who was only yesterday the oppressed, the slave'.

A loftier tone is taken in *Intruder in the Dust*, his most didactic novel. Lucas Beauchamp, a proud Negro farmer whose grandfather was white, has for years been a thorn in the flesh of the people of Jefferson on account of his refusal to acquiesce in the traditional inferiority of his race, adopting the servile attitude to whites expected of him. When a murder is committed and Lucas is framed there can be no doubt in the white mind of his guilt. Lucas's innocence is eventually established by the efforts of the sixteen-year-old boy, Chick Mallison, Chick's negro companion and seventy-year-old Miss Eunice Habersham. Chick is horrified by a society that can set aside the law when its victim is a Negro, and undertakes the gruesome assignment of digging up a dead body in order to prove Lucas innocent. The experience prompts him to turn a hectically critical eye on his own people towards whom he now feels revulsion, though he does still think of the North as 'outland'. He is reconciled to his people by his uncle, Gavin Stevens, who associates defence of the modern South against the North with what amounts to a policy of gradualism:

> Someday Lucas Beauchamp can shoot a white man
> in the back with the same impunity to lynch-rope or
> gasoline as a white man; in time he will vote anywhere
> a white man can and send his children to the same
> school anywhere the white man's children go and
> travel anywhere the white man travels as the white
> man does it. But it won't be next Tuesday.

The Civil War failed to secure the Negro's equality, and legislation can't, because legislation is an imposition from outside. The South must be converted from within; she must undergo her own process of moral regeneration and accomplish her own expiation. Man must cooperate with time: 'Yesterday today and tomorrow are Is: Indivisible: One'.

If there's something of the mugwump in Faulkner's moral position here, his scrutiny of the South acquires weight, as in *Absalom, Absalom!* by biblical overtones. In 'The Bear', the most complex story in *Go Down, Moses*, he relates the white man's sin of slavery to his rape of the land in a context that evokes the Fall. In the beginning the South is wilderness, waiting like a new Eden. Indians roam the wilderness, but can't possess it because the land has a quality of permanent inviolability and can't be passed down in ownership from generation to generation. The white man comes and buys the land from the Indians; but the purchase is an illusion, as Ike McCaslin eventually realises of the land he inherits. The bear of the title is Old Ben, 'shaggy, tremendous, red-eyed, not malevolent but just big'. His foot has been maimed in a trap but he is apparently bullet-proof and 'absolved of mortality'. He symbolises the spirit of natural freedom and the soul of the wilderness in his endurance and elusiveness. His human counterpart is the wise woodsman, Sam Fathers, Ike McCaslin's tutor and spiritual father. Sam's death coincides with the death of Old Ben when the bear is finally brought down by Lion, a wild Airedale cross Sam has trained. Sam's mixed heritage of the bloods of three races makes him an embodiment of the racial entanglement of the South. Crimes have been committed against both the land and the Negro and Ike realises he must seek redemption for the sins of his forefathers who bequeath him, with his inheritance, a legacy of guilt. Tracing the history of the McCaslin plantation in ledgers kept by his father and uncle, he discovers his grandfather's incestuous relations with a Negro slave who was his own daughter and finally relinquishes his claim to the plantation, thus hoping to expiate his family's crimes against both land and Negro.

There are awkward ambiguities in 'The Bear'. Given the symbolic value of Old Ben as an admirable embodiment of the inviolable freedom of the land, how are we to judge his killers? This is partly a story of initiation, but Ike — 'a boy who wished to learn humility and pride in order to become skilful and worthy in the woods' — is as intensely initiated into a cult of death as he is in the crafts of the woodsman. Hunting is presented as manly, sometimes heroic, yet it sets the characters in a destructive relationship with the wilderness. The story is divided into five parts; the most evocative writing is in parts one to three, dealing with the pursuit of Old Ben. Part four is a conversation between Ike and his cousin, McCaslin Edmonds. Heresy as it may be for confirmed Faulkner enthusiasts, it must be admitted that this part is difficult to read because Faulkner overloads the narrative with detail while indulging his taste for breathlessly long, convoluted sentences, as he also does in *Absalom, Absalom!* His message, however, is accessible enough and crucial for understanding his interpretation of Southern history. We are clearly meant to see the McCaslin family chronicle as the story of the South in microcosm: 'that chronicle which was a whole land in miniature, which multiplied and compounded was the entire South'. Transactions in which the land and the Negro are treated as objects to be bought and owned can bind neither land nor Negro. They are untouchable, immune, and embody a prime Faulknerian virtue, Old Ben's power of endurance.

It's the white man who is enslaved. The illusory binding of the Negro by the white man's law and custom may continue for some generations, but it can't last for ever, 'Because they will endure. They are better than we are. Stronger than we are. Their vices are vices aped from white men or that white men and bondage have taught them: improvidence and intemperance and evasion – not laziness: evasion: of what white men had set them to, not for their aggrandisement or even comfort but his own.' Both Ike McCaslin and Chick Mallison learn that they can't repudiate their own. Ike realises that his pursuit of personal redemption for the sins of his forebears will be meaningless if it separates him from the people of the South who have given him identity, and Chick Mallison associates the same kind of belief with the notion that the South must cure itself. The final emphasis, of course, is morally suspect, implying that it's better to sink together in shame than be shown by someone else how to navigate differently, though the professed moral realism of Faulkner's position, if misguided, is its own defence. But this must be seen in the context of his basic concern with the human bond and the need for life in true community.

In *Light in August* the community is the villain. Joe Christmas looks white but is purported to have Negro blood. He believes himself racially mixed. The janitor who is eventually revealed as his grandfather, the duplicitous dietitian he accidentally witnesses fornicating while he's stealing her toothpaste, and the children at his orphanage call him nigger; the Negroes he meets at night in Chapter Six take him for a white man. He craves the life of a white. Passing a house in the white part of town he watches a card game in progress on a lighted veranda:

> ... four people sat about a card table, the white faces
> intent and sharp in the low light, the bare arms of the
> women glaring smooth and white above the trivial

cards. 'That's all I wanted', he thought. 'That don't seem like a whole lot to ask'.

We're told that his skin is the colour of parchment. He imagines taunting Mrs McEachern, his foster mother, by daring her to tell her fiercely bigoted husband, 'That he has nursed a nigger beneath his own roof, with his own food at his own table'. He tells Bobbie, the prostitute waitress, 'I got some nigger blood in me'. The end of Chapter Fourteen focuses on his perception of his 'black shoes smelling of Negro: that mark on his ankles the gauge definite and ineradicable of the black tide creeping up his legs, moving from his feet upward as death moves'. He oscillates between white and black. As District Attorney Gavin Stevens puts it, his blood 'would not be either one or the other and let his body save itself'. Faulkner, as narrator, doesn't confirm his 'black blood' until the passage describing his death and apotheosis at the end of Chapter Nineteen. Others choose his race for him, including Joanna Burden who has become erotically savage in her lust for Joe as Negro before losing her sex drive and trying to persuade him to train as a Negro lawyer. His life is a series of flights from racial categorisation; but his murder of Miss Burden gives the community its way with him by conforming to the expected formula: a white woman has been raped and killed by a Negro. Definition is thus forced on him as the consequence of an act by which he sought to escape it. A scapegoat for communal racist hatred, he is made to carry all the connotations of 'black', defined into evil since childhood by other people's imposition of evil upon him.

The ultimate triumph, however, is his. During his seven-days' flight from everything, he feels outside time and beyond the fury and mire of human involvement, achieving a transcendence in which he finds himself at last. Finally, he deliberately re-enters human time and community because only within their framework will his life have meaning. He gives himself up, then escapes to surrender himself sacrificially to Percy Grimm, Faulkner's brutal Nazi clone, who represents 'a belief that the white race is superior to any and all other races'. Joe allows Grimm to shoot him, whereupon Grimm castrates him so that he will 'let white women alone, even in hell'. But Joe has not only given Joanna Burden her expiation; he has indirectly caused the Reverend Gail Hightower and Byron Bunch to be jolted out of their isolations and brought a measure of peaceful closure to Mrs Hines, his long-suffering grandmother. He is, thus, not only scapegoat but redeemer too. He is certainly not to be equated with Christ, but he is Christ-like – a sacrificial offering for the sins of Southern humanity, remembered 'forever and ever', his face 'musing, quiet, steadfast, not fading and not particularly threatful, but of itself alone serene, of itself alone triumphant'. His apotheosis is a far piece from the Joe Christmas of the orphanage, the McEachern farm, the Jefferson planing mill and Joanna Burden's bedroom.

'The only folks in the South who are not lonesome', says the protagonist of Robert Penn Warren's novel *Flood*, 'are the coloured folks . . . That is the heart of the race problem. It is not guilt . . . It is simply that your Southerner is deeply and ambiguously disturbed to have folks around him who are not as lonesome as he is. Especially if they are black folks'. Only the black folks achieve community in *The Sound and the Fury*. Entering, in the first three sections, the minds of the Compson brothers, Benjy the 'idiot', Quentin and Jason, the reader is trapped in three subjectivities which are sealed off from the objective world, all deficient in a sense of community. Benjy's section is the 'tale told by an idiot, full of sound and fury'. Locked in a timeless present he can convey his feelings only by howling, whimpering or remaining placid. The second section belongs to Quentin and reveals the thoughts and images which flash through his obsessed mind on the day of his suicide. Quentin is spellbound by the past and his sister, the vanished Caddy, while Jason, neurotically mean, is obsessed with the future, with time as money. In the fourth section Faulkner switches to third person narrative, presenting Dilsey the Negro cook who single-handedly has kept the Compson family precariously together by acting as a buffer to its warring factions. Through Dilsey the novel reaches its climax in the Negro church where she takes Benjy and Frony, her daughter. In a magnificent cadenza, one of Faulkner's most vivid passages, the Easter service is taken by a visiting preacher, an insignificant, dwarf-like man who nevertheless commands the congregation's attention by his virtuosity. There is a hymn, then the main part of the Easter sermon:

Then a voice said, 'Brethren'.

The preacher had not moved. His arm lay yet across the desk, and he still held that pose while the voice died in sonorous echoes between the walls. It was as different as day and dark from his former tone, with a sad, timbrous quality like an alto horn, sinking into their hearts and speaking there again when it had ceased in fading and cumulate echoes.

'Brethren and sisteren', it said again. The preacher removed his arm and he began to walk back and forth before the desk, his hands clasped behind him, a meagre figure hunched over upon itself like that of one long immured in striving with the implacable earth, 'I got the recollection and the blood of the Lamb!'

In this last section of the novel, after the hermetic darkness of the brothers' monologues, Easter and the promise of Resurrection, 'the recollection and the blood of the Lamb' are located in a Negro church. The reiterated, ecstatic affirmation of 'Yes, Jesus!' is infinitely more in this context than a bit of folksy characterisation. As they watch the 'worn small rock' of the preacher's body the Negroes are consumed with him, by his chanted expression of faith beyond reason, into a community that transcends the need for words.

Towards the end of his speech of acceptance on the award of the Nobel Prize for Literature in 1950, Faulkner said: 'I believe that man will not merely endure: he will prevail. He is immortal, not because he alone among creatures has an inexhaustible voice, but because he has a soul, a spirit capable of compassion and sacrifice and endurance'. It's under the name of Dilsey, the Negress, that he writes 'They endured' in the Appendix to *The Sound and the Fury*. It is she alone who displays compassion and is capable of sacrifice; she alone who sees the first and the last, the beginning and the ending. And although in the matter of human rights Mississippi remained for decades the most backward of the States, and despite many setbacks in the march to Martin Luther King's promised land, it seems reasonable to suppose that, had he planned this Appendix today, he might have written, 'They prevailed'.

6. Blackadder

The next object is a red diary. The two principal characters it represents are the girl who kept the diary and her father. Nellie Grassam was eleven when she accompanied her father, John Grassam, on a voyage from London to Brisbane in 1895-6. My great-uncle by marriage, John Grassam of Spalding, Lincolnshire, was Captain of the clipper ship *SS Blackadder*, 900 tons, registered at Lloyds. His officers for this voyage were Chief Officer, Mr Lloyd; 2nd Officer, Mr Holden. There were four apprentices. The number of able-bodied seamen is not recorded.

First, the girl.

Extracts from Nellie's intermittent red diary:

2nd February 1895. I got up nice and early this morning and then I went on deck. I saw some dolphins. They are lovely and the colours are always changing. At one moment they are blue & the next moment they are red. We tacked ship.

3rd February. Today I have begun to work really hard at my lessons. I started at 9 a.m. and finished at a quarter to 12. We tacked ship after dinner and I helped. I hauled on the top gallant and royal braces.

4th February. I did my lessons as usual this morning but did not do many as I felt ill. Mr Lloyd and I had a quarrel but we made it up again when I went to bed.

5th February. Today I felt very poorly and I did not do many lessons but I lay on my father's settee and read a book called The Three Musketeers by Alexander Dumas. (I gave it to father in Brisbane on his birthday.)

6th February. I feel ill again today. Mr Lloyd thinks I am shamming and so does Mr Holden as I ate four and a half pancakes for dinner. I did not do any lessons however.

19th February. We went 306 miles today.

6th March. Today we are 600 miles from the Lizard. We have got a fair wind too.

7th March. Today at noon we were 360 miles from Lizard. We have a nice spanking breeze and the ship is bowling along merrily at 9 knots per hour.

8th March. As today is Sunday I did not do any lessons this morning. Father expects we shall be in the Channel tomorrow. We have to depend on dead reckoning as the sun is not out.

9th March. Saw the Scilly's lights last night at 2.15 a.m. Sighted the Lizard at 9.30 a.m. this morning. We saw 3 tugs & 3 pilot boats and some steamers. The pilot came aboard & brought papers and took telegrams. Thick weather.

26th June. Moderate N. winds. Smooth sea. I now hold the log-glass while they heave the log, that is telling how fast we are going.

2nd July. Variable airs and calms. Saw flying fish for the first time. I steered at the wheel from 6 p.m. to 8 p.m. It was lovely.

9th July. Smooth sea. It is very hot. Saw some more flying fish. Mr Lloyd and I had a quarrel but we are reconciled.

15th July. Light South-east wind. Smooth sea. I am now taking my turn in the watch as third mate.

25th July. I got up at 20 minutes past 6 a.m. Mr Lloyd and I are the best of friends. It was my watch on deck from 4 p.m. to 6 p.m. and I did do a lot of work. It is a head sea & wind.

Middle row: Chief Officer Mr Lloyd, Captain John Grassam, 2nd Officer Mr Holden, Nellie Grassam with apprentices

26th July. I saw a lot of Cape Pigeons. They are very pretty. They hardly ever move their wings but fly with them quite still. There is a large white spot on their wings.

29th July. About a quarter past 11 a.m. this morning I saw a whale. They are monsters! It rose to the surface to blow and it did make a noise. There are some Cape Pigeons about the ship.

31st July. The ship rolled so much last night that I could not get to sleep for a long time; it kept waking me up through the night. It is considerably colder today. We tacked ship at 6 p.m. & she is pitching.

1st August. One of the crew caught a Cape Pigeon but he let it go again.

3rd August. There are a lot of Cape Pigeons, Molihawks, Cape Terns and other birds about us. They look very pretty flying about the ship.

5th August. Early this morning about 4 a.m. there was a very rough sea. There came a mountain wave & washed the apprentices' house. All of the apprentices got their clothes very wet.

11th August. I have not been up on deck all today as it is very bad weather & the cabin doors are shut as waves keep coming on the deck.

22nd August. It is a strong wind to a fresh gale today & the cabin doors are shut, in fact they have been shut for the last 3 or 4 days.

25th August. We have broken the record today. For the last few days we have been going very fast.

4th September. We passed Wilson's Promontory at midnight last night.

8th September. This afternoon we had a narrow escape of getting on shore. About 2 p.m. we could see the land, but could not see it plainly, so we thought we were a long way off, but in reality we were very near. It was very misty.

9th September. About 3 p.m. father went below and had a read. A short time later Mr Lloyd came down & told father we were close to land. Father went on deck & we were nearly ashore.

10th September. Yesterday we tacked just in time or in another 5 minutes we should have been ashore.

11th September. This evening we were off C. Morton & we burnt blue lights for a pilot. He came at last. I did not go to bed till 11 p.m. tonight.

12th September. We were waiting for a tug but none came for us. However we managed without one but now it is a calm.

13th September. We anchored.

14th September. I stayed at Mrs Brown's and played with Jacky. I am going to stay with Mrs Brown all the time.

15th September. This morning I went to church with father and I walked all the way back by myself. I was hot. There is a drought in Australia now. I had a bath.

19th September. This morning I made mud pies with dear little Jacky. A Chinese vegetarian came to the door & as soon as he saw me he put down his basket & said, 'You come China with me?'

24th September. Father and I have got an invitation to go up country to Mr Nutt & Mr Nutt said he has a nice quiet pony for me to ride on. We accepted the invitation.

27th September. Hurrah! I am up country. I got up early this morning at 5 o'clock and saw them milk the cows & feed the calves.

1st October. I expect father is coming up tonight. I am going to meet him in the horse and trap. On our way to the station Mr Nutt and I yarned away & he told me all about Australia.

2nd October. Father came last night. I got up early and went out shooting with Mr Nutt and father. We went in some thick scrub. We shot a bear & jackass & a diver. I ran to pick them up.

3rd October. This morning we went into some very long grass and had a shot at some snipe but could not hit them. I was afraid of snakes in that long grass. I was busy raking the hay & I rode on top when the cart was full.

4th October. This morning, sad to relate, we returned to town. The trains are so slow. It is only 42 miles but it took the train 3 hours to get there.

7th October. I like Mrs Brown more and more every day. She is very kind. Agnes, Mrs Brown's servant, gave me some nice doll's toys. Mr Brown is very nice too.

9th October. I often think about dear old Spalding. As I sit here pen in hand and think over my past life, I think how kind people in general have been to me & I thank them for it.

18th October. Today I went to Sandgate. It is a fashionable seaside resort. I went with Mrs F. Brown, Jacky and Mrs C. Brown. We had such a lovely bathe but did not go out far as we were afraid of sharks. We made our own fire and boiled our own kettle & it was lovely.

22nd October. I had a lovely shower bath this morning. Jacky had one with me too. I was so glad he did. He is such a funny little fellow. He splashed about ever so in the bath.

23rd October. This morning I said to Jacky, 'Do you love me?' He said, 'Yes'. I said, 'Where do you love me?' He said, 'In my little heart'. I said, 'How much do you love me?' He said, 'Two stone and a half'.

30th October. Miss Brown is going to give a party to a lot of people on Friday and she wants me to go and sing my songs. I accepted.

1st November. The party came off tonight. There were about thirty people there & I felt rather shy. However Miss & Mrs Brown pressed me to sing and all the people laughed as if they would go to pieces.

26th November. All the good-byes are said & today the Blackadder left Brisbane wharf. Mrs Brown & Jackie came to see us off. We went down Brisbane river & anchored. We are going to sea tomorrow.

3rd December. Directly I had finished my lessons this morning I went on deck & saw the boys fishing for albatross and molihawks. I did not work as it was not my watch on deck.

5th December. Today I saw them making rope. It is made in this manner. Some rope yarns are stretched from one end of the ship to the other, then the yarns are gathered up & a wheel turns & the yarns twist into a rope.

6th December. Today I did my lessons. Mr Lloyd is more of a tease than ever & he promised me he wouldn't tease me too. One of the apprentices caught an albatross & gave the steward its head.

13th December. Today we had horrible dried fish for dinner, pea soup & pancakes. I can't eat the fish or pea soup but I like the pancakes.

14th December. Father says we shall have 2 Sundays or eight days in a week. Is it not funny?

18th December. As I was lying down on father's settee this morning reading a big rat ran right over me to get to its hole. It ran so fast it made me jump ever so. The cabin doors are shut today.

19th December. The cabin doors are open today so I went on deck as it is nice and sunshiny. I can make the figure 8 knot and the sailor's knot and reef knot.

25th December. Today it is Christmas Day & a nice fine day it is too. I got up at 7 o'clock this morning and gave father, Mr Lloyd and Mr Holden my Christmas. Dinner was turtle soup, roast (fresh) pork and redcurrant pie.

1st January 1896. My New Year's Day did not begin very nicely for at breakfast I had a quarrel with Mr Lloyd. Then I did my lessons rather badly so that I was rather cross the rest of the day.

2nd January. Today I did not feel at all cross & I am friends with everybody. I went into Mr Holden's berth tonight and we had a nice yarn.

3rd January. Today it is a moderate E.S.E. to strong S.S.W. & S. gale with heavy squalls. I am lying on father's settee but at 2 bells I am going on deck as Freemantle (my favourite sailor) is at the wheel.

4th January. There was the sad death of the pig this afternoon so we shall have some pork tomorrow. Fresh pork I mean.

18th January. We are bonding sails today. I really have done such a lot of work what with hauling and pulling ropes, singing out and running about. My legs and arms ache ever so.

24th January. Today we have tacked two or three times & I pulled on a lot of ropes. I nearly hauled the top-gallants and royals yards all by myself. Was I not strong, dear diary?

25th January. Today we saw a barque with a skysail. We are passing her though we have a head wind.

Diary ends. The final stages of homecoming are not recorded.

Now the father.

His story as told in the obituary by my grandfather, Harry Walker, printed on 24th January 1933 in the *Lincolnshire, Boston and Spalding Free Press*.

UNLUCKY SHIP
Reformed by Old Spaldonian

LATE CAPT. GRASSAM'S
ADVENTURE WITH PIRATES

One more link with the England of clipper ship days is severed by the death at the age of eighty-four of John Grassam, an old Spaldonian, late captain of the clipper ship 'Blackadder'. This iron ship was built in 1869-70 for the China tea trade by Maudsley, Sons and Field, and was the only one of his fleet of twenty-two ships — which included the famous 'Cutty Sark' and 'Tweed' — that John Willis of London, and a Scotsman, retained to the day of his death.

'I shall keep her', said he to Captain Grassam, 'as long as you remain in command of her'.

In the course of her career in the tea trade the 'Blackadder' gained an unenviable reputation as an 'unlucky ship', and never did ship better deserve the epithet. Part of her misfortunes were undoubtedly due to the inexperience of her builders; part to the incompetence of her captains; but in the main they were attributable only to that misfortune which seems to dog some ships as well as some men.

During the whole period of Captain Grassam's command (from 1888) the 'Blackadder' was engaged in the Australian wool trade, and became a reformed character. She now established a contrary reputation, made some very smart passages, and became a centre of interest in shipping circles both in London and Australia. In her voyage (1897) from Brisbane to London in 79 days, she beat the record. Her best four days' run was accomplished in 1899 from Port Chalmers (New Zealand) to Hobart, approximately 300 miles a day. Other runs to her credit were one for 37 days, when she achieved an average of 240 miles a day; and another for 24 days when she averaged 250 miles a day.

PUT IN IRONS

Some remnant of the evil reputation which clung to the 'Blackadder's' tea trade experience was responsible for trouble when Captain Grassam first assumed command. The ship left London on June 26, 1888 and on July 2 the crew demanded that the ship be put back on the plea that she was not seaworthy. In an interview the captain intimated that there was one of two courses open to the men, to go to Brisbane or to go below. Every A.B. then refused duty and was put in irons. For four days the ship was handled by the officers, apprentices, cook, steward, carpenter and sailmaker. On the tenth day one A.B. 'turned to', to quote from the captain's log. Next day only 9 A.B.'s are logged as off duty, and this number was gradually reduced until on the 23rd day of the voyage only two men were still in irons. There they remained until the ship arrived in Brisbane, when they were handed over to the civil authorities and were sentenced to three months' hard labour for refusing duty. An interesting sidelight on the 'Blackadder' and her master is afforded by the fact that on the arrival of the ship at Brisbane after her next voyage, one of these two men came aboard with the request to sign on for the voyage home.

'No', was the reply. 'My ship is not good enough for you!'

SURROUNDED BY PIRATES

Captain Grassam's early career was not devoid of interest and excitement. On his first voyage the Liverpool ship in which he was apprenticed ran ashore in a typhoon off the island of Formosa. When dawn broke she was seen to be high and dry on a sandy beach and surrounded by hundreds of Chinese pirates. After consultation with the crew the captain decided to abandon ship as the one chance of saving their lives. The Chief Officer volunteered to be the first to leave the ship. The vessel had a heavy list and the officer was soon lost (underneath her bow) to the sight of those on deck. After a time he appeared again at a distance from the ship beyond the ring of pirates, stark naked. One by one the crew descended and were despoiled, though not all so drastically as the unfortunate mate. Our apprentice was allowed to retain boots, socks and trousers, and a gold watch the pirates had overlooked. After some days of wandering, during which they existed on wild sweet potatoes, the sailors were taken to the local mandarin, who transferred them to the nearest British Consul.

DAY AND NIGHT AT PUMPS

Captain Grassam's first command (1881) was John Wallis's barque 'Laurel'. In this barque he carried coolies on several occasions between Madras and Natal. The 'Laurel' was a teak ship and leaked abominably. On March 8th 1886, the log reports, 'Commenced to blow a hard gale, with high seas S.S.E., which continued till noon of the 11th. Hands employed constantly at the pumps; at times the water gained on us, but after veering round on starboard tack, after four hours' pumping with all hands, the water was just able to keep free'. During the entire voyage the men worked at the pumps in day and night shifts. Colombo was reached on 15th June and on 9th August the same weary pumping began again when the barque left Colombo for Madras, Mauritius, back to Madras, thence to Natal, back again to Madras, and once more sailed for London.

But there is a limit to human endurance. The men refused duty and the Captain was obliged, much against his will, to put into Mauritius. 'Get her home if you can', had been the instruction of old John Willis. At Mauritius the Seamen's Union summoned the Captain for sailing in an unseaworthy ship and in 1887 the case was brought before the High Court of Mauritius. The Master's cross-examination lasted for two hours and a half. He lost his case, as he knew he would. In summing up the Judge remarked on the conduct of the Captain that while the bravery of the British seaman was proverbial, the action of the Master in this instance savoured more of fool-hardiness than bravery. And that was that!

The 'Laurel' was sold at Mauritius and broken up. Captain Grassam sailed for Europe in a French liner and was met by John Willis with the remark, 'You lost your case. That's all right. The 'Blackadder's' waiting for you'.

LAST VISIT TO SPALDING

Until Captain Grassam retired from the sea he resided in Spalding. He always took a great interest in his native town, and his last visit was in October 1931. He married Miss S. Draper, the eighth child of the late Thomas Draper of Spalding, who at the time of her marriage was a teacher at the Wyggeston School at Leicester. This was in 1881, and thus they celebrated their golden wedding last July. There are two daughters of the marriage — Mrs R. Holloway [Nellie], who is a head-mistress in London and whose lectures in various parts of the country have earned her a great reputation; and Miss E. Grassam who holds an important position with Messrs. Ginn and Co., the world-known scholastic publishers.

Captain Grassam was laid to rest on Monday last in New Southgate Cemetery amid many manifestations of sympathy.

So ended the interesting career of one of Spalding's sons.

H.W.

7. Shakespeare's Comic Object

Do Shakespeare's comedies make you smile? Do you laugh? What is the comic object, the comic vision? For Aristotle, uncomfortably, comedy involved what he saw as a kind of ugliness:

> As for comedy, it is...an imitation of men worse than the average, worse however, not as regards any and every sort of fault, but only as regards one particular kind, the Ridiculous, which is a species of the Ugly.

And, well into the eighteenth century, the word for what makes us laugh is the 'ridiculous'. Laughter is derision. Thomas Hobbes wrote:

> Laughter is nothing else but sudden glory arising from some sudden conception of some eminency in ourselves, by comparison with the infirmity of others, or with our own formerly.

Doesn't this account for the pleasure we take in the spectacle of a humiliated Titania, a stripped Shylock, a routed Malvolio? In *Much Ado About Nothing* we can see the gulling of Benedick or Beatrice as comic because we do have an 'eminency' as compared to their 'infirmities'. We're aware that a trick is being played on Benedick while he is not; but surely there's something more to it than this, surely it's something in Benedick's behaviour and in his response to life, that we find comic. If we enjoy comedy only because it gives us a sense of eminency and makes us feel superior, then the comic vision might be morally dangerous breeding pride if not contempt. Unless, of course, the comic object is ourselves and we're laughing at our own infirmities, which could be healthy.

In 1900 a book was published in England which more than anything written before or since offers a systematic account of comedy and the comic, a translation of *Le Rire* by Henri Bergson. Bergson says comedy is the spectacle of the mechanical intruding into human conduct. Our behaviour issues from choice. Bergson suggests that we laugh when human beings reject choice, when a person behaves like a jack-in-the-box. A simple example is the meeting of man and banana skin. Picture someone walking along the street, nose in air, with an air of well-dressed self-importance. He slips on a banana skin and tumbles to the ground. We laugh. Why? Not just because we have a sense of eminency, not just because we feel superior to the crumpled heap on the pavement, but because our supposedly autonomous person has been in an instant transformed from a human being flaunting his command of the universe and himself to a mere thing without choice, at the mercy of a mechanical law. This is what Bergson describes as '*la méchanique plaquée sur le vivant*' — the mechanical encrusted on the living.

Our Bergsonian figure is a very physical example, and it's crucial to mark the discrepancy between his air of self-possession and his abrupt dispossession by the banana skin. We wouldn't laugh at a physically challenged or elderly person, mindful of hazards and stepping carefully until brought low by a regrettable accident. The element of come-uppance is part of the comic object. When a man, believing himself in complete control of himself and his life, behaves automatically or when his response to life becomes mechanical, he is comic, fundamentally because he is manipulated by something external, or living by formulae instead of by true animation. Ben Jonson's comedy is based on his depiction of ready-made types; characters behave mechanically under the domination of qualities or humours indicated by their names, e.g., Knowell, Brainworm, Downright — a plain Squire, Justice Clement — an old merry magistrate, Madam Would-be, Lovewit, Littlewit, Zeal-of-the-Land Busy — a Puritan. Not in Shakespeare's class for subtlety, but illustrating the idea that the comic is something mechanical. Other instances abound. There is Pope's illumination in *The Rape of the Lock* of the habitual (the mechanical) in the comic juxtaposition on Belinda's dressing table of 'puffs, powders, patches, Bibles, billets-doux'. In 'or stain her honour or her new brocade', and 'Not louder shrieks to pitying Heaven are cast, / When husbands or when lap-dogs breathe their last' he exposes an habitual (and comical) confusion of values by this use of a single verb (stain, breathe) for two such disparates. There's Don Quixote, his mind turned, quite out of control because he is ruled by his habit of expecting life to be the same as literary romance. So, by gazing on the fixed star of his obsession, Don

Quixote falls down the well of reality. Jane Austen's Catherine Morland nearly does so, too, in *Northanger Abbey*.

One of my favourite examples of the way in which literature can inculcate a comic mechanism of ideal notions of behaviour is in the novel *Look Homeward, Angel*. Thomas Wolfe's young Eugene Gant 'entombed himself in the flesh of a thousand fictional heroes', and Wolfe gives us some fruity examples:

> ... They stood silently a moment in the vast deserted nave of Saint Thomas. Far in the depth of the vast church Old Michael's slender hands pressed softly on the organ-keys. The last rays of the setting sun poured in a golden shaft down through the western windows, falling for a moment, in a cloud of glory, as if in benediction, on Mainwaring's tired face.
>
> 'I am going', he said presently.
>
> 'Going?' she whispered. 'Where?'
>
> The organ music deepened.
>
> 'Out there', he gestured briefly to the West. 'Out there — among His people'.
>
> 'Going?' She could not conceal the tremor of her voice. 'Going? Alone?'
>
> He smiled sadly. The sun had set. The gathering darkness hid the suspicious moisture in his grey eyes. 'Yes, alone', he said. 'Did not One greater than I go out alone some nineteen centuries ago?'
>
> 'Alone? Alone?' A sob rose in her throat and choked her.
>
> 'But before I go', he said, after a moment, in a voice which he strove in vain to render steady, 'I want to tell you ...' He paused a moment, struggling for mastery of his feelings.
>
> 'Yes?' she whispered.
>
> '... That I shall never forget you, little girl, as long as I live. Never'. He turned abruptly to depart.
>
> 'No, not alone! You shall not go alone!' she stopped him with a sudden cry.
>
> He whirled as if he had been shot.
>
> 'What do you mean? What do you mean?' he cried hoarsely.

'Oh, can't you see! Can't you see!' She threw out her little hands imploringly, and her voice broke.

'Grace! Grace! Dear heaven, do you mean it?'

'You silly man! Oh, you dear blind foolish boy! Haven't you known for ages — since the day I first heard you preach at the Murphy Street settlement?'

He crushed her to him in a fierce embrace; her slender body yielded to his touch as he bent over her; and her round arms stole softly across his broad shoulders, around his neck, drawing his dark head to her as he planted hungry kisses on her closed eyes, the column of her throat, the parted petals of her fresh young lips.

'Not alone', she whispered. 'Forever together'.

'Forever', he answered solemnly. 'So help me God'.

The organ music swelled now into a triumphant paean, filling with its exultant melody the vast darkness of the church. And as old Michael cast his heart into the music, the tears flowed unrestrained across his withered cheeks, but smiling happily through his tears, as dimly through his old eyes he saw the two young figures enacting again the age-old tale of youth and love, he murmured,

'I am the resurrection and the life, Alpha and Omega, the first and the last, the beginning and the end'.

The stereotyped romantic postures and emotions make for a mechanical idealism. Eugene, to the degree that he is involved with this literature, is in a very real sense 'entombed' — comically lifeless. The comedy is heightened by the fact that Wolfe has endowed Eugene with so much vitality, the element of discrepancy again. This part of *Look Homeward, Angel,* therefore, evinces the two ingredients that Bergson insists must be present in the truly comic moment: a sense of the elasticity, the livingness of life (Eugene's established vitality), and the mechanical (the clichés of his reading).

Samuel Beckett provides more sophisticated examples. In his novel, *Molloy,* Beckett juxtaposes implausible but irrepressible vitality and clichéd expectation. Finding ourselves in a forest, like Beckett's tattered and disabled protagonist, and aware of our Western cultural traditions we might expect to hear Wagner's forest murmurs. Nothing of the kind in the world according to Beckett, no Wagnerian rustlings, no wood-bird to guide this unlikely Siegfried to the perfect woman in a magic circle of protecting fire. The comic absurdity is Molloy's inappropriately cultivated expectation of horn and huntsman. Nothing doing, but from time to time, something decidedly incongruous:

> But before I go on, a word about the forest murmurs. It was in vain I listened, I could hear nothing of the kind. But rather, with much goodwill and a little imagination, at long intervals a distant gong. A horn goes well with the forest, you expect it. It is the huntsman. But a gong! Even a tom-tom, at a pinch, would not have shocked me. But a gong! It was mortifying, to have been looking forward to the celebrated murmurs if to nothing else, and to succeed only in hearing, at long intervals, in the far distance, a gong.

The two Bergsonian ingredients of vitality and mechanism are richly present in the famous opening words of *Twelfth Night*:

> *Duke*: If music be the food of love, play on,
> Give me excess of it, that, surfeiting,
> The appetite may sicken and so die. —
> That strain again. It had a dying fall;
> O, it came o'er my ear like the sweet sound
> That breathes upon a bank of violets,
> Stealing, and giving odour. Enough, no more.
> 'Tis not so sweet now as it was before.
> O spirit of love, how quick and fresh art thou,
> That, notwithstanding thy capacity,
> Receiveth as the sea. Nought enters there,
> Of what validity and pitch soe'er,
> But falls into abatement and low price
> Even in a minute. So full of shapes is fancy
> That it alone is high fantastical.
> *Curio*: Will you go hunt, my lord?
> *Duke*: What, Curio?
> *Curio*: The hart.

Two things happen here. Shakespeare means us to feel how rich it must be to live in such a way as to be granted images like this — what rich emotional life. He also intends us to exclaim, 'How corny' — as corny as Eugene Gant's pulp romances in Thomas Wolfe's novel. Orsino's poetic balloon is pricked by Curio's prosaic, 'Will you go hunt, my lord?' and the subsequent pun on 'heart'. We are not only intended to envy such emotional richness, but also to think, here is the old romantic lover in all his formulaic excess. In *A Midsummer Night's Dream* Theseus wraps up Shakespearean comedy in his juxtaposition of 'the lunatic, the lover, and the poet'.

Three scenes in *The Merchant of Venice* show us the true nature of Shylock. The first, I,iii, presents his indignation and reveals its quality; the court scene, IV,i, shows him to be an incarnation of malevolence. But the middle scene, between Shylock and Tubal, III,i, exposes Shylock as a Bergsonian object. His first words in I,iii mark his habitual preoccupation:

Shylock: Three thousand ducats — well.

A few lines later he observes:

Shylock: Antonio is a good man.
Bassanio: Have you heard any imputation to the contrary?
Shylock: Ho no, no, no, no! My meaning in saying he is a good man is to have you understand me that he is sufficient.

'Good' is a financial word for Shylock: Antonio is 'good' for 3,000 ducats. Shakespeare gives Shylock the habit of attributing to other people vices which are his own: 'How like a fawning publican he looks', he says of Antonio:

I hate him for he is a Christian;
But more, for that in low simplicity
He lends out money gratis and brings down
The rate of usance here with us in Venice.

Antonio's art of generosity makes him more hateful to Shylock than his Christianity. This is the real Shylock speaking, the usurer who interprets 'good' in terms of money and who hates Antonio because he doesn't lend at an extortionate rate of interest. *The Merchant of Venice* is based on the antithesis of gold and silver against love and friendship, and Shylock acts as a machine under the control of his own greed for gold and silver. He is a truly comic figure, a Bergsonian character who has relinquished his freedom to become the plaything of the mechanical law of avarice. He is impelled by the law of avarice to confuse money with living beings: 'My daughter!' he wails, 'O my ducats! Justice! the law! my ducats and my daughter!' (II,viii). No wonder he's mocked by the youth of the town. His house is a house of death: no wonder his daughter leaves it.

The sympathy we are tempted to feel for Shylock enhances the portrayal of a man acting as a machine. Shakespeare puts the mechanism of Shylock into a context of '*le vivant*', and those parts of the play in which we feel the shadow of humanity in Shylock serve to accentuate his machine-like quality. His remark to Tubal, for instance, about the ring Jessica has given away for a monkey:

> *Shylock*: Out upon her! Thou torturest me, Tubal.
> It was my turquoise; I had it of Leah
> when I was a bachelor.
>
> (III, i)

This gives us a sudden glimpse of Shylock when betrothed, a human Shylock in contrast with the avaricious automaton he has become.

What about Shylock's great 'moral issue' speech in III,i — 'Hath not a Jew eyes? Hath not a Jew hands, organs, dimensions, senses, affections, passions?' You may argue that here if nowhere else he is speaking for the oppressed minority. Yet these are dramatic words spoken as a plea for humane treatment by a man who violates the humane. Further, the scene in which he speaks these words is the one in which he is most vividly a comic character. Through Tubal Shakespeare manipulates Shylock like a puppet. Tubal tells Shylock the report of Antonio's losses and teases him into cries of joy; then a flick of the dialogue, mentioning Jessica's spending four-score ducats in one night in Genoa, sends him crashing to despair. Through Tubal Shakespeare plays with Shylock the machine and demonstrates that greed is the machine's *modus operandi*.

Shylock exploits his Jewishness in an attempt to explain away his hatred of Antonio by giving it biblical justification. When he says, 'Sufferance is the badge of all our tribe' he is dishonestly, though craftily, seeking moral shelter behind a general truth. It's not Shylock the Jew who has suffered but those Christians who have been lured by him to destruction. In III,iii Antonio says:

> He seeks my life. His reason well I know:
> I oft delivered from his forfeitures
> Many that have at times made moan to me.
> Therefore he hates me.

Shylock harps on his Jewishness because he is trying to rationalise his hatred of Antonio away from its true motivation to elevate it to a moral principle. If we allow our sympathies to rush out to an oppressed Jew we are being taken in, and instead of seeing a man who acts as a machine we are responding as a mechanical audience.

On the level of plot, the form of *A Midsummer Night's Dream* accords with the medieval definition of comedy, the movement from woe to weal. By the law of Athens, if Hermia won't accept the lover of her father's choice, the alternative is death or its Elizabethan surrogate, 'the livery of a nun'. The shadow may be only nominal, but it's there and the play moves from potential woe, through real confusion, to its happy ending. Two sets of lovers are opposed to the world, to the authority of father and state, and the end of the play, reached through the agency of the love-juice, is the reconciliation of the lovers and the world. So the last Act consists of an amateur theatrical show in which the lovers sit side by side with authority and share laughter at a play about romantic love. The device of the love-juice is Shakespeare's method of high-lighting the capriciousness of romantic love, and there is nothing more Shakespeareanly comic than the symmetrical change of partners — passion and mechanism brought together. Shakespeare is guying romantic love from the standpoint of Theseus, yet Theseus himself is undermined because he mechanically substitutes law for the living fact of human love, 'being over-full of self-affairs' to bother with the living issue. In spite of his protestation, 'Love, therefore, and tongue-tied simplicity/ In least speak most, to my capacity', he has shown little in the way of real concern for love in Act I — apart, that is, from his own; and he took his Hippolyta by storm:

> Hippolyta, I wooed thee with my sword,
> And won thy love doing thee injuries;
> But I will wed thee in another key,
> With pomp, with triumph, and with revelling.

Perhaps Theseus's technique of courtship explains why, backing father Egeus, he is so out of sympathy with the knacks and nosegays of Lysander. The war veteran has little time for the devotee of flower power. But Theseus's practicality aligns him with the rude mechanicals: he is an upper-class Bottom, and if we laugh at the lovers from the viewpoint of practicality, then that viewpoint itself becomes a comic spectacle as Bottom and the mechanicals show worldly practicality running away with itself.

Of course Shakespeare uses comedy to realise serious issues. His method in *Measure for Measure* is the juxtaposition of a number of bits of life each claiming to be the whole. Against a natural way of behaving there must be law: appetite must be regulated. Accordingly, there are two embodiments of rigorous law: the austere Puritanism of Angelo and the chastity of Isabella. The course of the play puts both Angelo and Isabella into corners where their laws are untenable, thus exposing their inelasticity, their mechanical adherence to rigid absolutes. Dickens's novels teem with caricature mechanisms in the service of social satire. In the twentieth century mechanism is the butt of Mikhail Bulgakov's mockery in his masterpiece, *The Master and Margarita*. Bulgakov's satire of life in Soviet era Moscow is deadly serious, but he uses the devices of comedy as well as magic realism to make his points against atheism and the corruptions of Stalinist bureaucracy.

No play more clearly illustrates all the levels of Shakespeare's comedy than *Much Ado About Nothing*. The plan of the play is based on three different modes of behaviour, three different levels of awareness, or three different worlds. There is, firstly, the enamelled world of conventional chivalry, of social manners. Chief inhabitants of this world are Don Pedro, Claudio, Leonato and Hero. Secondly, there is the world of Beatrice and Benedick who are determined to stand outside the conventional proprieties. And thirdly, there is the woolly world of Dogberry: low, confused, a model of sublime immunity to sense. The main contrast is between the suave behaviour of Leonato, Don Pedro and Claudio and the sparring between Beatrice and Benedick.

It's obvious that Claudio behaves mechanically, first as a man in love with the role of lover, later as the lover wronged. The course of the play educates him from being a poseur into true loving. But if Claudio takes his behaviour off the peg, Beatrice and Benedick are determined that theirs shall be off the cuff. It's clear that they are all but in love with each other from the start. Beatrice's first words are a question that indicates real curiosity under cover of scorn, and we sense the instant response of their personalities to each other. Benedick has had time for only four lines before Beatrice feels compelled to launch her first dart:

> *Beatrice*: I wonder that you will still be talking, Signior Benedick. Nobody marks you.
>
> *Benedick*: What, my dear Lady Disdain! are you yet living?
>
> (I, i)

Beatrice openly contradicts herself for she marks Benedick all too closely. By the same token, Benedick's words turn in on themselves — she *is* his 'dear Lady Disdain'. Though not yet a marriage, this is already the engagement of true minds and the abiding interest of the play is the way in which impediments are dissolved. As against the conventional, social behaviour of Don Pedro and company, Beatrice and Benedick are determined to remain individuals: they will not be pressed into marriage and out of themselves. Benedick will have nothing to do with marriage, a situation in which one has, at best, only partial control: there is no danger of a bachelor's becoming a cuckold. Yet for all his resolution, he has 'fallen from his faith' as he excuses his inconsistency to himself: 'No, the world must be peopled. When I said I would die a bachelor, I did not think I should live till I were married'. But if we examine his soliloquy after the exit of Don Pedro, Leonato and Claudio, their gulling successful, we see that this bit of sophistry comes at the end of a speech in which he tries to persuade himself that he has taken the decision to love Beatrice, that he is still in control, with all his wits about him. This is why we find the speech comic. They have, of course, both lost control and surrendered it to Cupid and the sexual puppeteers of Messina.

So, too, Beatrice is resolved to maintain her free vitality as an individual against the forms of society. She will not be mastered by any man: 'Would it not grieve a woman to be overmastered with a piece of valiant dust? to make an account of her life to a clod of wayward marl?' (II,i) Even when she has been tricked by the conversation between Hero and Ursula, she deludes herself into believing that she still holds her own strings:

> *Beatrice*:... Benedick, love on; I will requite thee,
> Taming my wild heart to thy loving hand.
> If thou dost love, my kindness shall incite thee
> To bind our loves up in a holy band;
> (III,i)

Thus Shakespeare allows Benedick and Beatrice to build themselves up in their vaunted independence and self-sufficiency before their comic Nemesis overtakes them. Bergson points out that we laugh most when we are reminded of the livingness of life contrasted with some habit. Accordingly, in *Much Ado About Nothing*, we laugh most of all at the manipulation of Beatrice and Benedick: we laugh most of all when the two most alive characters in the play take the infection and fall in with the Messinian habit of deception and self-deception, reduced from their flashing vitality to a pair of mechanicals.

There is truly comic paradox even in Act IV, scene i where concern for Hero makes detachment impossible for Beatrice and where she scores her supreme victory over Benedick in making him promise to fight a duel with Claudio, for Beatrice and Benedick have refused above all to dwindle into stock romantic lovers. The first stage of their comic Nemesis is their gulling; the second stage is in this scene in which they sink into convention. Benedick cries: 'Come, bid me do anything for thee', and Beatrice answers, 'Kill Claudio'. From being individuals vibrant with independent life, these two fall into the most blatant clichés of the romantic situation. While they are at their most involved they are at their most stereotyped. 'O God, that I were a man! I would eat his heart in the market place', cries Beatrice with fine romantic excess. It's the old routine: the mechanical knight-lady cliché imposed on the living issue.

Language ought to be a free, unpredictable mirror of an elastic mind. When we have stiffness in words we have material for laughter. Like Claudio's language on a different level, Dogberry's is made up of clichés, but clichés he gets wrong. His language is not free and alive, but mechanical: 'Comparisons', he says, enunciating a cliché — but the cliché falls flat on its face — 'are odorous'. W. H. Auden points out that 'Words are man-made things which men use, not persons with a will and consciousness of their own'; but Dogberry's words have more will and consciousness than Dogberry. He is mastered by his language, and his language makes him say what he doesn't mean. Lawrence Durrell plays with this kind of linguistic anarchy in his story 'Frying the Flag' from *Esprit De Corps — Sketches from Diplomatic Life*. The story tells of a newspaper, the Central Balkan Herald, gloriously mis-edited by a pair of elderly spinsters, Bessie and Enid Grope. We are treated to examples of the paper's flair for misprints in its headlines:

WEDDING BULLS RING OUT FOR PRINCESS
QUEEN OF HOLLAND GIVES PANTY FOR EX-SERVICE MEN
BRITAIN'S NEW FLYING-GOAT

We don't laugh merely at the absurdity of substituting Bulls for Bells, Panty for Party, Goat for Boat, but at the ludicrous possibilities suggested. So when Dogberry says to Borachio: 'O villain! thou wilt be condemned into everlasting redemption for this', we laugh because he should have said 'damnation', we laugh at the linguistic confusion, the inanity; but we also laugh at the crazy sense the confusion makes. There is the diabolic notion that Heaven might be something to be 'condemned to'. It's the notion considered by Moran in Beckett's *Molloy*: 'Might not the beatific vision become a source of boredom in the long run?' Again Dogberry's language obviously has more will or consciousness than he has in III,iii:

Dogberry (addressing the Watch): First who think you the most desertless man to be constable.

and then, to neighbour Seacoal: You are thought here to be the most senseless and fit man for the constable of the watch.

Dogberry's language has accurately defined the gentlemen of the Watch — to be a fit member one must be desertless, senseless. Stupidity is the criterion of worthiness. Dogberry is at the mercy of his language just as our self-important, Bergsonian personage was at the mercy of physics and a banana skin. His language, of its own volition, tells the truth about him and his companions. In Act III,v Dogberry says to Leonato:

Goodman Verges, sir, speaks a little off the matter — an old man, sir, and his wits are not so blunt, as God help I would desire they were.

In other words, Verges is not perhaps quite stupid enough to take his rightful place among his fellow-fools. Dogberry looks down on him from the height of his superior foolishness. Truth breaks out again in the comic irony of language when, in IV,ii Dogberry asks: 'Is our whole dissembly appeared?' 'Dissembly' perfectly defines this parcel of fools. So an ingredient in our laughter at Dogberry's linguistic nosedives is our seeing the misguided sense in the words.

The play moves through its confusions, its momentary woes to end in weal. It illustrates the triumph of life over ingredients in life that try to take over. And it enacts the triumph of love over rejections of love (Beatrice and Benedick's initial rejections, and the formal rejection of love in the church scene). The last words of the play are those of Benedick, the all-but married man, to the musicians: 'Strike up, pipers!' and the curtain falls on a communal dance, signifying the achieved harmony. Or, as Eliot puts it in 'East Coker':

The association of man and woman
In daunsinge, signifying matrimonie —
A dignified and commodious sacrament.
Two and two, necessarye coniunction,
Holding eche other by the hand or the arm
Which betokeneth concorde.

In the final dance, before the 'necessarye coniunction' of Hero and Claudio, and Beatrice and Benedick, we applaud the concord which has supplanted confusion. The vision with which Shakespeare leaves us is endorsed by the reverential view of comedy expressed by Kipling in his poem, 'The Necessitarian':

Yet, it must be, on wayside jape
The selfsame Power bestows
The selfsame power as went to shape
His Planet or His Rose.

The scene is Western Kentucky University at Bowling Green (Motto: 'The Spirit Makes the Master'). It's 26th June 1969, approximately 3.20 p.m. I've finished speaking about Shakespearean comedy to a full auditorium and question time has been lively. In his introduction to my talk the 'Moderator' has remarked, to my acute embarrassment, that 'a literary love for the bard' has led me 'to investigate the background of Shakespeare and turn out a thesis of a sort for his type of comedy'. Ouch. Just as he is about to bring proceedings to a close, another hand goes up. A lady at the back of the hall stands and clears her throat with intent. My thesis-of-a-sort may be in some danger.

'Doctor-Professor, Mr Walker, sir', she begins, a lady clearly steeped in Southern courtesies, 'I have so much enjoyed your most enlightening appraisal of William Shakespeare's charming comedies'. She pauses.

'Thank you, madam. You are very kind'.

'May I ask you, Professor, a question about that beautiful comedy, *A Midsummer Night's Dream*?'

'Certainly, yes, please do'.

'You were telling us today about the fascinating thoughts regarding comedy put forward by Mr Henry Bergson?'

'Yes, indeed'.

'And I believe Mr Bergson had thoughts about the mechanical?'

'Quite right'.

'Well, Professor-Doctor, I noticed in *A Midsummer Night's Dream* that William Shakespeare calls some of his delightfully amusing characters *rude mechanicals*?'

'Yes, that's what Puck calls them when he's telling Oberon how he gave Bottom an ass's head'.

'Professor, this is a most interesting coincidence. Do you believe that William Shakespeare **read** Mr Bergson?'

This time the pause is mine. Like the hero in Eugene Gant's awful romance, I struggle for mastery of my feelings.

'Thank you. It's an interesting idea, madam', I reply. 'Unfortunately, I'm afraid, chronology is against it'.

Mercifully, nobody laughs.

8. Eyes

A letter nearly a hundred years old. My mother and her sisters attended Woodside School in Glasgow. The letter dated 18th June 1914 is to my grandmother from one of the teachers. My grandmother had written to the teacher thanking her for kindnesses to her girls.

Dear Mrs Mitchell,

Thanks very much for your kind note and good wishes for the holiday.

I have been so sorry for Nora, as she has suffered greatly by having those headaches so often. I just trust the new treatment may be perfectly successful. She is an exceedingly clever girl and so kind and helpful. I hope you will pardon me saying so but I cannot help remarking on the very admirable manner in which you train your girls. They are so strong mentally and physically and so self-reliant, quite fearless in expressing their opinions yet without a trace of forwardness. I must say it has been a great pleasure to have had Nora. Teachers do appreciate girls of the Mitchell type!

Trusting you may have a very pleasant holiday,

Believe me

Yours sincerely,

Jessie J. Hendry

Whatever the new treatment for her eyes amounted to it involved taking Nora out of school at age eleven. Reading was forbidden. Four years later her diary for 1918 records regular, often disabling headaches. Her myopia was progressive. She became the family's chief housekeeper, serving breakfast, making up the fire, baking, shopping. She ends every entry in her diary with 'Tra-la!' The headaches couldn't keep her down, neither could the housework.

She was always a non-conformist, often impish. On my way home from school one day I met her carrying three shopping bags, one in each hand and a third in her teeth. Pretentiousness in people used to give her fits of giggles. She'd try to keep a straight face while shaking internally, and usually turned scarlet before extricating herself from the situation. On her birthday one year the phone rang early in the morning. Blithely assuming a call from a well-wisher, she picked up the phone and sang, 'This is my lovely day...' She wasn't the least fazed when the caller turned out to be the coal man, ringing to say his deliveries were running late.

Her father was one of 21 passengers killed in the Elliot Junction railway disaster near Arbroath in December 1906, and in May 1917 her twenty-three year-old brother, Marshall, was reported missing in action with the Scottish Rifles on the Salonika Front. For missing read killed. Nora and her older sisters, Mary and Jessie, were brought up by their resourceful mother, according to legend largely on porridge, semolina and practical jokes. Money was very tight. Marshall wrote in his last letter from the front on 4th May 1917: 'Nora must continue with her swimming at the baths, for the exercise will do her an infinite amount of good in every way'. Whatever good the swimming did her, it didn't improve the eyesight. She minded babies, took a course in high-class cookery and at twenty-four set herself up as what used to be called an elocution teacher. There's a 1926 newspaper advertisement in which 'Nora K. Mitchell begs to intimate the opening of her studio for VOICE CULTURE'. Offerings include 'Elocution, Voice Production, Dramatic Instruction'. She helped people with speech impediments and other voice problems. For example, she might be approached by a young teacher with a stutter or a budding minister of the Presbyterian Church who lacked confidence about projecting his voice when preaching a sermon. One of her pupils was the Scottish actress-writer, Molly Weir, who wrote about her in *Best Foot Forward*, the second volume of her autobiography, as 'this beloved teacher':

> Beautifully dressed, with soft brown wavy hair, rosy cheeks, good teeth, and, best of all, a lovely voice. I had expected a good voice, of course, but this was a deep, warm, carrying voice which sent tingles down my spine...Oh, if only I could learn to speak like Miss Mitchell...I began to respect my mother's values when she used the words, 'She's a real lady'.

She embarked on a short career as actress and, in a small way, a pioneer of Scottish Broadcasting. She belonged to a group of performers – a concert party for radio – called 'The Radioptimists', broadcasting from Belfast, Newcastle and Dundee as well as Glasgow. In 1928 they gave what may have been the first outside broadcast in Scotland from a houseboat on Loch Lomond. Other members or associates of the troupe were Martyn Webster who went on to produce the BBC's 'Paul Temple' detective series and David McCallum who became Sir Thomas Beecham's leader in the Royal Philharmonic Orchestra. A guest artist was Tommy Handley with the wartime fame of ITMA still to come. He christened my mother 'Wee Nora', which stuck, and showed the performers something new in radio technique at that time by standing close to the box-shaped microphone and speaking into it very quietly.

In 1933, after a well-reviewed portrayal of the name part in Somerset Maugham's *Lady Frederick* and a successful film test, she gave up her career and her name in favour of Harold Walker, a Chartered Accountant of Yorkshire origin who went to Scotland at the age of twelve and had the intelligence to stay there.

My mother, Nora Kennedy Mitchell or Walker

I inherited her myopia and the headaches. For my first five years everything was foggy. People were blurs with smells and voices. Of course I didn't know my world was foggier than other people's, but wondered why everyone else navigated with such confidence. Why didn't they bump into things like me?

'Look where you're going', my parents said.

On the way home from my first day of school with Peter from next door he stopped and waved.

'Who are you waving to?' I said.

'Look over there, it's your mother'.

My mother was wearing a coat in bright green and white checks. I hadn't seen it. Grown-up talk began about my eyesight. I tripped on the steps at our front door and split my forehead. More talk, but mainly about my clumsiness. My father took me fishing. When he watched me cast a Greenwell's Glory into reeds instead of to the side of them where the trout lay he decided I couldn't see well enough to do important things and an appointment was made with Dr Garrow, oculist. His methods were old school, which meant that he under-corrected short sight in the belief that this would keep the eyes making an effort, encouraging them to grow stronger. Full correction would result in lazy eyes. The fog lifted a little, but my navigation still left much to be desired.

A jaunt to Edinburgh with my mother was intended as a treat. First the Zoo, then we'd visit the Castle. We worked our way slowly from the Aquarium to the monkey cages. Children were feeding the perky little animals. A monkey hanging on the fence accepted my offer of fruit gums. Another monkey was jealous, shot its hands through the fence and snatched my glasses. Without the glasses my limited vision meant I missed the rest of the action, but mother said the thief tried to put on the glasses. She succeeded in grabbing an arm and might have retrieved the glasses if astonished onlookers had helped her, but all they did was laugh while the monkey bit her thumb and she was forced to let go. Darting to the back of the cage the monkey broke the glasses across its leg and tossed the pieces over a shoulder. There were no keepers in sight. When we reached the exit and reported the incident the attendant insisted on dressing mother's thumb. Apparently the bite was poisonous. We abandoned the Castle and Edinburgh, now for me, thanks to monkey tricks, next to invisible.

When Dr Garrow retired I was taken to an eminent new specialist with the title, 'The Queen's Eye Specialist in Scotland'.

He gave me fuller correction, a more detailed world and a brief surge of new confidence before putting the boot in. He asked me what I wanted to be when I grew up. I wanted to be a doctor.

'That's out of the question', he said. 'You'll be blind by the time you're twenty. Think of something you can do when you can't see. Be a grocer'.

My new lenses were thick, like milk-bottle bottoms and my eyes looked tiny through them, like a pig's. The frames had to be thick, too, to carry the weight of the lenses. Boys at school called me 'Piggy', 'Specky' or 'Four Eyes'. Some teachers were kind, others contemptuous. The English teacher was acid. He was commenting on Polonius's advice to Laertes in Act I of *Hamlet*:

> Costly thy habit as thy purse can buy,
> But not expressed in fancy; rich, not gaudy;
> For the apparel oft proclaims the man.

This led to a discussion about the relation between appearance and character.

'For example', he said, 'I distrust a person who wears spectacles with heavy frames'.

Heads turned to stare at me. I kept my eyes down on my desk and tried not to breathe.

'An attempt to add an air of distinction to an otherwise featureless face', he said.

The class sniggered.

When it was time to learn about rugby the games master ordered me off the field. I couldn't see the difference between my side and the opposition and got in everybody's way. Nor was I to be allowed cricket. The ball might smash my glasses; the school couldn't take responsibility.

Mr Adams, the music teacher, came to my rescue. He had already won my gratitude for ever by introducing me to the music of Sibelius, now I was even more indebted to him. Realising I'd be alone and aimless when the other boys were at their sports, he asked me if I'd like to spend the free time developing my music appreciation. Keys for the gramophone room would be mine every sports day, with access to the school's sizeable collection of classical music records. The weekly day of limbo was transformed into pure delight. Mozart's *Jupiter* Symphony, Beethoven's

8th, Tchaikovsky's *Romeo and Juliet Fantasy Overture*, Elgar's *Cockaigne* and *Introduction and Allegro*, Sibelius's *Karelia Suite*. Soon I knew all the titles in the collection and could plan my solitary concerts in advance.

The Queen's Eye Specialist in Scotland said that while waiting to go blind I should keep my eyes closed as much as possible. A limit was put on reading. So my growing appetite for books would need to be satisfied by stealth. I had no wish to vex my anxious parents by openly disobeying doctor's orders, so I acquired a stout torch with a strong beam. In bed, knees up to make the sheets into a tent, I read voraciously by torchlight in defiance of eye-strain headaches and whatever other damage I might be doing. Jeffery Farnol and Ian Hay from my father's bookshelf. All the Sherlock Holmes novels and short stories as well as Conan Doyle's *Tales of Pirates* – renowned for Captain Sharkey, of the 20-gun pirate barque, *Happy Delivery*, a man of grim pleasantries and inflexible ferocity – *Tales of Blue Water, Tales of Terror, Tales of Twilight and the Unseen*. Edgar Wallace for *Sanders of the River, The Four Just Men* and *The Admirable Carfew*. Most of John Buchan and Kipling's *Plain Tales from the Hills*. New batteries required for the torch. Robert Louis Stevenson. *The Count of Monte Cristo*. Guy de Maupassant. Simenon. Somerset Maugham. Raymond Chandler. The outer limits of my world were selling programmes for the Saturday concerts of the Scottish National Orchestra at St Andrew's Halls in town and, courtesy of my BBC Aunt Mary, performances in their Glasgow studio by the BBC Scottish Orchestra under their conductor, Ian Whyte, my boyhood hero. Core reality was the school music room and my literary tent of nocturnal rebellion, but suddenly school was over and the question loomed: what next?

After school the orthodox middle-class destination was university. It was also the way to turn a passion for books into a degree and a meal-ticket. I psyched myself into the enrolment hall at the University of Glasgow and signed on for English Literature. The Queen's Eye Specialist was wrong. I didn't become a grocer and I didn't go blind. Progression of the myopia slowed down and headaches were alleviated by Aunt Jessie's typing my lecture notes on green paper. And I used green ink. Green was said to be less taxing on eyes. There was a chance meeting between my father and the eminent oculist.

'Oh yes, your son', said the eminence, 'he was one of my mistakes'.

9. Being Kinder to Ahab

Lassie for a collie, Pooh or Paddington for a bear, Bambi for a deer and Moby-Dick for a whale; but how many know the book that made Melville's whale everybody's whale? Not so many, outside the academy. It's not surprising. The language is richer than we're accustomed to, especially when Ahab's doing the talking; there are many digressions, and much critical discussion of the novel cheats it of its story, making it a symbolic treatise or a weighty critique of American Transcendentalism. Flesh and blood disappear into a conspiracy of themes. We hear about the book's formal idiosyncrasies or Melville-Ahab's philosophical quarrel with God, and human concerns are lost in the metaphysical implications of cetology. Ahab is explained away. Yet the book begins with the warmth of human contact, a man speaking to men, to the reader, in the button-holing immediacy of 'Call me Ishmael', and Ahab's godlike godlessness commands the imagination only because he is human before he is anything else. Perhaps, then, we should abandon readings which reduce the book to a grid of symbols or a philosophical essay on the themes of solipsism and ambiguity. Perhaps we should put the characters back in place, returning in particular to Ahab himself, looking again at his predicament and his torment, the anguish of his consciousness and his universality. He is, after all, one of us.

It's the force of his personality that empowers him to take the men of the *Pequod* with him, and that power is coincident with his anguish. The worthiness of conservationists and subscribers to Greenpeace can swing the interpretative beam too far in favour of the enigmatic whale, to the disadvantage of the *Pequod*'s all-too-human captain. Compared to the madly driven energy of Ahab, isn't Ishmael's pallid appeal that of the *voyeur* who watches, rather than plays the game? Of course Ishmael performs the function of narrator, but he takes to sea because of his 'hypos', to drive off the spleen and get through the 'damp, drizzly November' in his soul. He needs a vacation, a change of scene. Ahab roars off into the unknown because he is a consciousness in pain, demoniacally possessed by the compulsion to avenge himself on the creature who dismasted him. Cool Hand Luke signs on for a trip with King

Lear; Luke survives, but it's surely the King who should bear our hearts away.

Ishmael moves from alienation to redemption, democracy, perception, balance and sole survival. What, then, of Ahab, who moves from alienation to monomania, dictatorship and death? Before he dies, we may say, he creates himself, an example of Emerson's self-reliance gone mad. Can we feel nobility here? Consider the proposition that Ahab's obsession degenerates into a justification for moulding the crew of the *Pequod* to his own diabolical will as Napoleon and Hitler, Stalin and Mao Zedong moulded armies and nations. It's easy to judge Ahab a sinner who sacrifices others for the sake of vengeance on the whale, and to deplore the egotism by which he interprets creation solely in terms of personal experience. But he has no ease, no *dacha*, no Eagle's Nest, no *Berchtesgaden*. The evident pain of his voyage to self-destruction might enjoin us to more sympathy than he often gets. Let's try to understand him as a specific yet representative consciousness, and then consider to what extent we should be moved by him. So, let's read the wonderful book again.

In 'The Quarter-Deck' chapter Ahab first gives us his conception of the whale: 'That inscrutable thing is chiefly what I hate'. From the beginning it's clear that Ahab is ungodly. His name alone establishes this. The name was applied to two Old Testament characters, one a false prophet, the other the seventh king of Israel who 'did evil in the sight of the Lord above all that were befor' him' and 'took to wife Jezebel the daughter of Ethbaal, king the Zidonians, and went and served Baal, and worshipped ' Elijah the Tishbite was the prophet who thrice warned Kir – hence the parallel in 'The Prophet'. In the all-male cas' *Dick* Fedallah is to Captain Ahab what Jezebel was inciting him to evil. King Ahab was defeated in ba' Ahab is defeated in his battle with the whale since 'the old squaw Tistig, at Gayhead said th somehow prove prophetic'. The Captain, h prophecies and omens whether heavenly the first lowering), human (the encou' the *Jeroboam*), or marine (the grea' himself the 'Fate's lieutenant' he r fatality. There's a kind of heroic : Captain Peleg tells Ishmael, 'a gran.

Towards the end of 'The Sermon' Father Mapple says: 'Delight, – top-gallant delight is to him who acknowledges no law or lord, but the Lord his God, and is only a patriot to heaven'. Ahab is without delight. Father Mapple had said earlier: 'And if we obey God, we must disobey ourselves; and it is in this disobeying ourselves, wherein the hardness of obeying God consists'. Ahab obeys only himself; yet this becomes obedience to God simply because, as the *Pequod* draws nearer in time and space to the climactic chase, Ahab and God become synonymous in the eyes of Ahab. This is the extent of his monomania, his blasphemy ritualised in the dedication ceremony of 'The Quarter-Deck'. Notice the irony of the *Pequod*'s setting out on its 'heaven-insulting purpose' on Christmas Day; the description of Ahab as a martyr, 'a man cut away from the stake'; his response to irresolute Starbuck: 'There is one God that is Lord over the earth, and one Captain that is Lord over the *Pequod*'. Remember the daring of his apostrophe to 'the clear spirit of fire' in 'The Candles':

> I own thy speechless, placeless power; but to the last gasp of my earthquake life will dispute its unconditional, unintegral mastery in me. In the midst of the personified impersonal, a personality stands here.

Intent on establishing among his crew 'that certain sultanism of his brain' he relinquishes given modes of navigation, smashing the quadrant, virtually abandoning the first log and line and accepting the turning of the compass by creating a new one: 'I crush the quadrant, the thunder turns the needles, and now the mad sea parts the log-line. But Ahab can mend all'. Mighty Ahab, indeed, but devilish Ahab too, for he dares God out of His heaven, and his assumption of Godhead is explicit in 'The Quarter-Deck': 'I'd strike the sun if it insulted me...Who's over me?'. The satanic quality of his presumption reaches a new climax in 'The Forge'. In a second ritual, like a Black Mass, he consecrates his newly-fashioned harpoon in the heathen blood of Tashtego, Queequeg and Daggoo 'Ego non baptizo te in nomine patris, sed in nomine diabili!' – the words of medieval witches in their renunciation of God. Similarly, in 'The Honour and Glory of Whaling', Ishmael enrols himself as a whaleman in an emblazoned fraternity that includes

Perseus and St George, maintaining that the English dragon was a whale. Thus the narrative of the hunt for Moby-Dick is associated with the seminal myth of a hero who, to save others, destroys in single combat the powers of wickedness embodied in an evil monster. But Ahab is exactly the opposite of men like Perseus and St George. Where they were divinely inspired, he pursues a private revenge, self-inspired; where they were saviours of their fellow-men, he enlists his crew in his own ruin. He is a kind of latter-day Prometheus, hurling his defiance at God, yet ultimately bound to the God incarnated in the whale by the harpoon ropes that bind him to Moby-Dick as Prometheus was bound to his rock. The difference, of course, is that the agony of Prometheus arose from his efforts to help mankind, while Ahab would carry mankind down with him to destruction. Yet in his battle with the whale he sees himself as the lordly avenger confronting the tangible shape of evil:

> ... all truth with malice in it; all that cracks the sinews and cakes the brain; all the subtle demonisms of life and thought, all evil to crazy Ahab were visibly personified, and made practically assailable in Moby Dick.

That the demonism which obsesses Ahab does exist in the human situation is beyond doubt. As part of the great Immanence, part of the indwelling truth, God, or over-Soul it shares a central position in Melville's moral world, and, we dare say, in ours; but the fact of demonism is no more the whole truth than the Edenesque absence of 'cares, griefs, troubles and vexations' in Melville's paradisal *Typee* is the whole truth. Ahab's 'torn body and gashed soul [have] bled into one another; and so, interfusing, made him mad', and in his madness he attempts to stand outside human limitation and to wage war on the permanent order of the universe. This is the upper level of his sin, his *hubris*, witness his soliloquy at 'Sunset', following 'The Quarter Deck':

> What I've dared, I've willed; and what I've willed, I'll do! They think me mad – Starbuck does; but I'm demoniac, I am madness maddened! That wild madness that's only calm to comprehend itself! The prophecy was that I should

be dismembered; and – Aye! I lost this leg. I now prophesy that I will dismember my dismemberer. Now, then, be the prophet and the fulfiller one. That's more than ye, ye great gods, ever were.

In 'The Chase — First Day' Moby Dick swims away 'divinely' and is invested with 'a mighty mildness of repose in swiftness'. There is more to the world than demonism and there is more to the whale than malice: there is Whiteness which expresses the intimate relationship between innocence and malignity. In the absolute purity of the whale's whiteness lies its absolute terror. 'It was', says Ishmael, 'the whiteness of the whale that above all things appalled me'. The colour is 'Made the emblem of many touching, noble things – the innocence of brides, the benignity of age'…'in the higher mysteries of the most august religions it has been made the symbol of the divine spotlessness and power'. Yet: 'there lurks an elusive something in the innermost idea of this hue, which strikes more of a panic to the soul than that redness which affrights in blood'. Ishmael cites the terrifying associations whiteness can have: there is the Polar Bear, whose 'irresponsible ferociousness…stands invested in the fleece of celestial innocence and love'; there is the white shark; the repulsion of the Albino man; the White Squall; the pallor of the dead; the desolation of the Antarctic and so on.

For Melville, to see only beauty and beneficence in nature was culpably naïve. He described himself as 'neither pessimist nor optimist', though he confessed to preferring pessimism as 'a counterpoise to the exorbitant hopefulness, juvenile and shallow that makes such a bluster in these days'. Moby-Dick is clearly associated with the Transcendentalists' immanent God, for, according to some superstitious whalemen he is 'not only ubiquitous, but immortal (for immortality is but ubiquity in time.)' And Moby-Dick is Twoness, an incarnation of the fact of polarity – good and evil, beneficence and malignity, with the blessing and curse of his colour. He is both heavenly and infernal rolled into one enormous One, intermingling and indivisible. Ahab divides the One, splits the moral atom and blows himself up.

In his relationship to Moby-Dick, Ahab is like the Narcissus whose legend Melville puts at the core of his book in Chapter One:

...Narcissus, who because he could not grasp the tormenting, mild image he saw in the fountain, plunged into it and was drowned. But that same image, we ourselves see in all rivers and oceans. It is the image of the ungraspable phantom of life; and this is the key to it all.

The parallel between Narcissus and Ahab is made plain in 'The Chase – First Day'. Moby-Dick has sounded. An hour passes. Ahab looks over the side of the *Pequod*, and, like Narcissus, sees the image of himself in the water:

> ...suddenly as he peered down and down into its depths, he profoundly saw a white living spot no bigger than a white weasel, with wonderful celerity uprising, and magnifying as it rose, till it turned, and then there were plainly revealed two long crooked rows of white, glistening teeth, floating up from the undiscoverable bottom. It was Moby Dick's open mouth and scrolled jaw; his vast shadowed bulk still half blending with the blue of the sea.

He has so thoroughly forced the whale out of its ambiguity, out of its expression of fusion, of the doubleness of truth and into the strait-jacket of his own woe that it becomes his reflection. (The way has already been prepared for this by the end of 'The Symphony', where Ahab looks over the side: 'but started at two reflected, fixed eyes in the water there. Fedallah was motionlessly leaning over the same rail'. The Bad Angel has won.)

Even on the last day of the Chase, it's not too late for him to abandon his destructive course. Moby-Dick has run amok among the boats. Swimming out from them, he turns and reveals the torn body of Fedallah, lashed to his flank by the tangle of harpoon lines. Thus, the last prophecy in the book is almost fulfilled. Then, as if giving Ahab a chance to escape from his self-appointed destiny, the whale:

> ... seemed swimming with his utmost velocity, and now only intent upon pursuing his own straight path in the sea.

'Oh! Ahab', cried Starbuck, 'not too late is it, even now, the third day, to desist. See! Moby Dick seeks thee not. It is thou, thou, that madly seekest him!'

But Ahab too consumingly hates the image of himself which is so fixed for him that he cannot see in the whale's swimming away a sign of that other part of Moby-Dick's symbolic value, the bright side, the beneficence, and the whale's remoteness from the personal engagement on which he has postulated his solipsistic enterprise. To the end he will impose himself on the hump of his chosen adversary. Like Narcissus he seeks and finds himself. The discovery kills him.

Moby-Dick is an epic, and it has, in the rescue of Ishmael by the *Rachel*, the traditional happy ending of the epic form. For Dryden *Paradise Lost* failed as an epic because its ending is unhappy. This misreading of Milton's poem arose from Dryden's belief that Satan is the hero. Satan is unsuccessful in *Paradise Lost*, the argument goes, so the ending is unhappy, and the typical, formally expected epic conclusion is therefore absent. Now while I believe this view to be mistaken, there is certainly a good deal in Milton's Satan with which we may be tempted to sympathise. He wouldn't be much of a devil if he couldn't seduce; and there is even more in Ahab to command our sympathies. Ahab is more of a truly tragic figure; he even bears an outward and visible sign of his tragic flaw, what the Greeks would have called his *hamartia*:

> Threading its way out from among his grey hairs, and continuing right down one side of his tawny scorched face and neck, till it disappeared in his clothing, you saw a slender rod-like mark, lividly whitish. It resembled that perpendicular seam sometimes made in the straight, lofty trunk of a great tree, when the upper lightning tearingly darts down it, and without wrenching a single twig, peels and grooves out the bark from top to bottom, ere running off into the soil, leaving the tree still greenly alive, but branded.

Ahab's mark splits him in two, as he insists on splitting into its two components the paradoxical fusion of Moby-Dick. 'Moody stricken Ahab' shows 'a crucifixion in his face; in all the nameless regal dignity of some mighty woe'. Such a figure must appeal to our compassion; we almost grant him his egoism, anything to buoy him up in the predicament he has chosen. There's a reminder of Milton's Satan's 'plain heroic magnitude of mind' in his colossal presumption. In the midst of his iron, he has, as Captain Peleg says of him, 'his humanities'. He has, too, the self-awareness, the capacity for self-analysis of a Shakespeareanly tragic figure. This comes out in his soliloquy in 'Sunset':

> Gifted with the high perception, I lack the low enjoying power; damned, most subtly and most malignantly! damned in the midst of Paradise.

This, then, is wounded, mad Ahab in his anguish of torn body and gashed soul, and it's time for the hard sell. Can we be true to our own 'ambiguity-tolerance' deficiencies and withhold our compassion from him? Do we dare to confront our own egotisms and disavow a man who becomes a slave to his? Are we so lacking in narcissism that we can disconnect from Ahab's? Are we deaf to his primal scream? Are the philosophical claims of the novel so strong and are academic accounts of it so intimidating that they crowd out our sense of this immense, tragic figure, who crucifies himself and all but one of his crew on a failure of perception caused by his refusal to accept the relentless complexity of life? Can he be forgiven for demanding that the world be other than it ambiguously is, for being inconsolable and titanically angry? Have you seen the lapel badge or the greetings card bearing the legend, 'Life's a bitch, then you die'? Dismasted ourselves by the condition of being merely human, would we not rail and storm at the constrictions of the world if we were not so civilised and inhibited? Aesthetically, morally and emotionally, should we not be kinder to Ahab?

10. Jessie

Auntie Jessie was the younger of my mother's two elder sisters. There were rumours of a boyfriend lost in the First World War. If so this would seem to have been her first and last fling. She stayed spinster, guarding her preoccupations with writing and smoking and, from Coronation Day in 1953, television and smoking. She contributed short, whimsical poems to Glasgow newspapers. Her most signal achievement was a story printed in *The People's Friend* on July 7th 1934 under the title 'He Fell in Love at Rothesay Pier'. It was illustrated by a wooden drawing of a brilliantined young man in blazer and tie leaning on a fence while leering at a smitten damsel in a flowered dress. The caption read: 'You look sweet with the sun in your eyes...Good night, dear'. I loved Jessie not just because she took me on holiday to Carnoustie for the thrills of hypothermia by immersion in the North Sea when my parents thought I needed a bit of diversion and they could use a break from me. Not just because she typed my university notes on green paper to help ease my eye strain, but for her combination of sharp sense and blatant sentimentality. She was a keen observer of the ways of children and she could write in Scots with a nifty punch line.

The Fall

Wee feet scliffin' on the flair,
Doon he gaes, my heart is sair
Tae hear the dunt.
I haud my breath – it seems an 'oor –
Will he greet, will he be dour?
Siccan dunt!

Syne he grins, 'O dearie me',
Glowers at his scartit knee,
His stourie claes,
Till his lip, stuck oot a mile
Curls in a douchty smile
An' aff he gaes.

The road is lang an' aften wae,
Ye maun traivel till ye're grey
An' humpy-backit.
Whiles ye canna help but fa',
There's nae shame in that ava!
It's hoo ye tak' it.

Jessie had worked as a secretary before WWII, but when it got serious and we evacuated to the South Side it was decided in plenary session of the family that she would look after Granny and the house, keeping them safe while everyone else worked in the

Jessie with someone else's fish

wider, anxious world, her sister Mary at the BBC, my mother as an elocution and reading teacher and my father in his Ayr and Glasgow accountancy offices. She seemed happy with this arrangement which catered to her writing and taking an interest in her nephew. She was a rare comrade. Many years later, when I lived in the top flat of a Glasgow tenement, attempting to provide for six children on a university lecturer's salary, she would climb the stairs every Saturday morning after she'd done her shopping. She brought comics and sweets for the children and a big packet of toilet rolls. She'd sit for a while, chatting, and smoke a cigarette. Before she left she'd crush a five-pound note into my hand. Meat for the week. Did I ever thank her enough?

She thought seriously about politics and world affairs, leaning to the left. Curiosity took her to Germany in August 1937. She snapped men in Potsdam exchanging the 'Heil Hitler' salute, but she didn't write directly about the War. She noticed how it affected people at home in domestic situations and how, obliquely, it could change lives. She was perceptive without being heavy. So the next object is one of her unpublished short stories. It's about the impact of wartime evacuation. It's slow-moving, soft writing you might say, in need of editing, but there's fluency, a worthy purpose and a telling conclusion. Her big heart's in it, and her fidelity to Scottish ways of feeling.

Aggie's Laddie

In the friendly atmosphere of the village Aggie McMaster stood out like a sore thumb. Hard-faced and close-fisted, she went about her business accepting kindness from no one and giving none. As Dossie Ferguson of the wee shop said, 'I'm willin' tae believe that Aggie's got her guid points but she winna let a buddy see them'.

Then there was the business of Lizzie Chalmers. Aggie and Lizzie had, strangely enough, been good friends and loved the same man. Lizzie had got him. No wonder, for Lizzie was the pretty, gentle type, while Aggie, even as a girl, was determined and awkward although not unhandsome. When Alex Chalmers died, Lizzie, who had never taken to city ways, hankered to come home again and because she was ill at the time instructed her solicitor, for Lizzie was bein [well off], to get her a house in Corbreck.

Well, the man had done his best but when Lizzie came to the tiny house at the head of the Big Brae she found that her one and only neighbour was Aggie McMaster. Lizzie had tried to make friends again but Aggie would have none of it and so they lived, Lizzie pitied by the entire village and Aggie increasingly unpopular.

Then came the War and evacuation.

'I'll not have strange bairns mucking up my house, I tell you'. Aggie faced Mr Todd the schoolmaster who was billeting officer for the village. 'I'm too old for that sort of nonsense'.

'But I'm afraid', replied Mr Todd, 'there's no alternative. You'll only get one child as you've but the one spare room with a single bed in it – and remember, there's a war on'.

'Am I likely to forget it! And what about Lizzie Chalmers? Is she not getting an evacuee?'

'Dr Scott says she's not strong enough to manage a child. She's got a weak heart, you know'.

'More like a weak head', snapped Aggie McMaster.

Lizzie Chalmers watched the boy kicking his heels in Aggie McMaster's back garden.

'What's your name, laddie?' she enquired gently.

'Tam'.

'Are you hungry, Tam?' Aggie had been out all afternoon.

'Aye'.

'Would you like a piece?'

'Aye'.

'Well, come on over and I'll see what I can do for you'.

The boy scrambled over the fence and followed her into the house.

'Sit yourself down'. Lizzie, her thin face alight, fetched bread, butter and jam and a glass of milk.

'There, do you like that?'

'Aye'.

He was about twelve with a thin, red face and fiercely defensive blue eyes. His hair was unkempt and his clothes had seen better days.

When he had finished, Tam wiped his mouth with the back of his hand and got to his feet.

'Let's be friends, Tam. I like boys'. Lizzie held out her hand.

'She', he jerked his thumb towards the cottage next door, 'doesna like ye'.

Lizzie flushed but she met his eyes bravely.

'I know – but can't *we* be friends?'

He shook his rough head and without another word took his leave.

'Oh dear!' Lizzie dropped into a chair and the tears came. 'If only Aggie would forgive and forget. I never ran after Alex, it was he who picked me. And – and I did so want an evacuee'.

Tam soon became notorious in the village. Mr Prosser, who prided himself on his fine apple trees and guarded them jealously, caught Tam red-handed helping himself to his very best apples. Infuriated, he tackled Aggie.

'That laddie of yours', he began angrily.

'He's no laddie of mine', disclaimed Aggie acidly, 'and if he's been up to anything you can deal with him yourself. You're a man aren't you – or aren't you? You can tell anybody else he bothers the same thing', and she slammed the door in his face.

Well, others were bothered and feelings ran high against Aggie and Tam. Lizzie, trying to pour oil on troubled waters, met with no success.

'Whit way d'ye stick up for Aggie?' asked Dossie Ferguson. 'She's no freend o' yours'.

'No', agreed Lizzie with a sigh, 'but I wish she was'.

'Weel', went on Dossie, as she measured rice into a poke, 'I'm kind o' sorry for the laddie tho' he is a wee deil, livin' in that hoose o' Aggie's'.

'Oh, it's a nice house, Dossie', Lizzie said.

'Aye, it's a nice wee hoose but it's no' a hame. Clean as yin o' thae operatin' theyaters and aboot as cheery. She mak's that Tam tak' aff his buits afore he comes ben the hoose on a saft day. Aye, and Mr Todd tells me he hadna muckle o' a life in Glesca, the puir bairn. Lived wi' an aunt wha's a reg'lar besom an' glad to get rid o' him when the war came. I wish you'd had him. You'd hae gotten that queer ticht look aff his wee rid face afore noo'.

'I wish I had, Dossie, but he'll not be friends with me although he eats my pieces'.

'Him and Aggie are a right pair', concluded Dossie Ferguson.

74

But even Lizzie's pieces ceased to be. One day, when she was escorting Tam out of the back door clutching a large scone thickly spread with syrup, she came face to face with her neighbour over the fence that divided their gardens.

'Come over here at once, Tam Henderson, and as for you, Lizzie Chalmers, you've no call to be feeding that boy. He gets all he needs from me'.

'Aggie!' Lizzie Chalmers cried pleadingly, but the other woman had turned her back.

Lizzie had hoped that perhaps the boy might heal the breach between them, might soften Aggie herself. Alas, the contrary had happened. And yet one day she thought she caught a glimpse of something quite different. Tam was going off to school and a cold wind was blowing. From her window Lizzie watched. Suddenly she heard Aggie's hard voice.

'Tam, put on that scarf this minute. I've had enough of coughing and sneezing about the house'.

She held out a woollen scarf and as the boy dourly wrapped it round his neck there was a look on her face, a tenderness one would have called it in anybody but Aggie McMaster.

After the incident of the last piece Aggie was even colder towards Lizzie and often downright rude. Lizzie's slow pride took up arms and she didn't defend Aggie any more when others criticised. Now Aggie stood alone in the village.

Soon after this Dossie Ferguson remarked to Aggie, 'Weel, Aggie McMaster'll nae be bothered with her evacuee muckle longer. Mr Todd telt me this morning that Tam's auntie has died sudden like and Jamieson o' Blains has offered to tak' the laddie for guid. He'll be richt handy on the fairm when he comes on a bit, Jamieson haein' nae bairns o' his own. Aggie'll be weel pleased noo. Nae mair glaur on the kitchen flair and nae extra mooth tae feed'.

'That's right, Dossie', said Lizzie, 'She'll likely start her Christmas cleaning the minute Tam's over the door'.

Lizzie walked home with strange feelings in her heart. Well, Aggie couldn't complain any more, as she had been doing incessantly since Tam came, and they two would settle down in an eternal blackout of bitterness, for somehow she knew that in the boy lay her only hope of breaking down Aggie's resistance to her longing for reunion in friendship. She, Lizzie, had grown fond of Tam despite his dourness. There was something appealing about his lonely little figure and he had a good eye in his head. A little love, she felt, could melt his reserve. Probably his termagant of an aunt had bred a stubborn defensiveness in the boy and damped down any natural instinct to respond to kindness. He had had a hard life, Dossie had said.

'She's an auld sourock is Aggie McMaster. Ma mither says...'

Lizzie stopped dead on the road. The voice came from the little park with the War Memorial. She crept up to the hedge between the road and the park.

'She's no", cried a fierce young voice. Lizzie recognised Tam's. 'Miss McMaster's a bonza wumman. Tak' that'.

There was a scuffle and the sound of blows. Lizzie peered over the hedge. Tam and Willie Rodger, a big bullying boy of fourteen, were swaying back and forward on the gravel path, locked in each other's arms.

The timid little woman, normally terrified of any sort of conflict, found herself smiling. She opened her mouth to expostulate but remained silent. The tough city sparrow was more than holding his own and there was something fine in the sight of the unwanted wee evacuee playing knight to his hard-hearted hostess.

She left them to it and hurried home, panting up the Big Brae. When she saw Mr Todd disappearing into Aggie's door she knew why she had been urged on. With him was big, grim farmer Jamieson of Blains. Aggie would never get Tam back once Jamieson got hold of him. Thinking of that sturdy, battling little figure in the War Memorial park, she kept going. She believed in the look of something like tenderness she had glimpsed in Aggie's eyes, but Aggie would hand the boy over, hiding any qualms she felt, because of her hard pride. Tam, like Aggie herself, had kept his feelings under cover and she would have none of him when he only tholed her like the people in the village.

Even as it was, she might refuse to keep him, but Lizzie decided, suppressing her own *amour propre*, Aggie must have her chance. Aggie and Tam, both. It might make no difference between them, but it just might be Aggie's salvation. Lizzie sped round to her neighbour's back door. Aggie McMaster glowered at the woman she hated.

'What do you want, Lizzie Chalmers? I've Mr Todd and Jamieson of Blains in bye going to take Tam off my hands and I'm busy'.

'Oh, Aggie, don't let him go'.

'What right have you to interfere with me?' Aggie began to shut the door.

'But', cried Lizzie desperately, 'he'll be so unhappy. Tam – Tam likes you so much'.

'Likes me!' Aggie shook herself. 'You're blethering, Lizzie Chalmers. That laddie doesn't care a hoot for anybody', but Lizzie had her attention now.

'No Aggie, you're wrong. As I was coming home I saw him fighting Willie Rodger because he'd called you a – a sourock. Tam gave him a great bash and cried out, "She's no'. Miss McMaster's a bonza woman"'.

Something was happening to Aggie McMaster. Her face took on a queer blurred look.

'Willie's much bigger than Tam, but he was getting the worst of it', Lizzie said.

'Come in, Lizzie', Aggie opened the door wide. Lizzie followed her into the small sitting room where Mr Todd and the farmer were waiting impatiently.

'I've changed my mind', Aggie announced. 'I'm keeping Tam myself'.

'But Miss McMaster', protested the schoolmaster, 'you've been asking us to remove him, day in, day out and you know you only took him under protest. I don't understand. Mr Jamieson here is very anxious...'

'I can't help that', said Aggie. 'He's my laddie. He's just proved it but I doubt if you men would understand. Anyway I'm going to be an auntie to Tam in place of the one he's lost, and I mean for good'.

Mr Todd, baffled, looked first at Aggie, then at Lizzie standing behind her.

'Well, it's beyond me but I sincerely hope it'll be all right'.

'It *will* be all right, Mr Todd', said Lizzie, 'Aggie and I will look after Tam'.

And with disapproving grunts from Mr Jamieson the two men left.

There was a sound at the back door. The two women hurried into the kitchen. Tam came in, his face streaked with dirt and blood from a long scratch on his cheek.

Standing near the door, Lizzie watched Aggie's back stiffen.

'You're late, Tam, and your face is filthy', Aggie said.

'Aye', said Tam, 'Me and Wullie Rodger were playin' in the Park an' I fell'.

Lizzie saw Aggie's back relax and knew the woman had been dreading what Tam might say. She would have kept him, of course, but if the boy had told her the real reason for his battered face something would have been lost between them.

'Come into the scullery and get yourself clean'. Aggie put a hand on his shoulder and Lizzie saw a light in the boy's eyes she'd never seen before. 'There's black pudding for tea'.

'Black puddin'!' cried Tam ecstatically, following Aggie into the scullery.

Lizzie slipped into the tiny hall and left them together.

Sadly she lay in her bed that night and thought of the pair next door. Well, she had given Aggie her chance and she had taken it. Aggie could be trusted now to tell the laddie of his loss and to make him feel secure for the future. All was well with them, but she was left out in the cold. She disliked black pudding but she'd have eaten pounds of it gladly if only Aggie had asked her to stay. That would have been enough. No words were necessary, but it seemed the leopard couldn't change its spots. When she fell asleep her pillow was damp under her cheek.

All next day Lizzie kept indoors. It was cold anyway, she told herself, and it was going to be a dark night with no moon. The winter, stretching ahead with its grim wartime blackouts and fears that compounded the fears of the lonely, was a long tunnel and she lost in it. She shivered as she set the tea table.

There was a knock on her front door. Tam stood on the whitened step.

'She', he jerked his thumb at the house next door, 'she wants you to come to tea'.

'Let me get my hat and coat'. Lizzie was radiant.

'It's no' black puddin' tonight', Tam said as they made their way down one garden path and up the other. 'It's Finnan Haddie'.

'I love Finnan Haddie', Lizzie almost sang.

Aggie was at her door.

'Tam, I've no pepper. Will you run to the shop and get two ounces. Here's a sixpence. The fish'll be ready when you get back'.

Tam sped off.

In the sitting room the table was bounteously set. Lizzie turned to her neighbour. 'I'm so glad to come, Aggie'.

'You would be. I know that now', Aggie held herself once again as stiff as a poker. 'I've been a fool. I've...'

'Oh, Aggie, please ...'

'Let me speak'. She faced the other woman squarely now. 'You see, I – I liked Alex Chalmers a lot – he was the only one I ever did – and when he chose you instead of me it – it was like a slap in the face. Done in public, too, for the whole village had seen me make up to him'. She winced. 'I was aye one to keep myself to myself as you know and as proud as blazes, and when you and Alex went off to Glasgow in what looked to me like a triumphal procession I seemed to sour like milk in thunder'.

Lizzie shook her head sadly.

'I know, I know, I told you I was a fool. When folk spoke kindly to me I thought they were pitying me and I barked back at them. Dossie Ferguson said, "Never mind, Aggie, there's as guid fish in the sea as ever came out of it". Well, that fair tore it'.

It was Lizzie's turn to wince.

'When you came back, a widow, and tried to be friends with me I said to myself, "Lizzie Chalmers is just wanting to gloat". But what you did yesterday opened my eyes. I couldn't have done it. Nobody mean or gloating would have done it – so, if you'll...' It was hard to say.

'Of course, Aggie'. Lizzie held out her hand and it was gripped in the other's hard fingers.

The front door banged shut.

'Have I no' been quick? Jimmie Todd gi'ed me a back step on his bike doon tae the wee shop an' back. Is the haddie ready?'

'Aye, it's ready, laddie', said Aggie McMaster.

Lizzie smiled as Aggie brought the haddie in from the scullery stove.

'It's good to hear that, Aggie. *Your* laddie'.

Then Aggie made the supreme gesture.

'*Our* laddie, Lizzie, our laddie', and all the hardness went out of her face.

Aggie McMaster no longer stands out like a sore thumb in the village. Her tongue can still be sharp at times but there's no sting in it and she lends a hand as readily as the next, though maybe a thought awkwardly. The village, with a war on and all, is doubly willing to respond. Tam is still lovingly supervised and has found a jolly laugh that rings out here and there in Corbreck, but you see him at his best in and about the houses at the head of the Big Brae or sitting down to tea with his two aunties.

11. Five-day Sergeant

The next object is a Royal Air Force luggage tag No. 64349 in the name of Cadet Sergeant G. M. Walker. Destination Berlin. It's accompanied by a tattered souvenir banknote for Eine Deutsche Mark and attached to a memo to Sergeant Walker from Flight Lieutenant J. W. Charman on behalf of Senior Air Staff Officer No. 66 (Scottish) Group. The memo is headed 'Overseas Flight – Briefing'. There are five marching orders:

> 1. You are to catch the 10.20 p.m. train to London (Kings Cross) from Edinburgh (Waverley) on 4/4/55
> 2. You are then to make your way from Kings Cross to Euston Railway Station, there to report to the R.A.F. Movements Section in the R.T.O's office by 0830 hours.
> 3. You must, at all times, wear your uniform, unless permission to wear civilian clothes is given by the Officer who is in charge of you.
> 4. You are to keep a diary of the trip, and give it to your Commanding Officer who will send it to this Headquarters.
> 5. You must on no account accept hospitality from nationals of the countries you visit without first obtaining the permission of the Officer who is in charge of you.

All of which I obeyed except for the ban on hospitality from nationals which, as will appear, I had no option but to accept. I duly kept the required diary, as follows.

Under instruction from Flight Lieutenant Charman, Flying Officer Brown, C.O. of our school cadet corps R.A.F. section, promoted me from Corporal to Sergeant for the duration of the flight. I was given a uniform with appropriate stripes. So that my elevation from Corporal might appear less recent, I rubbed ash from my father's pipe into the stripes.

On 4th April I took the 11 a.m. train from Glasgow to Edinburgh and proceeded by bus from St Andrew's Square to Hopetoun crossroads where I telephoned Flight Lieutenant Charman of 66 Group Headquarters at South Queensferry. A few minutes later a car arrived to take me to Flight Lieutenant Charman for briefing and I surrendered a postal order for 12/6d to cover my messing fees for five days. This was the total cost of the trip. Another car then took me to Turnhouse for a free meal. I dumped my kit in an empty billet cupboard, reported to the Guardroom, and armed with knife, fork and enamel mug, entered the Airmen's Mess for a plateful of liver, chips, peas, two slices of bread and butter and a mug of what was allegedly tea. As I was leaving the Mess a large, bulbous, ginger-haired Sergeant with a fiery complexion confronted me with some violence. Although only a mere six inches from my face he felt it necessary to shout, 'Who the hell told you to come and eat here?' 'Flight Lieutenant Charman', I replied, softly. 'Oh, well, of course', he said, backing off with a sickly smile, 'that's all right then'. I collected my kit from the billet and left the Camp to catch the bus back to Edinburgh.

When I reached town I made for Waverley station and learned I was too late to book a seat for the 10.20 to London. I killed time over an iced drink in a café and strolled along Princes Street enjoying the spectacle of Edinburgh by night before making my way to platform 11. There were empty seats in a compartment already occupied by a soldier and a sailor. I panicked a little when the train left the platform at 9.50 instead of 10.20 but was reassured on hearing that this train would arrive at King's Cross a few minutes before the 10.20. I had worried that it might be a very slow service which would stop at all stations on the line, making me late for my appointment in London. I slept quite well in a sitting position throughout the journey. The soldier, virtuoso of the f-word, seemed to pass the entire night telling stories as blue as my uniform. Whenever my sleep was briefly broken he was still talking. There were Irish and Polish stories and many stories featuring bishops and admirals. The sailor sat in his corner with a fixed grin.

On 5th April at 6.30 a.m. we reached London. I took the Underground to Euston Station where I breakfasted and reported to the R.A.F. Movements Section in the R.T.O's office as per my briefing. There I was given the job of tying luggage labels to the bags of the eighteen passengers for Berlin, most of whom were either R.A.F. personnel or government officials, e.g. the Queen's

Messenger, identifiable by an exceptionally elegant briefcase. At 9.10 a.m. I travelled in the passengers' bus to Northolt Aerodrome. A beaming officer conducted us through passport control and customs and we assembled in the passengers' buffet for briefing about the flight before proceeding to the plane, a Valetta. The Squadron letters were UWV (United Kingdom – Warsaw – Valetta) and this aircraft was Valetta VW 855. The crew were all N.C.Os: Flight Sergeant Krombach (Captain), Sergeant Spencer (Navigator), Master Signaller Ashcroft and Sergeant O'Brien (Quartermaster). I became a temporary member of the crew as Assistant Quartermaster, answerable to Sergeant O'Brien, my job being to advise passengers to fasten their seat belts and to serve lunch and tea.

Take-off was at 10.55 a.m. We climbed smoothly to 7000 feet, piercing ceilings of cloud. The Captain told us the temperature was one degree Centigrade, the weather fair to cloudy with no rain. This was my first flight in a comparatively large aircraft; previously I had only flown in Chipmunks, so it was my first experience of being above cloud cover, looking down on a vast carpet of white cumulus under a sky of perfect blue. Cloud prevented us from seeing much of the country below us, except for a small part of Belgium.

We touched down at Wildenrath aerodrome at 12.30 p.m. Here we had a wait of an hour and twenty minutes. Tea was available in the buffet. Wildenrath has mostly Sabre aircraft. As we were on the point of take-off we were told that two Sabres had crashed in the air, killing the crews of both planes. We left Wildenrath at 1.55 p.m. Cloud had thickened and as we approached our destination we ran into turbulence. One passenger was very sick. It fell to me to clear up the mess and supply him with brown paper bags. Sergeant O'Brien nicknamed him 'Fountain-face'. He was sitting beside a disconsolate Wing Commander. We touched down at Gatow at 3.46 p.m. The Captain made a bumpy landing and two young ladies screamed.

Accommodation at R.A.F. Gatow was centrally heated and otherwise excellent. I had my own room with bed, bedside table, wardrobe, table and chair. A towel was supplied. After a good meal Sergeant Pat O'Brien and I decided to go into town. I borrowed civvies from the Captain and Pat changed into a very suave blue suit. We prepared to set out but discovered that it was pouring with rain outside, so abandoned the project. We joined the rest of the crew in competitive table tennis and skittles. Members of the crew were often difficult to understand as they were all ardent 'Goon Show' fans and conversed as if they were characters from the show. We lingered in the Mess where cigarettes were a mere shilling for twenty and beer only sixpence a glass.

I slept well until 8 a.m. (now Wednesday 6th April) when I was rudely awakened by Pat, wearing his sharp suit. It was time to get ready for another attempt on the town. Indian by birth, Pat O'Brien was twenty-eight years of age, very dark-skinned. He said he had attended Cambridge University, which may have accounted for his extremely plummy English accent, but left to go into business. Eventually he had joined the R.A.F. and under its auspices had travelled far and wide. He was an intelligent, humorous man with a high opinion of Sergeant O'Brien, but very likeable. When we passed each other in the narrow aisle of the Valetta during the spell of turbulence he would say to me, *sotto voce*, 'Shall we dance?' His typical response to earnest questions from a seventeen-year-old cadet was, 'Oh, don't be so naïve', accompanied by a radiant smile.

After bacon and eggs, toast, marmalade and tea we were once more ready for the city. The early morning was foggy, but the sun appeared soon and a bright day ensued. We caught the bus from just outside the station to a place called Pickeldorf Platz – though I can't vouch for the spelling – and from there went by tram into the centre of the British Sector of Berlin. Many areas of the city were like lunar cityscapes, evidence of wartime devastation. On the Kurfürstendamm we passed a ruined church, the Kaiser-Wilhelm-Gedächtniskirche. Bombed in an air raid in 1943, it has been left in its severely damaged state as a memorial to the ravages of war. I felt painfully saddened and distressed by this tragic sight. To a British eye German buses look weird. They're much bigger than ours with very long bonnets which make them like giant moles. We window-shopped and entered the American Sector because Pat wished to visit friends in a hotel near Tempelhof aerodrome. He gave them several containers of what appeared to be Nescafé and I thought money changed hands. I admired a memorial to the Berlin Airlift. We returned to Gatow by the way we had come and dined at 3 p.m.

Sergeant Pat O'Brien

There was more table tennis in the afternoon, then I retired to my room to bring this diary up to date. Captain Krombach came to my room in his capacity as my controlling officer to check that I was comfortable, enjoying the trip and didn't have any problems. He proved to be an enthusiastic photographer so we had an amicable talk about cameras, the merits of different film formats and the art of photography in general. I decided to take a shower and asked him to tell me how to get to the ablutions block. The Captain granted me permission to go sight-seeing in Berlin that night provided I was accompanied by Sergeant O'Brien.

[The following passage was omitted from this diary when I gave it to Flying Officer Brown for forwarding to Flight Lieutenant Charman.

The ablutions block is an enormous concrete structure, starkly utilitarian and formidably grey and cheerless. If the day hadn't been warm with the sun shining I think I would have done without the shower; but a shower is so glamorous, a great luxury unless you're very rich. I don't know anybody at home with a shower in their house, so this was a rare opportunity. I chose at random one of the entrances to the block and came to one of several rows of curtained shower stalls. My footsteps reverberated and when I coughed the sound was amplified in the vast space of the building. I couldn't begin to imagine how many shower stalls there might be in this colossal echoing shell of a place. I deduced there was no one else there and undressed, picked a stall and switched on the light. There were pegs for hanging clothes just beyond the range of the shower. I closed the curtain, turned on hot and cold taps and got to work mixing hot and cold until I had achieved the ideal temperature. I stepped into the powerful spray from the shower head and began to soap myself. Bliss. But not for long. An unseen hand drew back my curtain. Captain Krombach, naked, entered the stall. He is a muscular man, tall, at least six feet. Now he had doubled his height and girth and I was shrinking.

'Hello, Sarge', he said, 'having a good, hot shower, eh?'

I froze. I had lost all saliva and couldn't speak.

'So how are <u>we</u> this afternoon?' he said, raising his arm to send his spade-like hand towards my genitals.

Mute, trembling with a fear I haven't tasted before, I stared at his towering bulk.

'You've got a nice big bag, haven't you?' he said, giving my testicles a flip with his enormous hand.

The next few seconds remain inexplicable. I seemed to act without conscious volition as some instinct of self-preservation took command. Now, only minutes later, I can replay the scene graphically. Krombach is standing very straight. I think he's an Orkney standing stone, big, hard and immovable. His arm extended, his fingers are moving on me. My mind is mush.

My voice says, 'I think you should stop that. Why don't you go back to your own shower, there's a good chap'. I have no idea where these words come from.

His fingers stop moving. As my voice speaks I put my hand on *his arm and press it lightly away from my body. There's a long pause. Neither of us moves. There's no sound except for the gush of water from the shower. He drops his arm. He makes a small, sad humming noise, turns and leaves.*

I quickly re-soaped and rinsed south of the equator, half dried myself, yanked my clothes on and ran back to my room. I'm writing this quickly, only minutes after the incident. I can hardly hold the pen. I'm still shaking.]

At 8 p.m., after a hearty meal of steak and kidney pie, Pat O'Brien requisitioned the station transport car to collect us. It would take us to see Berlin by night. Pat would telephone for it to pick us up when he was ready to return to the station. In the morning the city had seemed in part garishly new, partly shattered. Once a great city in the country of Beethoven, it was now beaten, bankrupt and under foreign rule. Memories of wartime Glasgow rushed into my mind. This broken place was what happened to the evil people who had sent us scurrying to air-raid shelters and bombed us in their attempt to dominate the world. They had killed my father's partner at Dunkirk and conquered France. It was because of them I had been given a gas mask, because of them I was terrified of the darkness and the warning howl of the air-raid siren. These were the people responsible for the death camps' living skeletons I had seen in newsreels in the cinema, grisly left-overs from the liquidation of millions of Jews. Now look at them. They had brought ruin on themselves, or had they? It was surely Hitler we had fought, not the German people. Instead of the venomous hatred I felt towards them during the war all I could feel now was pity. Yet at night their decimated city became a bright, vital place with its myriad busily flashing neon lights. With Pat's permission I asked our driver to take us to the famous Brandenburger Tor. At Tempelhof we branched off to the 'Unter den Linden' the road our driver said Hitler called 'The East-West Road', where he held military parades and where the German allies assembled on state occasions. We travelled slowly, our thoughts occupied with the violent past. As we neared the Brandenburg Gate we passed the Soviet War Memorial. There were Soviet guards beside it, rigid in the gloom. At the Gate itself were large notices printed in bold white letters:

YOU ARE NOW LEAVING THE BRITISH SECTOR OF BERLIN
YOU ARE ENTERING THE SOVIET SECTOR OF BERLIN

On the top of the Gate the red bulk of the Soviet flag flapped in the wind. On the other side of the Gate were more guards. Behind them the lights of the Soviet Sector pricked the darkness. We turned off down a road to the right into the Soviet Zone. At this part of the city a small stretch of Soviet ground lies between the British and American Sectors. We sped through a poor, ill-lit part of Berlin now; the people who passed us in the streets were badly dressed if not ragged, and dirty.

Once in the American Sector Pat asked the driver to drop us at a café called 'Hamburg Ahoi'. I had a Coca-Cola, Pat bought a beer. I have developed a taste for beer but decided that I had better forgo that pleasure on this excursion and keep my wits about me. The proprietor of the cafe was fat and friendly. He showed us German television. I thought the quality of their pictures superior to ours. After the 'Hamburg Ahoi' Pat and I walked to another café where we each consumed a large, spicy sausage with mustard. Very succulent. Then it was onward for further investigation of Berlin's night life; at least I suppose you might say I was investigating it; Pat knew all about it already.

Pat made it clear to me that he was hunting for 'Popsies' and I'd have to look after myself. I agreed. It would have been impossible for me to see the sights of Berlin on my own. I knew nothing of the lay-out of the city and might easily have wandered unwittingly into the Soviet Sector. The Berlin transport system is complicated. I could neither speak nor understand German and most Germans are not fluent in English. The only way I could visit the city was with a member of the crew, provided one should be kind enough to put up with a schoolboy cadet for a companion. Sergeant O'Brien's friendly attitude solved the problem of how to see something of Berlin but how was I to go out on the town with a man whose purpose was to find 'an enthusiastic amateur' and at the same time protect myself from harm in the Berlin underworld? Pat would only call the transport car to pick us up together and he'd probably keep going until the small hours at the earliest. However, as it was probably the only time I'd ever be in Berlin, I decided to take a chance on my ability to handle any situation that might arise. If I hadn't gone with Pat I'd have seen nothing except R.A.F. Gatow and I'd had enough of table tennis. I decided I'd stay with Pat in a pub or café until he had found his Popsy; then I'd accompany them to the hotel of their choice and book my own room, or pass the remainder of the night in a pub.

After relishing the spicy German sausage our next pub was 'The Manhattan'. Lights were low in the bar and a juke-box was playing. An American officer, perched on a high stool at the counter, held a glass of beer in one hand and a waitress in the other. Pat walked over to the juke-box and tried to operate it. From their corner three girls watched him and sniggered. One came over to Pat and showed him how to put money in the machine. When he had loaded the juke-box under her flirtatious supervision with enough coins to keep it playing for a while, he sat down with his beer at a table with me and my trusty Coca-Cola. He offered cigarettes to the girls. They giggled, pointed at us and whispered. More people entered and a couple danced to the juke-box. Pat bought drinks for the girls with special treatment for the girl who had helped him. She had earned a cognac and Coca-Cola, apparently the fashionable drink in Berlin. The girl then sat beside us. She told us her name: Illona. As soon as she finished one drink Pat bought her another. He asked me to buy him a beer, so I walked over to the bar counter. A blonde waitress appeared from nowhere and put her arms round my neck. I made silly noises, thinking my best defence was to play the idiot, but she tried to kiss me, tightening her hold on my neck. At some loss of dignity I managed to wriggle out of her grasp. In a voice cribbed from Marlene Dietrich she crooned, 'Please you buy me drink'. I did and promptly returned to Pat's table, leaving her at the bar. Illona was now embracing and fondling Pat. The blonde came to sit beside us. She said her name was Hannelora. I said nothing in response and concentrated on giving the impression of one who would remain for ever aloof and unapproachable. Eventually Hannelora withdrew to the other side of the room where she moped and sent savage glances in our direction. Illona said, 'The blonde, she like you verra much'. I drank my Coca-Cola in studied detachment.

Pat and Illona danced and continued drinking. More couples shuffled round the small dance floor. At length Pat told Illona they'd have one final drink and then take a taxi to a hotel. Illona nodded inebriated assent. Pat and I agreed that I'd go with them to the hotel and book a room for myself. The pair had their final drink and Illona became abruptly very drunk, obviously shamming. She nagged at Pat, entreating him to buy her one more drink but he refused, reminding her that what he was 'primarily interested in' was going away with her. She turned to me and wagged a finger, 'Why you not want a girl?' I confessed my sworn fidelity to Marilyn Monroe. Illona observed to Pat, 'You see he is so happy and yet he does not drink', then turned in her seat to face the other tables and sang, 'Bonga, bonga, bonga, I'm so happy in the jungle!' An American soldier, rather the worse for wear, shouted, 'You sure would make a good ape!' Pat seemed to realise his plans for a night of love with Illona were doomed. As we left the 'Manhattan' there was a final comic touch as Pat and Illona shook hands.

The cool air outside was a relief after the smoke-filled 'Manhattan'. Pat drew a defeated hand across his brow but proclaimed his intention to accept failure with a smile and continue the search for a compliant Popsy. It was now 1.15 a.m. on 7th April. We walked back the way we had come and turned an unfamiliar corner. We came on two women standing in the doorway of a shop. One woman looked middle-aged, the other, resplendent in a fur coat, young and attractive. At their feet children played on the pavement and in the gutter. One of the women called out something in German. I wished them good night and walked on, saddened by the sight of the children, but Pat stopped. It seemed he had met the older woman on a previous trip to Berlin. The younger woman said her name was Inge and asked us where we were going. 'To a café', said Pat. Inge said all the pubs would be shut now. Pat asked her where she was going. 'Looking for you', she replied. 'Let's go', said Pat, offering his arm. The older woman made for me but by this time the night had taught me to be a master of evasion. She looked as if she was decomposing rapidly, like an unstable compound. It felt heartless to abandon the children, but we had no means of helping them. There seemed to be no connection between them and the two women. It emerged that the object of our wandering was to find an all-night pub and buy cognac, but Inge appeared to be right: all the pubs and cafés we came across were closed. Knocking at the door of one dingy establishment Pat was greeted by a large nose poked out from a cautiously opened shutter. The nose scrutinised Pat, decided it didn't like him and slammed the shutter shut. It was decided that we would go to a flat to which Inge had access.

We walked along a dark street and entered the doorway of an apartment block. The walls were peeling with damp oozing from them. When Inge knocked at the door of a ground-floor flat the door was opened by a woman Inge introduced as her aunt. A small sitting room was dominated by a large sofa against one wall. I sat firmly on a chair against the opposite wall. Inge called me 'Baby-face' and said I talked 'like a chaplain'. She told Pat she knew of an all-night place nearby where they could buy cognac. She and Pat left on this mission, leaving me alone with the aunt who made what passed for coffee. In case I might be left by myself I had brought a paperback book: *The Little World of Don Camillo* by Giovanni Guareschi. I took the book from my pocket and pretended to read, though I continued to pay attention to how this situation was evolving, but the pretence of reading was a way of conveying to the aunt that my interests did not coincide with Pat's.

Pat and Inge returned bearing a large bottle of cognac and several bottles of Coca-Cola. They sat together on the sofa drinking cognac and Coke while I maintained the pretence of reading. Pat was busy trying to persuade Inge to sleep with him. As alcohol took effect she began winking at me and put her hand on my knee. I became 'Big Man Marshall' instead of 'Baby-face'. I picked up her hand and returned it to the rest of her. When the hand wandered back I told her I would read her future in her palm. Pat pressed his suit but whenever he told Inge what he was 'primarily interested in' Inge said that Big Man Marshall was telling her fortune.

Pat and I realised that Inge understood English better than we had thought at first. He hit on the idea of conversing in a broad Scottish or Irish accent which completely foxed her. When he appeared to be getting nowhere with her he said to me, 'Me boyo, I wonder if you would be after engaging the old Auntie in a spot of blarney while I have a stab at persuading the colleen to see things my way'. Accordingly I turned to the Aunt, suppressing a yawn as it was now 3.30 a.m., and asked Auntie, 'Parlez-vous francais, o tante d'Inge?' She giggled and replied, 'Un peu, monsieur'. I struggled along with a few every-day phrases but soon found that her 'peu' was a gross exaggeration. She babbled away in German, with me putting in the odd 'Ja', and showed me photographs of herself when young. She seemed to have been involved in cabaret and there was one picture of what looked like ballet. When I mentioned Tchaikovsky she nearly had hysterics.

They all became drunk with Pat working himself up into a frenzy over Inge who persisted in winking at me. When Pat left the room to use the bathroom Inge said to me, 'Why is his face so black?' I explained: 'His face is not black. He is a dark-skinned Indian gentleman'. 'Poof', she exclaimed, 'I not go with niggers'. It was clear that she was only intent on Pat's money in the form of drink and that she had no intention of letting their relationship develop into anything more intimate. When Pat realised this himself he suggested that I should stay in the sitting room with Inge while he and the aunt went to the only bedroom to sleep together. I said that I didn't mind waiting for him in accordance with our agreement. Luckily Inge was completely drunk by this time and interested in no-one. She thought she was going to be sick. Pat and the aunt went out to buy another bottle of cognac, having agreed they would sleep together. Inge gave me no trouble. I read a little *Don Camillo*.

When Pat came back with Auntie they all had another drink and Pat took Auntie to the bedroom. I heard raised, drunken voices. Pat burst into the sitting room and said, 'Come on. Let's get out of here. I'm wasting my time'. He grabbed the now half-full bottle of cognac. The two women tried to stop us from leaving and the aunt began calling Pat 'Bertie, darling'. When pleading failed they resorted to weeping and wailing, but Sergeant O'Brien had made up his mind and led the way out of that dark and dirty dwelling.

Pat had telephoned for the transport car when he was out procuring cognac with the aunt. It was to collect us at 7 a.m. It was now 6 a.m. on Thursday 7th April. We walked up the street to an open bar and there Pat had his final beer. Even at that hour the place was busy. Many of the customers attempted to engage us in conversation. Pat shrugged. I was too tired to explain that I understood not a word of what they were saying, so I merely nodded as if in agreement with an occasional 'Ja, oh, ja' when it looked as if I was expected to comment. After we'd been in the bar for ten minutes the door opened and in tottered Inge with Auntie.

Inge pointed at me and proclaimed loudly, 'He is my man'. This was obviously her way of making it clear to everyone that she had nothing to do with the dark-skinned Indian gentleman. I had had more than enough of the night by this time, so went out into the street, leaving Pat to finish his beer and insult the women who had turned him down. After a few minutes Inge followed me outside and implored me to give her some British money. I shook my head. She pretended to be sentimental and asked for my address. I made up something. She promised to write and 'Tell me all about everything'. I went back into the pub to see how Pat was faring.

At exactly 7 a.m. the transport car arrived. I shook hands with Inge and said good-bye. 'Gimme a remembrance of you', she demanded, probably expecting at least a fiver. I presented her with a horseshoe nail I'd been given by a farmer on Mull and carried with me for luck. She ordered me to kiss her. I pecked at the air beside her cheek and got into the car with Pat. As we drove away I was struck by a sense of sadness in the lives of Inge and her Auntie. In their grimy flat they were like bigger versions of the night-time children we had seen playing in the gutter. What could the future hold for all these waifs? We reached Gatow in good time for a wash before breakfast, after which we packed and were taken with the rest of the crew to the airfield. My Berlin night was over.

Again we boarded eighteen passengers, some of whom had flown with us on Tuesday. Take-off was 10.38 a.m. It had been beautifully sunny on the ground, but by 11.10 we had run into dense cloud. I distributed lunch boxes and served tea in paper cups. We touched down at Wildenrath at 12.18 p.m. where we were scheduled to wait for an hour and a half but due to a problem with currency exchange were delayed until 2.05 p.m. Visibility was much better for this stage of the trip than it had been on the outward flight so we saw quite a bit of Belgium, the coast of Holland and the area about Dunkirk. We also had an excellent view of Margate Bay. We encountered turbulence as we approached journey's end but nobody was sick, though some faces took on a greenish hue. Visibility was very poor by the time we neared Northolt and we were brought in by G.C.A. from London.

We touched down in rain at Northolt at 4.10 p.m. After Customs and Passport Control I shook hands with the crew and thanked them. Pat grinned and said, 'Shall we dance?' and I replied, 'Oh, don't be so naïve. We did'. I returned to London in the passengers' bus and caught the 9.17 p.m. train from Euston to Glasgow, arriving home for breakfast on Friday 8th April. I had come to the end of my five days as Sergeant.

I wish to express my sincere thanks to the R.A.F. for an unforgettable, totally unpredictable experience.

****

That's where the diary ends, but not the story. Some weeks after the diary had reached Flight Lieutenant Charman at South Queensferry I received a message to the effect that Sergeant Pat O'Brien was accused of illicit trading in coffee with a hotel near Tempelhof. Had I witnessed this? I had mentioned containers of Nescafé and the possible exchange of money in my report. Would I be willing to give evidence against him? I declined. True, his search for an obliging Popsy had taken me into difficult, even hazardous situations and confronted me with many challenges, but without his willingness to put up with my presence I'd have seen nothing of Berlin. I was indebted to him for slices of life. It was the Captain, Flight Sergeant Krombach, who was the vexation. Pat, all things considered, was a comrade.

12. Burns

He's in the birthright of every Scot. We can probably still take it for granted that most of us know his name; but how many twenty-first century Scots really want him and how many know his language? In my boyhood, sixty-five years ago, Scots words were part of daily speech. They were not affected Scoticisms, chosen for histrionic effect though they might have taken precedence over English for expressive colour. They were part of who you were when you were at home.

For example, in English you might say: 'The day was dreary, grey and wet. We were thoroughly soaked but thirsty, so we went to a cosy little pub where everyone was going on about the commotion in the Middle East and saying how disgusted they were with the stupid politicians who were scoundrels for creating such a state of confusion. It was high time someone gave them a thrashing'. If you were a Scot that could be (admittedly at a pinch) more like: 'The day was *dreich*. We were *gey drookit* but *drouthy* so we went to a *couthie* wee pub where everyone was *blethering* about the *stramash* in the Middle East and saying how *scunnered* they were with the *glaikit* politicians who were *skellums* for making *sic* a *bourach*. It was high time someone gave them *laldie*'. Of course, you wouldn't have spoken like that at school; but if you can't already claim ownership of this vocabulary, try the words on your tongue. Admit that compared to dreich, drookit, stramash and scunnered, English's dreary, soaked, commotion and disgusted are pallid, lifeless creatures.

Despite the achievements of the poets, Ramsay, Fergusson, and Burns, Scots was an endangered language for a long time after 1707 when the Act of Union installed English as our official language. Southern English was written by Scots who wished to appear cultivated even if they still spoke their native language in informal situations. The most significant communication was now with London. Scots who visited the capital didn't want to be thought bumpkins because of their outlandish speech. The English language of government was the language of civilisation even if poets thought differently and the natural use of dialect was outlawed in Scottish classrooms. In William McIlvanney's novel,

Docherty, young Conn Docherty's teacher asks the boy what's wrong with his face:

> 'Skint ma nose, sur'.
> 'How?'
> 'Ah fell an' bumped ma heid in the *sheuch* [gutter], sur'.
> 'I beg your pardon?'
> 'Ah fell an' bumped ma heid in the *sheuch*, sur'.
> 'I beg your pardon?'
> In the pause Conn understands the nature of the choice, tremblingly, compulsively, makes it.
> 'Ah fell an' bumped ma heid in the *sheuch*, sur'.
> The blow is instant.
> 'That, Docherty, is impertinence. You will translate, please, into the mother-tongue'.

Standard English couldn't banish the Scots vernacular from homes and between friends, but the classroom was a formal situation where correct English was *de rigueur* and demotic Scots unacceptably vulgar. If you lapsed into the Scots of your upbringing away from your ain folk, you might be punished, like Conn, or looked at queerly as if people thought you were being contrary or trying to be cute. Burns got away with it, but he was an exception that proved the rule.

Every 25th of January, after the piper, the haggis and the earlier drams of the evening, celebrants of Burns Nicht all over the world toast the immortal memory. Regions south of the equator may commemorate the 21st of July, honouring the death instead of the birth where it's thought more appropriate to the bard's climate of origin to salute him in winter, or bagpipes and haggis are felt to be sensations too strenuous for antipodal summers. He has long been accorded the status of mythical hero, an apostle of liberty and equality all the more beguiling for his supposed resemblance to Giacomo Casanova. Birthday or death-day, the cult of the Burns personality comes to a head annually when a rendition of 'O my Luve's like a red, red rose' or a maudlin reminiscence of how Scotland failed to get him on a British postage stamp until 1966, ten years after the Soviet Union's issue marking the hundred and sixtieth anniversary of his death, will introduce another farraginous display of 'Scotch drink, Scotch religion and Scotch manners'. All too often the myth takes precedence over the poetry. Hugh MacDiarmid's excoriation of Burns cult bardolatry is still regrettably apposite:

> It has denied his spirit to honour his name.
> It has denied his poetry to laud his amours.
> It has preserved his furniture and repelled his message.
> It has built itself up on the progressive refusal of his lead in regard to Scottish politics, Scottish literature, and the Scottish tongue.

Every Hogmanay drink and sentimentality transcend accuracy in what Lewis Grassic Gibbon calls 'the sugary surge' of 'Auld Lang Syne'. It's been dubbed 'the song that nobody knows' because progress is so seldom made beyond the first quatrain and chorus to the lyrical perfection of what follows:

> We twa hae run about the braes,
>   And pou'd the gowans fine;   *pulled daisies*
> But we've wander'd mony a weary fitt,   *foot*
>   Sin auld lang syne.   *long ago*
>
> We twa hae paidl'd in the burn,
>   Frae morning sun till dine;   *dinner time*
> But seas between us braid hae roar'd,   *broad*
>   Sin auld lang syne.

The childhood that kept companions playing together on familiar hills has passed. Adult feet have taken their separate ways and the shared miniature waters of the burn have immersed in the vastness of sundering oceans. So let us commemorate the bonding, companionable burn of innocence that flowed, as it must, into the severing seas of distance, experience and time with a draught of good fellowship, the 'willie-waught' in our raised glasses, as we toast again the emotionally tenacious past from which the present has come. These are the implications by which Burns raises the power of an old song from facile sentimentality to universal sentiment.

'Auld Lang Syne' is essential Burns in its demonstration of his gift for poetry as song, his passion for the Scottish tradition, his talent for reworking folk material, his feeling for human connection, and his use of Scots. Lionised after the appearance of the Kilmarnock Edition in 1786, he might have given in completely to the Anglicised tastes of the *literati* if only to show that a ploughman could graduate from his rustic background and beat the English at their own language. Occasionally he succumbed, in the generally second-rate poems written in English; but he was never long deflected from his idiom. The most striking aspect of his character is his independence. This is the point of contact between the myth of Burns and his gift.

The myth is fed by colourful background and salty incident. There is his humble Ayrshire origin in 'the auld clay biggin', the two-roomed thatched Alloway cottage, now picturesque to tourist expectations ('O the flummery of a birth place!' Keats exclaimed on his visit to the house) but then rudimentary, built by his father, William Burnes, with his own hands. There are the unpropitious farms at Mount Oliphant and Lochlea where he helped his industrious but unlucky father until, with his brother, Gilbert, he took the family to Mossgiel in the parish of Mauchline. There is his attempt to rescue the family fortunes by learning the trade of flax-dressing, the scheme aborted by the burning of the Irvine flax-dressing shop, set alight by the drunken carelessness of his partner's wife and reduced to ashes, leaving Burns 'like a true Poet, not worth sixpence'. There is his plan to escape from personal and financial difficulties by emigrating to Jamaica with 'Highland' Mary Campbell, his hiding from the wrath of James Armour, father of pregnant Jean, then his decision to stand his ground in Scotland after the publication of the Kilmarnock Edition. There are all the women and the offspring. There is the largely epistolary affair with Agnes Craig McLehose, the 'Clarinda' to his archly Arcadian 'Sylvander' and the 'Nancy' of 'Ae Fond Kiss' which commemorates their final parting in the compact expression of Burns at his most intense, the rawness of impulsive attraction and the hurt of parting simply set down with the art that conceals art:

> I'll ne'er blame my partial fancy,
> Naething could resist my Nancy:
> But to see her, was to love her;
> Love but her, and love for ever. –

Had we never lov'd sae kindly,
Had we never lov'd sae blindly!
Never met – or never parted,
We had ne'er been broken-hearted.

There is his likeable disregard for money. Then there is the overworked exciseman, worn by a life of emotional, intellectual and sexual intensity, riding up to forty miles a day, incongruously a figure of the establishment but still temperamentally attuned to the free spirits on the other side of the line of his profession as he makes clear in 'The De'il's awa wi' th' Exciseman':

The deil's awa the deil's awa
  The deil's awa wi th' Exciseman,
He's danc'd awa he's danc'd awa
  He's danc'd awa wi' th' Exciseman.

We'll mak our maut and we'll brew our drink, *malt*
  We'll laugh, sing, and rejoice, man;
And mony braw thanks to the meikle black deil, *great*
  That danc'd awa wi' th' Exciseman.

It's said that in the search for illicit stills Burns would arrive at a door with his hat off. This made the visit unofficial, but was giving a sign that he'd come back shortly with his hat on, which would make it official. Finally, there is the disappointed tenant of Ellisland Farm near Dumfries, 'this accursed farm' as he called it, whose position on the river Nith was visually pleasing, but whose soil was too exhausted to yield profit from his crops. There are many amours and biographical details to be filled in, but they can wait until the poetry has been read, felt and sung.

What, then, of the gift and the message? What of the mixture of tenderness and bawdy, calculation and spontaneity, vulgarity and exaltation? Byron, reading Burns's letters in 1813, marvels at the contraries in the poet's make-up:

What an antithetical mind! – tenderness, roughness –
delicacy, coarseness – sentiment, sensuality – soaring
and grovelling, dirt and deity – all mixed up in that
one compound of inspired clay!

Byron catches the range and variety but Burns, of course, was no more or less 'inspired' or 'heaven-taught' than any other genius. His schooling, mostly supplied by John Murdoch, the Alloway teacher hired co-operatively by his father and four neighbours to educate their children, was essentially English, although he did learn to read French and acquired the basic elements of Latin. He went to Kirkoswald to learn mathematics from Hugh Rodger, the parish schoolteacher, making 'pretty good progress' until 'set off in a tangent' from his studies by Peggy Thomson (the 'lovely charmer' of 'Now westlin winds') who lived next door to the school. He read Shakespeare, Milton and Dryden, Richardson, Smollett, Sterne and Mackenzie, but the two books that galvanised him – were Blind Harry's *Wallace* and Robert Fergusson's *Poems*. The *Wallace* cast a patriotic spell: 'the story of Wallace poured a Scotish prejudice in my veins which will boil along there till the flood-gates of life shut in eternal rest'. The prejudice boiled over into the nationalist verse of 'Robert Bruce's March to Bannockburn' or, as we tend to know it, 'Scots wha hae'. Especially forceful are the central stanzas in which Bruce challenges any cowards in his army to flee the field:

> Wha will be a traitor-knave?
> Wha can fill a coward's grave?
> Wha sae base as be a Slave?
>   Let him turn and flie —
>
> Wha for SCOTLAND'S king and law,
> Freedom's sword will strongly draw,
> FREE-MAN stand, or FREE-MAN fa',
>   Let him follow me.

The raised consciousness of Scottish feeling instilled by *Wallace* was enhanced by Robert Fergusson's models of native expression and Burns was soon developing his own synthesis of diction from the Scottish tradition, English and the spoken language of Ayrshire, acknowledging Fergusson as 'my elder brother in Misfortune,/ By far my elder Brother in the muse'. He commissioned a stone to be erected on Fergusson's unmarked grave and in the verse epistle, 'To W. S*****n [William Simson], Ochiltree' extols Fergusson's virtues, cursing the Edinburgh gentry for their neglect of the talent in their midst. He was a dab hand at the art of vituperation:

O *Ferguson!* thy glorious *parts*,
Ill-suited *law's* dry, musty arts!
My curse upon your whunstane hearts,   *whinstone*
   Ye Enbrugh Gentry!
The tythe o' what ye waste at *cartes*   *cards*
   Wad stow'd his pantry!   *would have filled*

At fifteen he 'first committed the sin of RHYME; in 'O once I lov'd', a song praising Nelly Kilpatrick who initiated in him 'a certain delicious Passion, which in spite of acid Disappointment, gin-horse Prudence and bookworm Philosophy, I hold to be the first of human joys, our dearest pleasure here below'. The piece is fluent like other early poems written in an English tinged with Scots, and mannered in its pious focus on the girl's moral character rather than on the physical attributes which doubtless attracted the young Burns and which he can be hilariously ribald about in his bawdy versifying:

A gaudy dress and gentle air
   May lightly touch the heart,
But its innocence and modesty
   That polishes the dart.

Believe that if you like. A year and a girl later love and poesy advanced to the technically maturer and emotionally convincing song, 'Now westlin winds', an early masterpiece in which the gentleness of love harmonises with the clear evening, blue sky and skimming swallow in contrast to the turbulence of the rough westerly and the murderous guns of autumn sportsmen. Landscape and love suffuse each other in 'I love my Jean' and in the haunting song, 'Ca' the yowes to the knowes'. In 'My bony Mary' neither war nor the 'roar o' sea or shore' holds danger equal to the pain of parting:

The trumpets sound, the banners fly,
   The glittering spears are ranked ready,
The shouts o' war are heard afar,

The battle closes deep and bloody.
It's not the roar o' sea or shore,
  Wad make me langer wish to tarry;
Nor shouts o' war that's heard afar —
  It's leaving thee, my bony Mary.

In 'The Banks o' Doon' the beauty of nature, impervious to the poet's unhappiness, expresses, like W.H. Auden's 'Musée des Beaux Arts', the exacerbation of anguish by a world that goes heedlessly on:

Ye banks and braes o' bonie Doon,
  How can ye bloom sae fresh and fair;
How can ye chant, ye little birds,
  And I sae weary, fu' o' care!
Thou'll break my heart, thou warbling bird,
  That wantons thro' the flowering thorn:
Thou minds me o' departed joys,
  Departed, never to return.

The connoisseur of love's joys and pangs is also in his element as a satirist. If his subtlest satire is in 'Tam o' Shanter' his funniest is 'Holy Willie's Prayer', a dramatic monologue in which the speaker unwittingly reveals the unsavoury truth about himself to us and to God. In 'The Twa Dogs' Caesar, the laird's dog, exposes the futilities and cruelties of his class of humans while the ploughman's collie, Luath, testifies to the resilience and talent for contentment of the poor. In 'The Holy Fair' true holiness is the pagan sanctity of life itself. 'Address to the Deil' cuts Satan down to size, calling him 'Auld Hornie', 'Nick' or 'Clootie' in mock-heroic contrast to Milton's 'great Personage' in *Paradise Lost*.

That leaves three of his greatest hits, three poems no Scot should be without: 'To a Mouse', 'To a Louse' and 'Tam o'Shanter'. The genius of 'To a Mouse' and 'To a Louse' is in the steady eye Burns keeps on the creatures. The most famous lines in 'To a Mouse, On turning her up in her Nest, with the Plough, November, 1785' arise from the apprehension of a miniature fellow-mortal in a moment keenly felt. Breaking up the mouse's 'wee-bit housie' prompts the expansion of sympathy into regret that 'Man's dominion/ Has broken Nature's social union'. The vanity of the mouse's foresight warrants the renowned truism that 'The best laid schemes o' Mice and men/ Gang aft agley', and the poet's focus on the mouse's predicament leads to a final comparison of their lives with a concluding sense of the crucial difference between them. Advantage, mouse:

> Still, thou art blest, compar'd wi' me!
> The present only toucheth thee:
> But Och! I backward cast my e'e,
>   On prospects drear!
> An' forward, tho' I canna see,
>   I guess and fear!

Again, in 'To a Louse, On Seeing one on a Lady's Bonnet at Church', while Burns is more obviously relishing the flavours of his language for their own sake, he refers to the 'crowlan ferlie' (the crawling prodigy) throughout the poem. It may be an 'ugly, creepan, blastet wonner' (ugly, creeping, accursed wonder), but it elicits the vanity of 'airs in dress an' gait', leading to the famous aphorism: 'O wad some Pow'r the giftie gie us/ To see oursels as others see us!'

Burns's own favourite of his works, 'Tam o'Shanter' is a mock-heroic variation on the theme of the homeward journey, with Tam crossing the 'mosses, waters, slaps and styles' between Ayr and Kirkoswald where his 'sulky, sullen dame' awaits to berate him once again for being a 'skellum', no Penelope to his Ulysses but, perhaps, a grumpy Calvinist Molly to his tipsy Bloom. Rapid motion starts in the opening lines, the rhythm of the octosyllabic couplets already anticipating Tam's hectic gallop through the night, propelling him from the convivial ingle with Souter Johnny into the real storm he will face as a prelude to the 'gathering storm' waiting for him at home. Ostensibly a warning against the evils of drink, the poem is a denial of its own feigned posture, being a visceral celebration of 'Inspiring bold John Barleycorn' which undercuts the po-faced moralising:

> Whene'er to drink you are inclin'd
> Or cutty-sarks run in your mind,
> Think, ye may buy the joys o'er dear,
> Remember Tam o'Shanter's mare.

This is ironic bathos. The reader is enjoined to repudiate the pleasures of the tavern, illicit adventures and a glimpse of a girl who can make the Devil wriggle all because a horse has lost its tail. The anti-climax of the conclusion turns the reader back into the life of the poem: the crackle of its witticisms, the fear of bogles, the piling-up of horrors on the 'haly table' in the Kirk-Alloway, the open coffins and the wild satanic dance to piped music from Auld Nick. That the moral is doomed from the beginning Burns makes clear by the comedy of pompous English couplets and pulpit gravity:

> You seize the flower, its bloom is shed;
> Or like the snow falls in the river,
> A moment white — then melts for ever;
> Or like the borealis race,
> That flit ere you can point their place;
> Or like the rainbow's lovely form
> Evanishing amid the storm.

After such a night Tam can have nothing to fear either from paltry homiletics or from his killjoy Kate. 'Kings may be blest', but Tam is still glorious, 'O'er a' the ills o' life victorious!' Maybe he did guess and fear when he looked into the future, but Burns's mock-heroic, like his work as a whole, is as affirming as the final 'Yes' of Joyce's *Ulysses*. In the digital age American idioms and globalisation have replaced young Conn Docherty's teacher as powerful deterrents from the usage, understanding and enjoyment of Scots vocabulary, widening the gap between us and the Scots of our greatest writer. We need teachers and a *literati* who will tend and nourish the birthright, both language and bard. Then we'll be in a position to say, with Wordsworth, 'Deep in the general heart of men/ His power survives'.

13. Favourite Reads?

The local newspaper was doing an occasional literary column, asking people about their 'favourite reads'. 'Favourite' is liberatingly subjective, shamelessly irresponsible. No donnish insistence on scholarly argument to justify 'Best' or 'Greatest', no need for defensive armour in readiness for critical slings and arrows. 'Favourite' solicits candour, unbuttoned, no stolid footnotes. Relax. We salute your allegiance to Shakespeare, Milton, Henry James, James Joyce; but, come on, what or whom do you curl up with?

So how about P.G. Wodehouse for omniscient, shimmering Jeeves, feckless Bertie Wooster, and Blandings Castle with Lord Emsworth's prize-winning pig, 'The Empress of Blandings'? How about Raymond Chandler, tough and hard-boiled but witty and lyrical, the romantic loner with 'a heart as big as one of Mae West's hips'? How about *The Tale of Mr Jeremy Fisher*, Beatrix Potter's epic of the piscatorial frog who lives in a damp house among buttercups?

> The water was all slippy-sloppy in the larder and in the back passage. But Mr Jeremy Fisher liked getting his feet wet; nobody ever scolded him, and he never caught a cold!

Impeccable prose: lucid, expertly cadenced. Proper words in proper places illustrated by Potter's delicate, lyrical miniatures.

THE TALE OF
MR. JEREMY FISHER

BY
BEATRIX POTTER
THE ORIGINAL AND AUTHORIZED EDITION
F. WARNE & Co

It's all here. Poling his lily-leaf boat into the pond to fish for minnows, Mr Jeremy Fisher is Ulysses, Ishmael and Siegfried. A hostile world fires its warning shot when a water-beetle tweaks the toe of one of his galoshes as he lunches on a butterfly sandwich. Instead of a minnow for dinner he lands a pricking, snapping stickleback. (How often has that happened to you?) A shoal of little fish put their heads out of the water and laugh at Mr Jeremy Fisher. (Common, contemptible *Schadenfreude*.) He's snatched from his boat by a great big enormous trout which carries him to the bottom of the pond but is so displeased with the taste of Mr Jeremy's macintosh that it spits him out, leaving our heroic frog to hop home, dress his fingers with sticking plaster and serve roasted grasshopper with ladybird sauce and salad to his classy friends, Mr Alderman Ptolemy Tortoise and Sir Isaac Newton. Mr Jeremy Fisher has come through.

And so does Pip in *Great Expectations*, wounded by love, manipulated by money, indoctrinated by snobbery, and finally processed towards redemption by the richest characters in the Dickens galaxy. The novel is a favourite among favourites, although anxiety about saintly Esther Summerson — please don't let her die from the smallpox — affection for John Jarndyce, contempt for Harold Skimpole, a hanky for Jo the crossing-sweeper, fear and loathing of scheming Mr Tulkinghorn and delight in Inspector Bucket make *Bleak House* a worthy competitor.

Richard Hannay, doyen of British action-men and amateur forefather of Ian Fleming's professional James Bond, is in pursuit of The Black Stone gang. A prominent politician is due to be assassinated. Time's running out. The stability of Europe is at stake. From the murdered American agent, Franklin P. Scudder's coded notebook, he deduces that 'the three cleverest rogues in Europe' will leave England for Germany from a place on the southeast coast where there are thirty-nine steps down to the sea. 'All this was very loose guessing', Hannay admits with the inbred, coy self-deprecation of the ex-colonial Anglo-Scottish gentleman – the Great War is coming and he is clearly officer material – 'and I don't pretend it was ingenious or scientific. I wasn't any kind of Sherlock Holmes'. So, in his best-selling 'shocker', *The Thirty-nine Steps*, John Buchan defers to Sir Arthur Conan Doyle, inventor of 'the most perfect reasoning and observing machine that the world has ever seen' ('A Scandal in Bohemia') and his bluff accomplice and foil, Dr Watson of limited 'frontal development', to whom nothing is ever as elementary as Holmes makes out.

Both Conan Doyle and Buchan were drawn to history, but it was crime and espionage that made them great entertainers worthy of inclusion in many pantheons of favourite reads. In Doyle's *The Lost World* Professor Challenger's journey into pre-history foreshadows Michael Crichton's science-fiction fantasy of genetically engineered dinosaurs in *Jurassic Park*; but it was the publication of *A Study in Scarlet* with its introduction of Sherlock Holmes (based on the forensic expert, Dr Joseph Bell, one of Doyle's teachers at Edinburgh University) that led to the stories in the *Strand Magazine* which made him and his detective famous by popularising the recipe devised by Edgar Allan Poe in such stories as 'The Murders in the Rue Morgue' and 'The Purloined Letter'. Poe's unflappably ratiocinative detective, Monsieur Dupin, and his narrator's role as a comparatively slow-witted intermediary between detective and reader, gave a model for the Holmes-Watson formula. His own skill in portraying memorable characters is more responsible for Doyle's success than the ingenious plots of his 'children's stories for grown-ups'. Holmes's 'cold, precise, but admirably balanced mind', his physical prowess and mastery of disguise, his violin, deerstalker, hypodermic and dottles smoked before breakfast guarantee a continuing readership for *The Sign of Four*, *The Hound of the Baskervilles* and all the stories leading up to the great confrontation at the falls of Reichenbach with his arch-enemy, Professor Moriarty ('The Final Problem').

The fertility of Conan Doyle's imagination is less widely recognised than it deserves to be because Holmes's unique magnetism as the world's 'only unofficial consulting detective... the last and highest court of appeal in detection' has deflected attention from the inventiveness of stories in which he doesn't appear. The variety of Doyle's interests is reflected in the headings under which *The Conan Doyle Stories* arranges its contents into Tales of the Ring, the Camp, Pirates, Blue Water, Terror, Mystery, Twilight and the Unseen, Adventure, Medical life and, his own favourite group, 'Tales of Long Ago'. He's an expert at the shock ending ('The Case of Lady Sannox'; 'How it Happened'), the tale of horror ('The Pot of Caviare'; 'The Striped Chest', (a gruesome variation on the *Marie Celeste* theme), and the mixing of scientific and supernatural ideas ('The Horror of the Heights'; 'Lot 249'). His Captain Sharkey of the barque *Happy Delivery* is an irresistibly villainous amalgam of insolent cunning, slicing wit and creative cruelty among those who 'hoisted the Jolly Roger at the mizzen and the bloody flag at the main, declaring a private war upon their own account against the whole human race' ('Captain Sharkey: How the Governor of Saint Kitt's Came Home').

John Buchan's fluent narrative style and personal conviction enliven his historical subjects and their times in *Montrose*, *Sir Walter Scott* and *Oliver Cromwell* but it's the characters he called his 'group of musketeers' who save him from becoming merely an honourable footnote in histories of Scottish and English literature. The popularity of *The Thirty-nine Steps* encouraged Buchan to follow it with a series of novels in which Richard Hannay reappears with his comrades – Pieter Pienaar, Sandy Arbuthnot (Lord Clanroyden), Sir Archibald Roylance, Sir Edward Leithen and John S. Blenkiron, the bulky American indebted to Hannay for the Turkish escapade in *Greenmantle* which cures his dyspepsia. If they now seem like humanoid editions of Kenneth Grahame's Mole, Ratty, Badger and Toad at play on a *Boy's Own Paper* riverbank, these are the 'puppets' who became for Buchan and the English-reading world, 'very real flesh and blood'. His retired Glasgow grocer, Dickson McCunn, is a more original invention than Hannay, but the novels in which he appears — *Huntingtower*, *Castle Gay* and *The House of the Four Winds* – are more loosely constructed than the Hannay books and less successful in projecting a coherent world for the reader to escape to.

The Hannay stories specialise in action – even if urgency is often jeopardised by Buchan's lingering too long in Hannay's decently prosaic mind – and compelling villains. Hannay's admiration for brutal Colonel Ulric von Stumm ('an incarnation of all that makes Germany detested...the German of caricature, the real German...I couldn't help admiring him'), and Hilda von Einem ('Mad and bad she might be, but she was also great') in *Greenmantle* and Dominick Medina ('a devil...but...a great devil') in *The Three Hostages* anticipates the sado-masochism pornographically deployed by Ian Fleming in his James Bond novels. The xenophobic racism of

Buchan's musketeers towards Jews, blacks and the Irish is more discomfiting than his smugly clubbable imperialism. Inadvertent self-parody is never far away:

> We met in a room on the second floor of a little restaurant in Mervyn Street...The Club had its own cook and butler, and I swear a better dinner was never produced in London, starting with preposterously early plovers' eggs and finishing with fruit from Burminster's houses. There were a dozen present including myself... Collatt was there, and Pugh, and a wizened little man who had just returned from bird-hunting at the mouth of the Mackenzie. There was Palliser-Yeates, the banker, who didn't look thirty, and Fulleylove, the Arabian traveller, who was really thirty and looked fifty. I was specially interested in Nightingale, a slim, peering fellow with double glasses, who had gone back to Greek manuscripts and his Cambridge fellowship after captaining a Bedouin tribe. Leithen was there, too, the Attorney-General, who had been a private in the Guards at the start of the War and had finished up a G.S.O.I....I should think there must have been more varied and solid brains in that dozen than you would find in an average Parliament.
>
> (*The Three Hostages*)

All he claimed for his writings was that they were 'pure minstrelsy', yet behind the butlers, plovers' eggs, country estates and jolly good fellows, Buchan writes as committedly as William Golding about the fragility of civilisation. A son of the Manse, he believed in human susceptibility to evil. As the urbane Andrew Lumley tells Edward Leithen in *The Power-House*, 'Civilisation needs more than the law to hold it together...Civilisation is a conspiracy...Modern life is the silent compact of comfortable folk to keep up pretences'. Sandy Arbuthnot's speech about Ram Dass's opinion of propaganda in *The Three Hostages* is to be taken seriously: 'He said that the great offensives of the future would be psychological, and he thought the Governments should get busy about it and prepare their defence...He considered that the most deadly weapon in the world was the power of mass-persuasion'.

An entertainer can also be a prophet.

If I were asked to nominate a novel to represent Scottish literature, or the Scottish soul portrayed in literature, it would have to be Lewis Grassic Gibbon's *A Scots Quair*. ('Quair' is an archaic word for 'quire', meaning gathered pages.) '*Oh Chris Caledonia*', exclaims Robert Colquohoun to his wife, '*I've married a nation!*' So the *Quair* would be my book of the nation. Of course this is cheating a little because the *Quair* is a trilogy: *Sunset Song*, *Cloud Howe* and *Grey Granite*. The trilogy moves from legend to history, emerging from the days of William the Lyon and Cospatric de Gondeshil, Knight of Kinraddie, 'when gryphons and suchlike beasts still roamed the Scots countryside', into a chronicle of the Scottish nation from 1911 to the General Strike of 1926 and the hunger marches of 1932. It feels like a single, unified work, mainly because Chris Guthrie is the point of moral reference throughout the three volumes, even in *Grey Granite*, where her son Ewan's political career provides the main story.

Gibbon's flowing style, derived from the vernacular of north-east Scotland, gives the effect of one speaker talking, the voice of Scotland itself. 'In all three books', wrote Eric Linklater, 'the rendering of the anonymous voice of the countryside is miraculously evocative and quintessentially true'. Gibbon's idiomatic humour, both acerbic and warm, palliates the work's essential austerity. He gives us a bottomless loch which is like 'the depths of a parson's depravity'; Mistress Munro who, suspecting an ill word about herself, would 'redden up like a stalk of rhubarb in a dung patch'; the ministers offering up prayers for rain 'in between the bit about the Army and the Prince of Wales' rheumatics'; the Tory who fights a bye-election 'with a funny bit squeak of a voice, like a bairn that's wet its breeks'. In *Cloud Howe* there is the Segget War Memorial, 'an angel set on a block of stone, decent and sonsy in its stone night-gown' and the story of Dite Peat and Jim the Sourock's pig. In *Grey Granite* the Reverend Edward MacShilluck is a caricature of church bigotry, another Holy Willie.

Each book of the *Quair* culminates in Chris's survival over the failures of others. *Sunset Song* focuses on the life of farming. Chris's love of her land and its folk alternates with hatred:

...two Chrisses there were that fought for her heart

and tormented her. You hated the land and the coarse speak of the folk and learning was brave and fine one day and the next you'd awaken with the peewits crying across the hills, deep and deep, crying in the heart of you and the smell of the earth in your face, almost you'd cry for that, the beauty of it and the sweetness of the Scottish land and skies.

The split of feeling in Chris matches Gibbon's own ambivalence towards the life of the Mearns. In an essay entitled 'The Land' he writes:

> *That* is The Land out there, under the sleet, churned and pelted there in the dark, the long rigs upturning their clayey faces to the spear-onset of the sleet. That is The Land, a dim vision this night of laggard fences and long stretching rigs. And the voice of it – the true and unforgettable voice – you can hear even such a night as this as the dark comes down, the immemorial plaint of the peewit, flying lost. *That* is The Land – though not quite all. Those folk in the byre whose lantern light is a glimmer through the sleet as they muck and bed and tend the kye, and milk the milk into tin pails, in curling froth – they are The Land in as great a measure...I like to remember I am of peasant rearing and peasant stock.

But a few lines later he says: 'Once I had a very bitter detestation for all this life of the land and the folk upon it'.

Chris's achievement in the first book of Gibbon's epic sequence is a capacity for joy that withstands a series of primal shocks as well as her moods of recoil from her environment: John Guthrie treats her mother 'like a breeding sow'; pregnant again and unable 'to thole it longer', Jean Guthrie poisons herself and her twins; Guthrie terrifies Chris with urgent demands for incestuous sex ('*You're my flesh and blood, I can do with you what I will, come to me, Chris, do you hear?*'); her husband, Ewan Tavendale, treats her like a recalcitrant whore when he comes home on leave from the First World War, 'the foulness dripping from the dream that devoured him', and is executed in France as a deserter who only wanted to go home to his farm, the cry of the peewits and his sleeping wife. In *Cloud Howe* Chris survives the failure of religion to make a better world either by her energetic second husband's practical Christianity or by his gloomily apocalyptic Christian mysticism. In *Grey Granite* she survives the failure of politics. Young Ewan replaces his step-father's God with the Communist ideal of freedom from capitalist controls. Beaten up by the police, he feels his identity melt into 'a hundred broken and tortured bodies all over the world' as Gibbon's anger builds a litany of contemporary injustices and political hypocrisies:

> ...in Scotland, in England, in the torture-dens of the Nazis in Germany, in the torment-pits of the Polish Ukraine, a livid, twisted thing in the prisons where they tortured the Nanking Communists, a Negro boy in an Alabama cell while they thrust the razors into his flesh, castrating with a lingering cruelty and care. He was one with them all, a long wail of sobbing mouths and wrung flesh, tortured and tormented by the world's Masters while those Masters lied about Progress through Peace, Democracy, Justice, the Heritage of Culture – even as they'd lied in the days of Spartacus, lying now through their hacks in pulpit and press, in the slobberings of middle-class pacifists, the tawdry promisings of Labourites, Douglasites...

Notwithstanding the righteous ecstasy of his own outrage, Gibbon understands the psychology of the political fanatic. Ewan is not to be idealised, although his character closely resembles Gibbon's. As a boy he collects Bronze Age flints. His mother watches him become 'rather like a flint himself...grey granite down to the core' . Chris may represent the Earth-Goddess, but Ewan 'is something deeper: mineral...still natural, but part of a different and slower time-process'. The rock-like purity of his political commitment is at once the source of his strength and of his cruelty to Ellen Johns – '*I can get a prostitute anywhere*', he tells her – when she leaves the Communist Party, tired and disillusioned. At the end of the Gowans and Gloag strike Big Jim Trease, the Party Agitator, says, '*A hell of a thing to be history, Ewan*'. He has become a personification of the concept of the Just Man in History; but a concept is in danger of remaining an abstraction, unreal as well as coldly inhuman. Ewan knows that his mother is still real: *'Didn't you know you were real, Chris, realer than ever?'* Gibbon knows that his [Ewan's] conception of life can neither compete with nor replace the reality of hers. Whether she would have kept her reality if she had not folded up her books and dreams 'and laid them away by the dark, quiet corpse that was [her] childhood' is an open question.

As the trilogy unfolds Gibbon is seized more and more by an overweening compassion for the broken, tortured bodies of Ewan's imagining, but Chris's reality is untouched by religious or political faction and impervious to the gossip which gives Gibbon's panorama its anecdotal vitality. Yet, 'SHE HAD NOTHING AT ALL', she thinks in *Grey Granite*, 'she never had anything, nothing in the world she believed in but change...Nothing endured'. The theme of change is a refrain throughout the three books. 'Nothing endures', she thinks when Marget Strachan instructs her in love-making; 'nothing ever stayed the same', she decides, observing her careworn mother's sadness. 'Nothing endured at all', she thinks again after the death of her father in *Sunset Song*, 'nothing but the land'. The land is what she has had from the beginning, 'her surety unshaken' in 'the moors and the sun and the sea'. It's the land that mortally calls her husband back from the insanity of war and out of his perverse attitude towards her. She can take pride in her grim, tormented father in relation to the land because he 'could farm other folk off the earth'. All the other characters in *Sunset Song* are subsidiary to Chris's evolution and nature's unbiddable variety from the June moors 'yellow with broom and powdered with purple', the 'shoom-shoom' of the sea by Bervie, the whistle of blackbirds in Blawearie's trees, the wail of peesies (lapwings), night coming over the Grampian Hills and the snipe crying in their hundreds, to rain on the roof, the batter of sleet, the lightning that strikes the barbed wire, killing Old Bob, and the rats she finds 'maybe kissing' on her wedding day. Gibbon's – and Chris's – song of the earth is muffled by Robert's intensities in *Cloud Howe*. In *Grey Granite* it is almost silenced, except in Chris's mind, by the urban life of Duncairn until her final return to Cairndhu. Her brother Will had been right after all:

Scotland lived, she could never die, the land would outlast them all, their wars and their Argentines, and the winds come sailing over the Grampians still with their storms and rain and the dew that ripened the crops – long and long after all their little vexings in the evening light were dead and done.

This 'unending morning' is Gibbon's best hope, but it is scarcely human. According to his wife he believed in the Golden Age of prehistory and was 'not unhopeful of a Golden Age yet to come', but at the end of the *Quair* Chris neither feels the rain nor hears the lapwings. She has become as the stones about her on which the rain also beats.

Jewish novels of the mid to late twentieth century by Bernard Malamud, Saul Bellow and Philip Roth are often impressively accurate diagnoses of the era, psychologically penetrating and culturally astute. In Saul Bellow's *Herzog* the theme of alienation gets its most thorough workout since Dostoevsky. The novel's eponymous hero opts out of a society which exacts heavy penalties for non-conformity: 'They'll put a meter on your nose and charge you for breathing. You'll be locked up back and front'. Professor Moses Herzog attempts a 'five-cent synthesis' of modern character, his mind focusing on himself before panning across the general condition:

> His own individual character cut off at times both from facts and from values. But modern character is inconstant, divided, vacillating, lacking the stone-like certitude of archaic man, also deprived of the firm ideas of the seventeenth century, clear hard theorems.

In the story of *Herzog* modern man is doubly Jewish: firstly by birth, secondly by virtue or defect of being an academic, always the Jew among Gentiles. Back-lit by philosophers from Hegel to Kierkegaard who have shaped contemporary ideas about the human condition, Herzog is a professional systematiser, a man of syntheses who becomes disenchanted with intellectual constructs and the reality systems represented by colleagues, friends and competitors. He's trying to find the clear, hard theorem of himself in resistance to the attempts of others to make him conform to their idea of what he should be. In obedience to his lover, Ramona's instruction to shop for clothes that will proclaim a brighter, still virile personality, he is conducting an experiment in becoming, the process that will be replaced at the end of the novel — as in Bellow's *Henderson the Rain King* — by the state of being. As he lies waiting for Ramona to come to him — she is decking herself for love — his mind moves outward, beyond self-preoccupation, to survey the epoch. His self-concern becomes simultaneous with concern for the world in one of the grandest, most humane passages in modern fiction:

> ...he let the entire world press upon him. For instance? Well, for instance, what it means to be a man. In a city. In a century. In transition. In a mass. Transformed by science. Under organised power. Subject to tremendous controls. In a condition caused by mechanisation. After the late failure of radical hopes. In a society that was no community and devalued the person. Owing to the multiplied power of numbers which made the self negligible. Which spent military billions against foreign enemies but would not pay for order at home. Which permitted savagery and barbarism in its own great cities. At the same time the pressure of human millions who have discovered what concerted efforts and thoughts can do. As megatons of water shape organisms on the ocean floor. As tides polish stones. As winds hollow cliffs. The beautiful super-machinery opening a new life for innumerable mankind. Would you deny them the right to exist? Would you ask them to labour and go hungry while you enjoyed delicious old-fashioned Values? You — you yourself are a child of this mass and a brother to all the rest. Or else an ingrate, dilettante, idiot.

This is not a typical anti-Utopian protest, despite its references to dark aspects of the modern state. Those aspects have had plenty of air time in Orwell's *1984* and Aldous Huxley's *Brave New World*. The world needs their warnings, but it also needs a balancing recognition of the benefits of Alphaville, the positive aspects made possible by the 'beautiful super-machinery opening a life for innumerable mankind'. It's a noble paragraph.

But the most favourite sentence of all, the noblest sentence in English literature, comes at the end of George Eliot's *Middlemarch*:

> ...the growing good of the world is partly dependent on unhistoric acts; and that things are not so ill with you and me as they might have been, is half owing to the number who lived faithfully a hidden life, and rest in unvisited tombs.

14. Glasgow

In the nineteenth century it was the 'Second City of Empire'.
Tobacco and cotton, coal and ships brought wealth, but also
bred slums and gangs and it's the slums and gangs that lingered
in the myth of Glasgow's decline from Victorian boom town to
archetypal slump town. Journalists from South of the Border who
perpetuated the myth have, for at least three decades, run the
gauntlet of reprimand from the distressed reader's letter:

> Sir, I am disgusted that a newspaper of your standing
> should once again seek to perpetuate the image of
> Glasgow as a hellish mixture of poverty, drink and
> violence.

> Sir, Glasgow has the best collection of art in Britain
> outside London...the largest civic-owned library in
> Europe...more than 70 public parks...an architectural
> heritage commended by Betjeman and Pevsner.

> Sir, I have lived in Glasgow for 85 years and never
> once been assaulted on the street. I am also a lifelong
> teetotaller.

> Sir, I moved to Glasgow from Bradford-on-Avon and
> never regretted it. Does your ignorant and prejudiced
> reporter not realise that the 'bonny, bonny banks of
> Loch Lomond' are only FIFTEEN MINUTES away by
> car. 'Haud yer wheesht', as we say in these parts.

'You can't call it life, not in Glasgow', said my Mancunian
friend, Tom, 'not unless you'll settle for Bingo halls, betting shops
and boozers'. There's no conviviality to be had in a Glasgow
pub, Tom says, only an obligation to get dourly fu'. It's different
in Manchester. There'll be people in the streets late at night in
Manchester. Chances are they'll be jolly, he says, but never brutal
with it. In Glasgow to be out at night is admission of a perverse
desire to get cut.

Shades of Matthew Arnold. Glasgow is like the bad bits in Burns – Scotch drink, Scotch manners and Scotch religion. The drink needs no identifying, the manners derive therefrom and the religion is either bigoted Protestant, bigoted Papist, or the transposition of these into the blue and the green, Rangers and Celtic, perpetually clashing armies of an eternal cultural night.

'What's your name?' we asked the boy who appeared in the kitchen with one of our less discriminating daughters after a youth-club dance.

'Mick', he said. 'But I'm no' one. That's my name but I'm no' one. I hate them. An' my Mum and Dad hate them as well'.

Daniel Defoe, himself a canny man, would have been shocked by all this. If he had been forbidden London but given his pick of other towns he might well have chosen Glasgow. Its principal streets – there were four in his time – its Tolbooth, its university, its thirteenth-century cathedral, its 'houses all of stone' and the substantial signs of advantage taken by its merchants of the new opportunities brought by Union made for a city not merely 'very fine' but for 'the cleanest and beautifullest, and best built city in Britain, London excepted'. Beautiful buildings have gone up since Defoe was there: Pollok House, Glasgow's finest eighteenth-century domestic building, designed by William Adam, completed by his son, John, containing the remarkable Stirling-Maxwell collection (two El Grecos and several Blakes) – a notable supplement to the treasures of the Kelvingrove Art Gallery and Museum. In its grounds stands the craftily designed, purpose-built home for the great art hoard of the late Sir William Burrell. Concentrating on works by living artists from Beryl Cook's roly-poly urbanites to paintings by contemporary Scots such as John Bellamy and the new generation of Glasgow Boys, the Gallery of Modern Art occupies a building dating from 1829. Alexander 'Greek' Thomson's Great Western Terrace is one of many later nineteenth-century buildings lauded by Pevsner and there's the city's architectural masterpiece, Charles Rennie Mackintosh's School of Art. There's further audacity to be enjoyed in the metallic 'Armadillo', an extension to the Scottish Exhibition and Conference Centre, reminiscent of the Sydney Opera House, and in Iraqi-born architect Zaha Hadid's Riverside Museum, housing the popular transport and travel exhibition. The City Chambers building in George Square has doubled in films for both the Vatican and the Kremlin.

The Tobacco Lords built grandiose mansions to the west of what is now the city's commercial centre. When the tobacco trade declined the Industrial Revolution brought the city the means of re-inventing itself as a centre for cotton manufacturing, shipbuilding and heavy engineering. Employment opportunities attracted incomers from the Scottish Highlands and Ireland, expanding the population from some 40,000 to over half a million between the 1780s and 1880s. With the influx of cheap labour came sordid, cramped living conditions for many families, hence the widespread construction of tenements. Life in the tenements fostered a strong sense of community, but the demise of shipbuilding resulted in serious unemployment with the poorest housing blocks turning into overcrowded slums. Sanitation was at best inadequate; disease and death were common.

Utopian attempts to revitalise the city by demolishing ill-maintained tenements and building multi-storey apartment blocks were well-intentioned but only partly successful. Voices were raised in protest.

'The people who talk about demolition are thinking only about bricks and mortar. We are thinking about people. That's what a community is. Why not improve the houses and leave the people where they are?'

Like other British cities Glasgow made mistakes. The high rises get most of the stick now, rather unfairly. With religious fervour the planners worked a partial miracle in the notorious Gorbals; but the uprooting impersonality of the tower blocks deprived people of their sense of community, stimulating a reactionary romanticising of lost squalor and the hopelessness that was the obverse of single-end cosiness. There was no easy fix. Edwin Morgan, a Glasgow man of European mind, committed to his city and his century – Scotland's first Makar, first First Poet or Poet Laureate – makes the point in one of his Glasgow Sonnets':

> From thirtieth floor windows at Red Road
> He can see choughs and samphires, dreadful trade –
> The schoolboy reading *Lear* has that scene made.
> A multi is a sonnet stretched to ode
> and some say that's no joke. The gentle load
> of souls in clouds, vertiginously stayed

above the windy courts, is probed and weighed.
Each monolith stands patient, ah'd and oh'd.
And stalled lifts generating high-rise blues
Can be set loose. But stalled lives never budge.
They linger in the single-ends that use
their spirit to the bone, and when they trudge
from closemouth to laundrette their steady shoes
carry a world that weighs us like a judge.

So, just a couple of weeks ago, the brave, notorious Red Road flats, the tallest apartment blocks in Europe, were demolished. But what about the stalled lives *not* raised above the city in a multi-storeyed block, trudging 'from closemouth to laundrette', left behind by the planners and condemned to stay on in one of the decaying old tenements? Edwin Morgan again:

A mean wind wanders through the backcourt trash.
Hackles on puddles rise, old matresses
puff briefly and subside. Play-fortresses
of brick and bric-a-brac spill out some ash.
Four storeys have no windows left to smash,
but in the fifth a chipped sill buttresses
mother and daughter, the last mistresses
of that black block condemned to stand, not crash.
Around them the cracks deepen, the rats crawl.
The kettle whimpers on a crazy hob.
Roses of mould grow from ceiling to wall.
The man lies late since he has lost his job,
Smokes on one elbow, letting his coughs fall
thinly into an air too poor to rob.

The worst mistakes were not the multi-storeys but the big schemes. In the west Drumchapel; in the east Blackhill, Easterhouse. Expanses of dun, identical blocks staring at each other across patches of ground where grass has given up trying, in denial of the Celtic *'glas cu'*, alleged origin of 'Glasgow', meaning 'dear green place'. These, with the remaining slums of an earlier generation, are the true urban wastelands, breeding agonies far more literal than T. S. Eliot's. A citizen who makes it in these parts deserves the freedom of a more humane city, a *croix de guerre*. There will be an element of truth in my friend Tom's image of Glasgow as long as such places exist to generate the desperation, fear and outrage which will seek oblivion in the boot, the blade and the fury that growls, back of the throat, in the Hampden roar.

In the seventies the planners began to listen to local people and realised they'd got it wrong. Conservationist pieties replaced post-war thraldom to the architecture of social progress. Clearance stopped and thousands of Victorian and 20th century tenements were refurbished. New ones were built, often on the sites of old ones beyond restoration. The city's image was re-packaged. Derived from Roger Hargreaves's 'Mr Men' books, a 'Mr Man' logo – the 'Mr Happy' smiling circle on a bright yellow background – punningly proclaimed, 'Glasgow's Miles Better'. Better than where? Sarajevo, Rio de Janeiro? Soweto? Mogadishu? An American-style PR campaign in the 1980s implied an English answer: maybe my friend Tom's Manchester, maybe Birmingham. Epidemics of scrubbing and planting made it cleaner and greener. Delicatessens and wine bars attract an expanding population of yuppies. There are sports centres and arts centres. New technologies prosper where factories, forges and shipyards died. It looks like a resurrection and with the Garden Festival of 1988 and the title 'European City of Culture' in 1990 it began to vie with Edinburgh as Scotland's first city of tourism. Glasgow chauvinism began to flower again, as it hasn't since the city ranked high among the industrial power houses of the world. It's all right to belong to Glasgow now, as long as you're middle class, even without a couple of drinks on a Saturday, but it's still better with them.

✳✳✳✳

The difference between America and Scotland is that America got Aleksandr Solzhenitsyn and Scotland, for a few days, got Ovidy – 'Call me Ovid' – Gorchakov. Comrade Gorchakov made it clear to those of us convened to meet him in Glasgow under the auspices of the Scottish Arts Council that he wasn't much interested in anyone 'who cannot help me with my project'. His project was a historical novel involving the Scottish forbears of Mikhail Lermontov. If this bespoke a singleness of purpose slightly at odds with the larger issues of cultural *détente*, there was, nevertheless, something undeniably imposing about Mr Gorchakov's conception of himself as a hero of his times. He wasn't as likeable as the two other members of the Soviet delegation – affable Mr Melnikov who did translations and sensitive Mr Petrosian, First Secretary of the Armenian Writers' Union, who wondered if anyone read William Saroyan these days – but he certainly talked big.

'I write altogether fourteen books', he said.

'Oh, my goodness me, that's an awful lot of books', said Lavinia Derwent, creator of Tammy Troot, a Scottish fish for children. 'How do you manage so many of them at the one time? Is it pills you take?'

'Naw', said Mr Gorchakov with a scoop of the head cribbed from Cherkasov's Ivan the Terrible, 'naw. We are socialist country, not capitalist country'.

'Of course', said Miss Derwent, seeing at once the connection between capitalism and decadent stimulants.

'In my country', said Mr Gorchakov, 'my books make fifty thousand, one hundred thousand copies'.

'Goodness', said Miss Derwent, imprecisely.

'Oh yes. All over the place. When I translate into languages of our many republics I get thirty per cent of original contract'.

'How nice'.

'Oh yes, oh yes. We are socialist country. If we were capitalist country, with all my books, I would be...I would be...already... MILLINER'.

****

It was good to work at a university in a town like this. Your calling ensured service to the subject; the location protected you from the hazards of the *tour d'ivoire*. It was not as challenging a situation as I knew in South Africa in the 1960s. There, literature, as a medium of values was a weapon constantly burnished in the fight to keep liberalism alive. The temptation was to apply everything to the local enormity. *Othello*, of course, was a gift – once you had revealed the quality of Iago's evil you had exposed the Immorality Act as devil's work. *Nostromo* was another: the silver of the mine was the gold of the Rand and the contamination of Gould's idealism by material interests illuminated the protectionism that kept apartheid going. Jo, Dickens's crossing-sweeper in *Bleak House,* was kin to little Alfred who always managed to be waiting for you with outstretched hand at the end of the day, although the police were for ever moving him on. Even old Edmund Spenser was defiled by relevance. What was his description of Lucifera in Book I of *The Faerie Queene* if not an allegory of South African politics:

> ...rightfull kingdome she had none at all,
> Ne heritage of native soveraintie;
> But did usurpe with wrong and tyrannie
> Upon the sceptre which she now did hold:
> Ne ruld her Realme with laws, but pollicie,
> And strong advizement of six wisards old,
> That, with their counsels bad, her kingdome did uphold.

You read that to your students and invited them to identify the policy and the wizards in the Nationalist cabinet. Literature wasn't pressed into quite this sort of life in Glasgow, though I confess a secret longing to be given *The Castle* to teach, primarily as an opportunity to alert my customers to the ways of the Inland Revenue, the Scottish Gas Board, Strathclyde Regional Council's Department of Education and the Kafkaesque conspiracy in which they were all demonstrably joined against the wellbeing of my family and friends. Nowadays it would appear that the sway of Management throughout our systems has bureaucratised universities into making Castles of their own. Relevance need not be so blatant, but the arts, to thrive here, must be news of life, not merely exercises in aesthetics.

****

Scotland has been rich in comedians. Dundee produced Will Fyffe; Aberdeen produced Harry Gordon; Greenock gave us Chic Murray and Glasgow is known for Jimmy Logan ('Sausages is the boys'), Stanley Baxter ('Parliamo Glasgow') and the ubiquitous, endlessly inventive Billy Connolly. The comedienne, Elaine C. Smith, joked that in the last census 74 per cent of Glaswegians thought they could be funnier than Connolly, while 9 per cent thought they were him. Less adept at the punch line than Irish or American comics, the Scottish penchant has been for situational comedy. Chic Murray often appeared in a double act with his wife, Maidie. He was 6'3", she was 4'11" so they were billed as 'The Tall Droll with the Small Doll'. Chic excelled in uncovering the absurd in the commonplace. Scene: a butcher's shop. Enter Chic.

'I'd like to buy five wasps, please', he says.

'I'm sorry, sir', says the butcher, 'we don't sell wasps'.

'That's funny', says Chic, 'you've got six in your window'.

There's humour everywhere in Glasgow. Take the drunk man on the bus. Asked by a ticket inspector to state his destination he says, 'Mars. Ahm gaun tae Mars, okay?' When the inspector demands to see his ticket he digs into his pocket and produces a Mars bar.

Let me take you to a wet and windy street in the Partick district. The rain is horizontal. In the teeth of the gale stands a clump of ovoid women clad in 'rain-mate' hats and plastic macs. They clutch bulging plastic shopping bags. Impervious to the battering of the elements, they are talking with dismal intensity. Their faces are ashen, with expressions of the utmost woe. As you walk past this dolorous knot of humanity, lashed by the rain, a single voice rises above the sound of the wind. Her tragic face lifted to the dripping sky, the woman wails, 'Aw, right enough, ah had tae laugh'.

Anyone who supposes that the yuppification of Glasgow is going to bring Glaswegians into conformity with accepted norms should heed poet, Tom Leonard, who uses the city's patois to flight his satire with comedy, demonstrating that the thickest Glasgow dialect can say things we need to know:

> this is thi
> six a clock
> news thi
> man said n
> thi reason
> a talk wia
> BBC accent
> is coz yi
> widny wahnt

mi ti talk
aboot thi
trooth wia
voice lik
wanna yoo
scruff. if
a toktaboot
thi trooth
lik wanna yoo
scruff yi
widny thingk
it waz troo.
jis wanna yoo
scruff tokn.
thirza right
way ti spell
ana right way
ti tokit. This
is me tokn yir
right way a
spelling. this
is ma trooth
yooz doant no
thi trooth
yirsellz cawz
yi canny talk
right. this is
the six a clock
nyooz. belt up.

15. Edwin Morgan: First Poet

'I'd like you to be my literary executor', he said over a coffee in the Glasgow University College Club. 'But I'm going to New Zealand next year', I said, 'I'll be too far away', and this was already mid-1980. 'That doesn't matter', he said, compounding the honour, 'I'd like you to do it anyway'.

It had to be yes. I had been his student when he shared an English Department office with Jack Rillie. They were the moderns, the now people. They were hip, risky. Intimate with existentialism and the Beats. We called them 'The Rillie-Morgan Axis'. From seventeenth-century prose to *The Faber Book of Modern Verse* Eddie made it all feel contemporary. He never talked down to his classes, commanding attention by a springy conversational style, clarity from inwardness with the topic. You always wished his lectures would keep going past the hour. They made you feel more alive. Later, as fellow member of staff, he was as much comrade as colleague, always with time for you no matter how junior you were, how far behind.

Now I was a declared fan and had worked joyously with him in the interview originally published in *Akros* 11: 32, reprinted in Hamish Whyte's indispensable *Nothing Not Giving Messages*. Finding that a working relationship in the Department of English had evolved into friendship, was the privilege of a lifetime, with happy hours spent in the book-lined eyrie of his flat overlooking Great Western Road with a window ledge for a seagull and a balcony for jumping into the sun or taking off for the moons of Jupiter or up the road to Loch Ness to hear the monster singing. Eventually, in 1992, he'd take off for my new home in New Zealand where I introduced him to a packed hall at Wellington's International Arts Festival and he read his poems in Hamilton on receipt of an honorary doctorate from the University of Waikato. Not long after the millennium I seduced the University's Department of Theatre Studies into staging *A.D.*, his trilogy of plays on the life of Jesus. 'The First Men on Mercury' and 'Little Blue Blue' were already campus hits.

I loved the whiff of sulphur about him as self-styled Demon, rattling the bars of convention and complacency. I loved his hyenas, centaurs, astronauts, Mercurians and Glaswegians, his Cinquevalli, hard-man Cyrano and his Beasts of Scotland. I loved his energy, his delight in risk, the devilish optimism of his curiosity, his peerless, nonconformist contemporaneity. I loved his internationalism and his inveterate Scottishness. He might be talking to himself in his translation of Attila József's 'Elegia':

> Here, and only here, you may smile and cry, and
> Here, here only, can your sinews endure,
> my soul! This is my native land

The poet should be himself a true poem? This one was. I loved the work and the poem that was the man. Didn't everyone? Of course it had to be yes.

Edwin Morgan

As literary executor, seeking to be of service, I undertook the job of doing what I could to bring work and man together for future biographers in a time-line of his life. So we settled into a rhythm of regular meetings when I would ask questions and he would ransack memory and consult diaries, allowing ourselves a single malt only when digging was over for the day. When I left for New Zealand there was still much to unearth, so whenever I returned to Scotland for research, or passed through en route for somewhere else, I stopped in Glasgow and we got back to work. Birth in Hyndland on 27 April 1920, then Pollokshields, Rutherglen, Glasgow High School, pacifism, Royal Army Medical Corps, Palestine, Glasgow University for History, Political Economy, French, English and Russian, Professor of English, innumerable readings at schools, coming out as gay when he was 70. Always writing towards Buckingham Palace for a surprise OBE and laureateship first of Glasgow, then of Scotland. He was our first First Poet and the time-line was there for James McGonigal who begins his masterly *Beyond the Last Dragon: A Life of Edwin Morgan* with the perfect summing-up: 'Edwin Morgan is Scotland's best loved poet since Robert Burns'.

For his eightieth birthday on 27th April 2000 Robyn Marsack, Director of the Scottish Poetry Library, and Hamish Whyte of Mariscat Press commissioned a selection of admirers to contribute to *Unknown is Best: A Celebration of Edwin Morgan at Eighty*. The book opens with 'At Eighty', a poem by Eddie himself which begins: 'Push the boat out, compañeros,/ Push the boat out, whatever the seas', and ends:

> Out,
> push it all out into the unknown!
> Unknown is best, it beckons best,
> like distant ships in mist, or bells
> clanging ruthless from stormy buoys.

I wrote him a letter.

Dear Eddie,
What a day it is for us all!
Your mother laughed when you danced round the house as a

boy, chanting your rhymes. At 80 you're still at it, singing to us of rhododendrons, love, gasometers and gulls. Then your father told you how steel is made, giving you a taste for power and danger. So down you went into the mere with Beowulf to fix shadow-lurker Grendel's monstrous mother with refurbished alliterations. Then up again to sing with Piaf, Columba, Vico, apples and Oban girls and the Beasts of Scotland. You're still living dangerously, consorting with demons and hi-jacking Jesus, showing him the way to Sepphoris for some shopping and a bit of a fling, bothering the church, torching us to wonder. Can't everyone see that curiosity is celebration of the world and all its messages, that experiment is optimism?

With a literal torch you pored under the bedclothes over sets of cigarette cards like 'Romance of the Heavens' and were equally fascinated by the romance and the facts. So you took us from your city balcony in an impeccable trajectory to the Domain of Arnheim and a home in space and showed us how to keep a voyaging generation voyaging. If you were to travel through space the total mileage you've clocked up taking poetry to schools since your retirement from the University of Glasgow in 1980 you would see Saturn or the moons of Jupiter for yourself as well as in your mind's eye. On holiday at North Berwick you discovered intense feelings about sea and sun, fields of poppies, the passing of time and the seasons. You bunched the feelings together, found love and said, 'We must jump into the sun'. So we did. We'd been waiting. You just had to say the word.

The child was father of the man. Boyhood determined the writer's fabric with its life-long strands of play and romance, its reverence for fact, its sensitivity to nature and human emotion, its energy, its delight in risk. You are, essentially, a futurist. You tell us in 'The Manifesto' that the futurists 'thought life a bobby-dazzler', and so do you. The futurists 'made heavy words go heady', and so do you. The futurists 'flew kites up up up endless', and so do you. Your kites are everywhere because there's a world-wide readership relishing the speed, the fun, the glide and crackle, the illumination of life's difficult corners, the authoritative chords and indefatigable freshness of your verse. To read you, or to hear you read, is to feel a contagion. We are touched. Of course some of us, wherever we are, can hear tunes and rhythms close to home because, for all your fine internationalism, there lies on the bone and pulse and muscle of your lines a quality of Scottishness like a radio-active dust that can't be blown away. A little of the same dust can settle on others too, like Yevtushenko, Pasternak, Quasimodo, Montale, Lorca, Brecht, Mayakovsky and Attila József when you translate them, giving them new lives among us, sharing your traveller's booty.

It wouldn't do to paint you like Dickens in his chair at Gad's Hill, dreaming about his characters. You'd be wide awake, watching yours to see what they'd do next: hyenas and centaurs, astronauts and Mercurians, Tarkovsky and Jack London, the mummy of Rameses II, the Loch Ness Monster and vulnerable Glaswegian city-boy Cyrano de Bergerac with his 'auld lang whang', daring 'each and ivry wan'. More likely they'd be watching you, spotlit on the high tops with your Blakean Demon, or up there on the high wire of your imagination like your Cinquevalli, defying gravity (both kinds), juggling enigmas and sealing your letters with a billiard ball. Wordsworth would have recognised in you his idea of the poet as one who 'rejoices more than other men in the spirit of life that is in him'. At the end of 'On John MacLean' you give the great socialist the words, 'We are out for life and all that life can give us'. He surely speaks for the joyful aesthetic and ecumenical morality of Edwin Morgan, 'kind and croose and guid tae ivrywan,/ Witty and free'.

Your story, like your Faust's, 'like a lightning-flash invades/The dark heart of complacency'. Your thoughts are green. Thank you for them all.

Poet, laureate, Glaswegian, friend. Happy birthday.

****

An *honnête homme* involved with books and humankind, he chose the occasion of his seventieth birthday in 1990 to confirm his position as a homosexual writer. The decision to publish an explicit interview and an autobiographical poem, 'Epilogue: Seven Decades', completed a coming-out process in which the habits of secrecy formerly required by law or enjoined by social convention yielded to his wish to 'record the truthful emotional basis of the poetry'. The forthright poem ends *Collected Poems* illuminating the constriction within which he had lived and suppressed, but always managed to work:

At thirty I thought life had passed me by,
translated *Beowulf* for want of love.
And one night stands in city centre lanes –
they were dark in those days – were wild but bleak.
Sydney Graham in London said 'you know
I always thought so', kissed me on the cheek.
And I translated Rilke's *Loneliness*
is like a rain, and week after week after week
strained to unbind myself,
sweated to speak.

The variety of his work includes love poems, concrete poems, Glasgow poems and Scottish sonnets, emergent poems – the most famous of these being the much-discussed 'Message Clear' evolved from the line 'I am the resurrection and the life' – poster poems, sound poems, science fiction poems and libretti. His critical writing is erudite without pomp and never sectarian. He is the most holistic, enlanguaged and internationalist of contemporary British poets. The internationalism is evident in his range of styles and in his translations of European and Russian writers. In the Second World War he joined the Royal Army Medical Corps – as MacDiarmid had done in the First – and served at the 42nd General Hospital at El Ballah in the Egyptian desert as quartermaster's clerk and stretcher-bearer. The liking he acquired for Arab culture is evident in his sequence of poems, 'The New Divan'. In 1992 his Glasgow-based Scots version of Edmond Rostand's *Cyrano de Bergerac* was staged to nation-wide acclaim at the Edinburgh Festival. Against stiff competition his 1952 translation of *Beowulf* has been called 'the most satisfactory of all the attempts to reduce *Beowulf* to modern English verse'.

He doesn't like 'systems of thought or systems of belief'. A Blakean prose-poem called 'The Fifth Gospel' says:

I have come to overthrow the law and the prophets: I have not come to fulfil, but to overthrow...
It is not those that are sick who need a doctor, but those that are healthy. I have not come to call sinners, but the virtuous and law-abiding, to repentance.

Hugh MacDiarmid had taken a similar position, adopting as his motto Thomas Hardy's declaration, 'Literature is the written expression of revolt against accepted things'. This anti-establishment strain is the anarchic side of Morgan's relish of life in its fullness. *Wi the Haill Voice* is the title of his volume of translations into Scots of poems by Vladimir Mayakovsky, and it is the wholeness of his own voice that best testifies to the amplitude of his imagination. It's the voice of a romantic and intellectual sensibility constantly alert to a world which is 'everything that is the case' ('Wittgenstein on Egdon Heath'). It speaks of the vitality of the city and of its pathos; yet even in works which present the dark side of urban life ('Glasgow Green') or the cruelties of mid-century South African politics ('Starryveldt') or the ironies of events in the Gulf ('An Iraqi Student') there is compassion in the poetry, between the lines or like a heartbeat under them to be felt as part of what Charles Olson calls the poem's 'energy-discharge'. With the break-up of the USSR and 'the body of socialism' dragged 'into a common grave' the '*novus ordo*' prompts 'A Warning' in *Hold Hands Among the Atoms*. The poem's fuse of feeling rises through an empathic choice of detail to a poise of sadness and irony in which political realism and humane concern are perfectly combined:

> ...Take your string bag. An orange
> for strippers. Don't feel bought, you're buying, buying.
> – And if, oh, any should stint the euphoria
> for a moment, watching the snow falling slowly
> over shot-pocked facades, there'd only be some
> muffled echo of the better life that
> never seems to come, like a faint singing
> heard in the pauses of snoring out of cardboard
> or waiters' shouts from bursting blood-red kitchens.
> They must listen so very hard, the freed ones!

Morgan's work offers the hope that comes from the intrinsic optimism of curiosity. For Robert Frost a poem gives 'a momentary stay against confusion'; for T. S. Eliot, in 'East Coker'; 'the whole earth is our hospital'; for Wallace Stevens 'reality is a cliché from which we escape by metaphor'. Confusion, hospital, escape – a doleful trio. Morgan's Glaswegian 'Trio' in the poem of that name, wind in their arms 'the life of men and beasts, and music,/laughter ringing them round like a guard', and for him poetry and life are not to be defined in negative terms. 'I think of poetry as partly an instrument of exploration', he says, 'like a spaceship, into new fields of feeling or experience (or old fields which become new in new contexts or environments)'. Neophiliac enjoyment of science and technology is evident throughout his writing, but the sonnet 'Computer Error: Neutron Strike' graphically faces the supreme peril of modern science. The demolition of the Berlin wall in 1989 signalled the official end of the Cold War, but the nuclear threat remains. The possibility of total annihilation is still the nightmare distinction of our time:

> No one was left to hear the long All Clear.
> Hot wind swept through the streets of Aberdeen
> and stirred the corpse-clogged harbour. Each machine,
> each building, tank, car, college, crane, stood sheer
> and clean but that a shred of skin, a hand,
> a blackened child driven like tumbleweed
> would give the lack of ruins leave to feed
> on horrors we were slow to understand
> but did.

His sense of fun can be whimsical as in the 'concrete' poems, 'French Persian Cats Having a Ball' and 'Siesta of a Hungarian Snake', or grotesque as in his guidance about the right way to throw a dwarf. 'Rules for Dwarf-Throwing' include:

> 4. If a dwarf is to be thrown across the path of an oncoming train, the thrower must previously satisfy the organisers that he bears no personal malice to the throwee.
> 10. It is strictly forbidden, in dwarf-throwing literature and publicity, to refer to dwarfs as 'persons of restricted growth' or 'small people'.

'The Hanging Gardens of Babylon (for John Furnival's 50th birthday)' deconstructs from 'the hanging gravids of babyland' via 'the hamfisted gasfitters of hyderabad' to a birthday compliment in 'the halcyon galleys of furnival' ('remains turn happy', endorses 'The Computer's First Birthday Card'). In 'Not Marble: A Reconstruction' Shakespeare is co-opted to give Wallace Stevens's Tennessean jar (in 'Anecdote of the Jar') a run for its jungle:

> A Sqezy bottle in Tennessee,
> if you want permanence, will press
> a dozen jars into the wilderness.

All W. H. Auden's conversations about art, Stravinsky observes, were 'so to speak, *sub specie ludi*'; creating poetry and music was a game to be played in a magic circle. Such a view can be meretricious if it consigns the arts to a zone of rarefied precocity, obscuring the fact that the arts are, somehow, news of life, not intellectual larks to be shared by members of an inner ring. But fun is what first commends a Carroll or a Lear and the surreal is a truth not only of the semi-conscious or nightmare kind Morgan writes about in the sequence 'Waking on a Dark Morning', but of the comic kinds he celebrates in 'The Computer's First Christmas Card', 'Little Blue Blue', 'The Glasgow 'Subway Poems' or in his *Tales from the Limerick Zoo*:

> A viper with contact lenses
> Was subject to murderous frenzies.
> He bit the Mackays
> From ankles to thighs,
> Thinking the fools were Mackenzies.

The fun can be sharp-edged. 'Rules for Dwarf-Throwing' strikes both at racism and the sanctimonies of political correctness. In 'Save the Whale Ball' trophy fetishism has made a huge ball of whalebones, 'a gigantic hyperborean scrimshaw/perched on a scarp at Angmagssalik'. The Whale Ball is crumbling, people are concerned, but too late, and the poem finally kicks in its reproach:

> Some would re-cast it in stainless steel; others
> would pulverise it for talismans.
> Some say we should have saved whales instead.

In the collection called *Instamatic Poems* Morgan shows his responsiveness to fact, the cool hand of the poet interfering with the material of news clippings only to adjust them into the surprises generated by their arrangement as verse. *Themes on a Variation* includes 'Newspoems', an earlier group of poems derived from newspapers where the whimsical effect largely depends on the poet's success in completing the unexpected message with an appropriate title or caption. 'Notice in Hell' is the caption for 'HALT COMMIT ADULTERY' and the title 'Joe's Bar' is just right for the wistful:

SORT OF PLACE YOU
   SORT OF
      YOU WISH
     until Midnight

The Styx will not easily regain its solemnity after 'Charon's Song'. Morgan's caption recalls Charles Murray's poem of the same title ('Another boat-load for the Further Shore,/ Heap them up high in the stern') but his Newspoem overgoes Murray's mordant whimsy with a jokey hint of necrophilia:

    'I place
    the
    dead
    ahead
    of me,
    and bong'

If the 'Newspoems' are a species of light verse, modern life on wry, they are also reifications of unexpected ideas, arrests of attention belonging to the same constellation of aesthetic and moral purposes as the concrete poems, epigrammatic inscriptions, sculptures and sundials with which Ian Hamilton Finlay has created the tangible question-marks of 'Little Sparta', his symbolic garden at Stonypath in Lanarkshire. The poems arise from Morgan's interest in the power of the media which he explores in the sequence of twenty-seven poems called 'From the Video Box' based on the technology by which viewers can record their reactions to television broadcasts. They comprise a study of the uses and impact of television through a range of individual reactions from that of a man prospecting in Patagonia who is infuriated by the image on his wrist-watch television of an astronaut probing for water and life on Mars ('Good God, we've got life galore – / twenty million sheep in Patagonia') to the disgruntlement of the owner of the biggest satellite dish in Perthshire. The 'Burning of the Books, in China/I don't know how many centuries BC' is compulsive 'first-class entertainment' for one viewer, while to another the burning of the Library at Alexandria is 'barbarous philistinism' foisted on a million homes. For a third viewer:

> ...the display of that conflagration
> which laid the new British Library in ashes
> must rate as quite unusually riveting.

The sequence considers the power of television to impose its own values on the material it selects. The opportunity to appear on television by way of the Video Box, to become authenticated by the ruling medium of the age, inspires a Glasgow flasher ('Big yin, innit?...Wave/goodbye, Willie') and brings hope to the owner of a lost marmalade cat called Robertson ('I know you won't mind if I use your box/for a *cri de coeur*'). Violence on the screen becomes gore in the living room as a television set oozes blood and the anonymous, controlling power of the medium is spoofed:

> ...what sort of programme was that
> and who lets these things happen?
> Look, I didn't wipe it off. See that, camera.
> You think I'm crazy? Think again.
> I know we get our mail through the set, bills,
> Bank balances, but blood is ridiculous.
> I want a clean dry screen from now on.
> Let them bleed elsewhere, whoever they are.

The capricious medium touches the heart in the seventh poem where the speaker tells of an abstract blue image which grows on the screen to 'kick-start hope racing forward/into I don't know what roads of years', and in the seventeenth poem a woman tells of her impression that her dead son has appeared in a blizzard of images:

> his fist in a revolutionary salute,
> a letter sticking from his pocket
> with writing I saw as mine.
> Oh how little we know
> of those we love!

His science-fiction poetry confirms Morgan as a futurist with MacDiarmid's faith in 'the third factor between Man and Nature —the Machine'. He takes 'a hopeful or even a *very* hopeful long-term view of the possibilities of the human race', relishing the capabilities of machines we've got — computers, space stations, modules, videos — and machines yet to come, like the de/ re-materialisation apparatus used in 'In Sobieski's Shield' or the demagnification banks in 'Memories of Earth'. In the second of his collected *Essays*, 'The Poet and the Particle', he recalls C.P. Snow's Rede Lecture on *The Two Cultures and the Scientific Revolution*, commenting: 'It is bizarre how very little of twentieth-century science has been assimilated into twentieth-century art'. If the poet is 'the man who traditionally finds links and resemblances, dissolves rather than erects barriers, moves among the various worlds of his time', how can the contemporary poet responsibly ignore technology? As shaman the artist has a duty 'to record what is happening, telling the tribe's history'. The tribe uses computers, goes up in rockets, lands on the moon, sends missions to Mars, links vehicles in space. It's time poetry rose to such occasions. The problem of technological language is no excuse for not trying. Two kinds of poetry might be produced:

> ...there could be a simple, even perhaps romantic kind of poetry of space exploration where things would not be described in technical terms...but there might also be a different kind of poetry which was more willing to use the specifics in the situation as far as possible and therefore to have to use technological language.

In 'A Home in Space' from the sequence, 'Star Gate' Morgan fuses these two kinds. The language is as technical as it has to be: lift-off, key-ins, food-tubes, screens, lenses, station, capsule. The jump of adrenalin in the astronauts as they agree to sever their connection with earth and launch themselves outwards in their mobile home is felt through the accelerating repetitions of the run-on lines:

> ...and it must be said they were –
> were cool and clear as they dismantled the station and –
> and gave their capsule such power that –
> that they launched themselves outwards –
> outwards in an impeccable trajectory, that band –
> that band of tranquil defiers, not to plant any –
> any home with roots but to keep a –
> a voyaging generation voyaging...

Anti-sexist humour goes into orbit in the 'Instamatic' poem 'TRANSLUNAR SPACE MARCH 1972' and 'The First Men on Mercury' shatters imperialist vanities by setting a pompous astronaut against a mind-bendingly superior Mercurian. The close-encounters situation opens with the earthman's stiff greeting:

> – We come in peace from the third planet.
> Would you take us to your leader?

Earthly self-importance vaporises to comedy when the Mercurian forces the earthling to swap languages:

> – I am the yuleeda. You see my hands,
> We carry no benner, we come in peace.
> The spaceways are all stretterhawn.

In rapidly mastered English the Mercurian tells the stuffy earthman to push off home, a sadder and wiser man now ironically fluent in Mercurian. The moral – don't condescend to the natives – is refreshed by Morgan's dramatising it in the comic interplay of languages. Already in the sequence of nine poems called 'Interferences' he had experimented with language in relation to alien existence. The idea for the sequence comes from the phenomenon of tektites, small glassy objects of unexplained origin and the science-fiction element is the analogously small linguistic disruption in each poem. The moments of interference include the flight of an arrow ('straight to its/targjx'), and a failed lift-off for a mission to Saturn ('wo de nat hove loft-iff'). The key idea of the poems – 'the conception "of other eyes watching" or intersecting worlds or planes of existence'– is the central notion in Morgan's three most haunting science fiction narrative poems: 'In Sobieski's Shield', 'From the Domain of Arnheim' which takes off from Poe's story, 'The Domain of Arnheim', and 'Memories of Earth'.

'In Sobieski's Shield' is based on the postulate that a person can be beamed through space by the method used in the television series, 'Star Trek'. Morgan uses the idea to trigger a meditation on change, identity and the relationship between past and present. Is the narrator the same person still, even with only four fingers on his left hand? Apparently he is. Despite his traumatic re-birth he continues, evincing in the alien context of his 'second life' the best of human qualities. Above all there is his resilience as he prepares to leave the protective 'dome' and fare forward into the unknown world of iron hills and lakes of mercury. We can adapt to what lies ahead, the poem says, life goes on even out there; we can, with a will, be masters of the universe. In 'Memories of Earth' Morgan achieves both astounding science fiction and an artistic hat-trick. It's a science fiction poem; it's a relatively long narrative poem; its verse, though free, is subtly braced by an iambic underbeat. As in 'From the Domain of Arnheim' with its 'fires of trash and mammoths' bones' and new-born child, it is recognisable earth which is the alien place and again it is the alien visitors who are chastened and enlarged by what they find. Beauty is to be seen in the sight and sound of Wordsworth musing upon Snowdon in the company of Robert Jones and the shepherd with his lurcher (the reference is to *The Prelude*, Book Fourteen), in the love that even Auschwitz cannot extinguish, in the frailty of a white butterfly, and in a canoe of Polynesians crossing the Pacific.

He plays with physics in the sequence of six 'Particle Poems'; in 'Memories of Earth' he uses the idea of the particle scientifically, given that even a complicated system like the earth may be treated astronomically as a particle. The invention of the poem begins with a shift in scale that makes the earth a sub-atomic stone particle. Signals emitted by the stone have been detected by the Council of a cold-blooded, authoritarian society. Like the crew of the 'Nostromo' in Ridley Scott's film, *Alien*, Hlad, Kort, Hazmon, Baltaz, and the narrator, Erlkon, have been despatched to investigate. Their instructions are clear:

> Keep your report formal, said the Council,
> your evidence is for the memory-banks,
> not for crude wonder or cruder appraisal.

So the explorers meet in secret, listen to the tapes of their expedition and 'study how to change this life', home safely but, like T. S. Eliot's Magi, aliens in the old dispensation. The imaginative power of 'Memories of Earth' is first felt in the narrator's effort to describe the miniaturisation that shrinks the Brobdignagian travellers to micro-Lilliputian size allowing them to enter first the stone, then the smaller entities inside it:

> The shrinking must be done by stages, but
> even so it comes with a rush, doesn't
> feel like shrinking. Rather it's the landscape
> explodes upwards, outwards, the waves rise up
> and loom like waterfalls, and where we stand
> our stone blots out the light above us, a crag
> pitted with caves and tunnels, immovable
> yet somehow less solid.

Once the travellers are inside the stone the narrative focuses on the conflict between the Council's demand for objective documentation and the pull of earth's gravity of beauty and passion. The special successes of the poem are the exactness with which Morgan describes complex processes and the victory over cold injunction of this spinning particle of earth, ambiguous, beautiful, violent, frail, self-tormenting and self-renewing.

In *Sonnets from Scotland* science fiction's malleabilities of time and space are used to give surprising perspectives of Scotland and the planet Earth. In 'The Coin' a visitor finds a One Pound coin bearing the head of a red deer and the words *Respublica Scotorum*. A machine has brought space travellers to land on the earth of a remotely future Scotland at a time when an independent Scottish state has been in existence long enough for a coin of its realm to have had its date rubbed off by successive fingers. The race is now 'silent', which suggests that the state may have had its day, but can we be sure? The poem ends:

> ...Yet nothing seemed ill-starred.
> And least of all the realm the coin contained.

A star suggests destiny, a future. Perhaps the race is only silent because the people are hidden. The visitors may look up from the well-worn coin to confront Scots whose 'yuleeda' will be waiting to try languages with them in Edinburgh. 'On Jupiter' offers a less sanguine prospect where 'a simulacrum, a dissolving view' of Scotland is found:

> ... as solid as a terrier
> shaking itself dry from a brisk swim
> in the reservoir of Jupiter's grim
> crimson trustless eye.

If the gods or people of Jupiter have made this Scotland, they have abandoned it to a 'sea of doubt, though the 'terrier' gives it vitality, implying that doubt is external to the country and self-doubt not necessarily the Scottish problem; but will the terrier catch the stick the untrusting 'launchers' have thrown, or will the prospect of such a possibility just dissolve like so many promises of Scottish self-determination, and if it does, who will be to blame? Again Morgan uses the idiom of science fiction to ask questions about the reality of Scotland, its gods, its people, the sea of doubt that encircles it and the questionable national will, 'the strong sick dirkless Angel' which groans and shivers in 'Post-Referendum'. In the last of the *Sonnets from Scotland*, 'The Summons', visitors to Earth are surprised that they find it difficult to leave the planet ('Despite our countdown, we were loath to go'). 'They have', says Morgan, 'become more involved than they thought they would. They don't understand their emotional reaction. They take with them perhaps a kind of love'. The love is Morgan's own commitment to his country and to the 'Earth...the favoured place' where 'nothing is not giving messages' and which he has made so vocal.

16. God

They said He knew everything. He watched everything and cared for everyone infinitely, though admittedly He seemed to care rather less for non-Christians and might even have it in for Jews and dusky infidels on the other side of the world. He was always beside you but you couldn't call him a comrade. Too lofty and, of course, invisible which made Him uniquely powerful. He was both invigilator and chief examiner, which felt a bit creepy given his constant propinquity. There was no hiding place. It was like being spied on. He was unquestionably male until militant feminism in the latter part of the twentieth century insisted that biblical use of 'Father' didn't preclude a She-God, or perhaps a hermaphrodite. You were obliged to pray to Him regularly, especially with petitions for the welfare of others, and could talk to Him quite freely when you felt the need, but don't expect a response. People appeared complacent about this state of affairs and God didn't become a vexation until you'd done a bit of growing up.

In childhood you knew Him as part of a system, a comfort zone for unexamined lives. He was ring-master of a cluster of authorities. There were your church-going parents and the church itself with its dog-collared minister who said that life without Jesus Christ was like lamb without mint sauce. There was school which began each day with a prayer and a hymn, with bracing moral sermons by the Headmaster on Fridays. There was the gracious and noble king or queen we petitioned Him to save in the national anthem, and the state whose laws, under Him, were upheld by various institutions and the police. Holding the bible and invoking His help when you swore to tell a court the whole truth were taken as the best assurance of probity because a lie would guarantee an afterlife in hell. There was the family doctor who was a church elder. There was the army which marched to war 'with the cross of Jesus going on before'. There were holidays at Christmas and Easter for which we were indebted to Him. Easter was more eggs than resurrection but Christmas was rejoicing and fun, giving each other presents because of the birth of Jesus and the presents he was given by the three wise men. There were stirring tunes: 'Hark the herald angels', 'O come, all ye faithful', 'Still the night, holy the night', 'Once in royal David's city', 'The first Noël'. You never got a row on Christmas day but some subjects were taboo. You wouldn't refer to the poor and destitute or the hungry millions in faraway places who could expect neither presents nor a blow-out at dinner time. Nor would you tastelessly speculate about the baby's virgin birth which began to bother you when intense interest in human biology came with adolescence. You went to church in the morning for the official Christmas story and for the rest of day focused on gifts, holly, mistletoe, Christmas crackers disgorging terrible jokes, microscopic plastic toys and paper hats. And then there was the big family turkey dinner. The bird was succulent, the bread sauce just the right consistency; the holy baby's sacrificial adult ending in unimaginable pain wasn't mentioned. Knocking back the bubbly and gulping down the Christmas pudding, you'd have been a party pooper if you'd recalled a tortured body nailed to a wooden cross, gentle Jesus forsaken by his heavenly Father.

With time God became more inscrutable and less manageable. School religion was dourly Presbyterian. The church for school services posted messages on a notice board under the heading 'The Wayside Pulpit'. On your way to school you could be accosted by stark information: 'Christ died for our sins', beginning the day with massive guilt. Then came bewildered resentment. You weren't aware of particular sins on such a scale of wickedness. Your life was rich in peccadilloes, but nothing commensurate with hammering nails into a remarkably decent human being, requiring him to wear a crown of thorns and jabbing a spear into his side. History was bringing you horror stories about the sins of the church itself, persecutions, martyrdoms, the torture chambers of the Inquisition and the internecine conflict in your own country between Protestants and Catholics. The comfort zone was breaking down.

Nobody had much to say about Jesus beyond the pages of the gospels though there appeared to be good evidence outside the Bible that he did exist. A biographical note might read something like this:

> The man whom we know as Jesus Christ was born during the reign of Augustus, the first Roman Emperor (63BC – 14AD), around the year 4BC. He was Jewish and brought up in Galilee, though he may not have

been born there. During the final years of his short life he became well known as a religious teacher in various parts of Samaria and Judaea including Jerusalem. The Roman Governor, Pontius Pilate, put him to death by crucifixion around the year 30AD.

Apart from that we seemed to know very little; but if he was the son of God the human side of him merited more attention than people were giving it, and there was virtually no speculation about his everyday life. You were expected to settle for the itinerant preacher in what Billy Connolly called 'the good dress and the casual sandals' dispensing beatitudes and working miracles. But what was he like as a teen-ager? Who were his friends? Where did he go? How did he acquire his understanding of human nature? What was his sexuality? Why did he think he could repair our deficiencies? How did he view the society of first-century Palestine under Roman occupation?

My father had been brought up as an Anglican which meant that in Scotland he joined the Episcopalian church. This is where I was baptised in infancy and where my mother and I went with him for services. The Episcopalians were less miserable than the Presbyterians, but by the time I was fourteen I was wrestling with post-war doubts about the God who had allowed the whole catastrophe to happen. When I was sixteen it was time to be confirmed. Dutifully, I attended confirmation classes, but before the course was finished I had made up my mind. Like Huckleberry Finn I'd go to hell. Much as I wanted to believe and conform, I couldn't vow allegiance to a religion so flawed or a God so elusive, capricious, mute and apparently deaf to entreaty. I was struck by the Scottish poet, Edwin Muir's revulsion from human life conceived as a menagerie of creatures moving inexorably towards animal death in a slaughter-house open for business round the clock; but given the hells on earth humankind had constructed found it impossible to believe in the existence of a Deity who cared what people did to each other. What sort of heavenly Father dispensed natural disasters from floods, droughts and earthquakes to epilepsy, Parkinson's disease, children born with cleft palettes and a nightmare range of incurable afflictions? We were learning the truth about Hitler's attempted genocide of the Jews. So much for Yahweh.

I was a lost sheep. My parents would have to be told. I dreaded the confrontation.

It was our custom to listen to records of classical music *en famille*, usually at the week-end, sometimes on a week night when my father hadn't brought the office home with him and I was free of homework for the next day of school. After the dinner things were put away and the dishes washed we'd make a semi-circle round the record-player – persistently, for us, still a 'gramophone'. There was nothing in the world as comfortable as sharing our Beethoven, Brahms, Tchaikovsky and Sibelius, transforming the tiny sitting room into an exclusive concert hall for three. Tonight was going to be different. Would we three ever gather again in such contentment? I was aware of the risk, but couldn't contain my awful secret any longer. I had to come clean. When the last movement of Brahms's Third Symphony had processed us from passion to peace I told them.

My mother grew pale, picked up her knitting, said nothing. My father exploded. Who did I think I was to break from the ranks of Christians world-wide, to find fault with the convictions of mature, wise people who believed? It was beyond his comprehension that I couldn't accept a system that was good enough for him, for my mother and for their social circle. Why couldn't I profess an uncomplicated belief in God, follow the teachings of Jesus and join the club? This was a kind of sickness, not healthily British. You were expected naturally to honour the Sovereign, revere your parents, swell with pride at the sight of the Union Jack and worship the Christian God. What sort of life could I expect as an unbeliever? Did I enjoy insulting my mother and him by rejecting their values? What sort of return was this for years of careful parenting? What did I expect to gain from my attitude? Was I just trying to be different, a kind of exhibitionism? If I was ever fortunate enough to win the love of a good woman I would know there was a God, but my chances were looking slim.

Tense, terrible silence next morning until my father broke it. He was taking mother away on holiday that afternoon; in a few days I would be heading off to an R.A.F. cadet camp. I'd have work to do while we were apart. Here were my instructions.

'You will write me a letter. You will begin by stating that you do not believe in God or Jesus Christ. You will tell me why. You will send me the letter by the end of the week'.

It was a tall order for a sixteen-year-old .

Dear Dad,

15th April 1954

I have done my best to write down what you asked me for and here it is. If I seem at any time the slightest bit glib I am very sorry. I am not glib about this (or, I hope, anything) because I have not sufficient conviction or self-confidence.

You asked me to head this statement by saying, 'I do not believe in God or Christ', but I am not an atheist. If any single word were to be applied to my attitude it would be 'agnostic', but I am so indefinite about the business that I would prefer not to have any such word applied to me. I do not firmly disbelieve in God or Christ and I hope that some day I shall be able to say with deep conviction that I do believe in God and all that His Church stands for. My attitude is one of suspended judgement and although I sometimes become cynical and my leaning is rather towards the atheistic viewpoint, I am seeking after truth and I hope I shall always do so.

My reasons for this attitude are many and various and have accumulated over a period of at least two years. I have not suddenly decided to be different. These reasons have arisen from my own experience (such as it is) and what I have learned about the experience of others. Some of them are clear-cut in my mind, others are very vague and nebulous. But it would take a long time to list them. I don't even know if I could list them, so many were more impressions which I felt at a certain time and now the impression has gone but not before contributing to my general feeling of doubt and uncertainty.

You seem to think I take something of a delight in adopting this attitude. Please try not to think that. People who firmly believe in God, or for that matter have faith in any religion, have a certain spiritual comfort and security which I crave and life is, or should be, for them, considerably simplified, but the agnostic has no such security. When he is alone he is completely alone. It would be an easy thing for me to say to you that I believed in God etc. and was consequently confirmed just to keep things running quietly and to

146

keep you and Mum unconcerned about my spiritual welfare, but surely this would be the very essence of insincerity – after all: 'This above all to thine own self be true'. I am honestly very sad that I cannot make you all happy by accepting these things and I do not wish to cause any distress whatsoever, but I think Shakespeare was right.

This is what Stephen Haggard said in *I'll Go to Bed at Noon*: 'Never take anything on trust. Try to test each piece of knowledge you may glean from other people in the intercourse of life against your own experience. Accept nothing, believe nothing until a belief forces itself upon you, forces its roots into every cavity of your consciousness, and becomes an integral part of your way of life'.

And later: 'Remain a sceptic for 10 or 15 years: crystallise your beliefs and your intentions at the age of 30'.

Maybe 30 is a little late, but I think there's a great deal in what he says.

You may have wondered about the effect of my attitude on my views of morality. The only times when I'm inclined to feel morals are pointless are when I let myself think that if there is no God, then Man must be an end in himself, and if that is the case life appears utterly pointless – and if life is pointless, why bother about morals? But of course, on closer inspection, this idea can't hold water. I still think Christianity is the highest code of ethics ever conceived and I shall do my best to adhere to it. Man *may* be only a 'somewhat ridiculous animal, shouting and fussing during a brief interlude between infinite silences', but if that is so, then, for the time being one can at least concentrate on making him a little less ridiculous.

Incidentally, Conan Doyle's idea of the impersonal God seems a feasible conception.

So I feel, at the moment anyway, conscientiously compelled to suspend judgement and to forego communion with the Church, though I don't think it's wrong for me to go to a church if I wish to.

'I am not ashamed to confess that with this' – for the time being anyway – 'virtual negation of God, the universe has lost, to me, its very soul of loveliness, and although from henceforth the precept to "work while it is yet day" doubtless gains an intensified force from the terribly intensified meaning of the words, "the night cometh when no man can work", yet when I think, as think at times I must, of the appalling contrast between the hallowed glory of the creed that once was mine, and the lonely mystery of existence as now I find it – at such times I shall ever feel it impossible to avoid the sharpest pang of which my soul is susceptible'. However, I firmly believe that if there is a God in heaven and providing I continue to seek the truth, He will, in time, show Himself in a thoroughly convincing way.

Marshall

Clumsy, naïve – how could it have been otherwise at sixteen? – and laughably pretentious ('I think Shakespeare was right'), but well-meaning and desperately sincere.

[*A word of explanation. My resolve to believe nothing until a belief forced itself upon me was reinforced by the actor, writer and poet, Stephen Haggard. A grandnephew of H. Rider Haggard, he studied for the stage in Munich and London, worked in English repertory and played in New York. During the Second World War he joined the British Army, served in the Intelligence Corps and was posted to the Middle East where he worked for the Department of Political Warfare. In the summer of 1940 his wife and two sons went to the USA. And through the night after they left, a night of London blitz, Haggard sat up writing at top speed. He told his wife: 'I've written straight off a long letter to the boys telling them what sort of a fellow I am, what I believe and what I have experienced for I feel I shall never see them again'. When the Egyptian woman he'd fallen in love with broke off their relationship he shot himself at the age of 31. His book,* I'll Go to Bed at Noon: A Soldier's Letter to His Sons, *was published posthumously in 1944.*]

My father's reply came by return. I knew right away that I needn't fear more chastisement because he used his nickname for me; but the letter broke my heart. He respected the reasons I gave for my position. The fault was his and my mother's. They had failed in their duty to bring me up a Christian. He hoped I might find my way to faith.

My dear Snooks,

Thank you very much for your letter for which, despite the fact that it was an order, I am very grateful. I had thought it might serve two purposes, to clear your thoughts as well as to reveal them to me.

It may be that your agnostical leanings are a blow to my pride – it makes me feel that I have failed so badly in your upbringing, perhaps I should say we, Mum and I have failed so badly. You see I haven't been very successful in life and I fall down once more in this very important matter. Successful, however, I have been in one vital thing – by the grace of God I loved the finest woman and she loved me and so you acquired the finest mother – never forget it (even though we think she can't dust!!!)

Faith is a queer thing – I wish I had more. I find I have had most when things were black, which seems rather mean in a way.

By all means dissect, but don't wait necessarily until you are 30, the flaw in the theory as you detected. Revelation may come tomorrow or at 50, who knows.

I know you are sincere and am thankful that you realise that the Christian is the only way.

Have a good camp – hope the parcel arrived safely.

Your affectionate

Dad

My father, Harold Walker

Enclosed with his letter was an extract from a poem, Robert Browning's dramatic monologue, 'Bishop Blougram's Apology'. A worldly Bishop is criticised by his guest, a rigid atheist, who argues that the Bishop is a hypocrite because he acknowledges doubt. A man who doubts has no right to be a priest. My father had clipped a passage from the Bishop's response:

> The common problem, yours, mine, everyone's,
> Is not to fancy what were fair in life
> Provided it could be, – but finding first
> What may be, then find how to make it fair
> Up to our means – a very different thing!
> No abstract intellectual plan of life
> Quite irrespective of life's plainest laws,
> But one, a man, who is man and nothing more,
> May lead within a world which (by your leave)
> Is Rome or London – not Fool's-paradise.

But the Bishop had more to say beyond my father's extract. I tracked down the whole poem, as my father knew I would, and found a passage which cunningly amplifies the Bishop's Rome or London of plain laws and practicalities. The churchman admits he has doubts, the atheist acknowledges none; but just how secure in his non-belief can the atheist be? Is an atheist more immune to doubt than the professing believer? There's equal risk on both sides of the line. The Bishop speaks again, this time on behalf of atheists:

> Just when we are safest, there's a sunset touch,
> A fancy from a flower-bell, some one's death,
> A chorus-ending from Euripides, –
> And that's enough for fifty hopes and fears
> As old and new at once as Nature's self,
> To rap and knock and enter in our soul,
> Take hands and dance there, a fantastic ring,
> Round the ancient idol, on his base again, –
> The grand Perhaps!

While pondering this wily Bishop's argument and his alluringly poetic imagery, I dreaded my parents' return at the end of their holiday. I had even become less certain about God's ethics. Kierkegaard had pointed out that He had required Abraham to commit a crime, the sacrifice of his child. Surely Britain's allegedly righteous wars contravened Christ's injunction to turn the other cheek? But turning the other cheek wouldn't have cut much ice with the monstrous Hitler, would it, and what was God on about, letting an obscenity like Hitler live in the first place? Right enough, He moved in mysterious ways. I saw no evidence of the meek inheriting the earth, rather the opposite. An inflexibly secular, materialistic interpretation of human experience seemed false to a life that included music and love, yet doubts multiplied, on and on, as I waited for the encounter to come. There wouldn't be anger any more, but how could I bear the guilt of so wounding my kindly parents by my defection?

I needn't have worried. It was all smiles as they set down their suitcases and handed me a package. Here was Beethoven's Violin Concerto courtesy of Yehudi Menuhin and Wilhelm Furtwängler, our re-union concert ready to go. Our sitting-room concert hall was safe. No more wrangling about God, no blame game, just four drum taps, a gentle woodwind melody, a *tutti* and the solo violin in an ascent of octaves with all the promise of enchantments to come. As wily as the Bishop, my father had brought me a sunset touch from Beethoven, a fancy from a musical flower-bell. He knew me better than I knew myself. Beethoven may have believed in God, maybe not, but his music believed in something. A clear win for my father and the Bishop. The ancient idol, the grand Perhaps, was on his base again.

On a pillar in the Los Angeles freeway system I found my favourite graffito. Spray-painted, supposedly, by a celestial aerosol which, given its purported source, doubtless scrupled to use no fluorocarbon, the message read: 'Nietzsche is dead, signed God'. But the best advice came from the American writer, Robert Penn Warren, in his poem, 'Masts at Dawn':

> We must try
> To love so well the world that we may believe, in the
> end, in God.

17. RLS

There was a time when Scottish childhood would have been unthinkable without him. *Treasure Island* first. No villain more sinister than Blind Pew inexorably tapping towards the 'Admiral Benbow' inn with the Black Spot for Billy Bones; no rogue with the raffish magnetism of Long John Silver. No novel with a punchier beginning and probably the only novel commemorated by the game of golf. Spyglass Hill Golf Course is located on the Monterey Peninsula in California. All the holes are named after characters and places from *Treasure Island*. The first hole is 'Treasure Island'; others include 'Blind Pew', 'The Black Spot', 'Captain Flint' and 'Long John Silver'. The course is ranked fifth among 'America's 100 Greatest Public Courses'.

Then *Kidnapped*. Another classic villain in David Balfour's clay-faced, cringing uncle Ebenezer, a homicidal Uriah Heep on miserly small beer and porridge. No *frisson* sharper than the flash of lightning which reveals David's peril in the dark tower of the House of Shaws. We teeter with him in horror over the void at the treacherous end of the unfinished stairs, frozen in the untaken step that would have sent him plunging to his death. Magic. But what about the rest of Stevenson? Where should we go from there? Did he keep the magic coming? And what of RLS the man?

Summing up Stevenson's career, his friend, Henry James, concludes: 'It has been his fortune (whether or not the greatest that can befall a man of letters) to have had to consent to become, by a process not purely mystic and not wholly untraceable – what shall we call it? – a Figure'. An author of fables, Stevenson became in his lifetime the most fabulous of Victorian writers, as vivid a figure in his century as Ernest Hemingway in the twentieth. Shortly before he died another friend, Edmund Gosse, wrote to him in Samoa:

> ...the gossip-columns of the newspapers pullulate with gossip about you that cannot be true, such as: 'All our readers will rejoice to learn that the aged fictionist L R [sic] Stevenson has ascended the throne of Tahiti of which island he is now a native'...Since Byron was in Greece, nothing has appealed to the ordinary literary

man as so picturesque as that you should be in the South Seas.

The sequence of events by which Stevenson grew into the legendary RLS began with a sickly childhood. Invalided to 'the land of counterpane' by the bronchial problems that plagued him all his life, he soon learned to live in his imagination. As a reluctant student first of engineering, he became what Anthony Burgess called a 'proto-hippy' in a velvet coat, frequenting the dives of old Edinburgh. He learned respect for women as much from prostitutes as from his gentle mother, Margaret née Balfour, and his devoted nurse, Alison Cunningham whom he called Cummy, 'the angel of my infant life'. When he escaped from the study of engineering by which his father, Thomas, a lighthouse engineer and Commissioner of Northern Lights, hoped he would find a profession, he ostensibly embarked on an alternative career in law. Passing his final exams for admission to the Bar, he celebrated by driving through Edinburgh in an open carriage, hailing all who cared to notice him, and by promptly abandoning law for good. 'Give me', he says in *Virginibus Puerisque* ('For Girls and Boys'), 'the young man who has brains enough to make a fool of himself'. His father was disappointed and both parents were deeply hurt by his turning agnostic, yet they recognised his true vocation and supported him in his early efforts as a writer, through his moves from Scotland to France and England in search of a healthier climate, and to America where in May 1880 in San Francisco he married his resourceful lover, Fanny Vandegrift Osbourne, an American born in Indianapolis, ten years his senior and the divorced mother of two surviving children, Lloyd and Belle. The quest for a benign environment took him to Strathpeffer, Davos Platz in Switzerland, Pitlochry, Braemar, Hyères, Bournemouth, Saranac Lake in the Adirondack Mountains and to the Pacific. After sampling the Marquesas, Fakarava, Tahiti and Hawaii he bought four hundred acres of land on the green lower slopes of Mount Vaea near Apia on the island of Upolu in Samoa and built his last home, Vailima ('Five streams', or, some say, 'Water in the hand'). To the watching world he had become as exotic as a character from *Treasure Island*.

RLS's home in Samoa, Vailima as it is today

In the balance of life and art, readers sometimes find the figure and the life more commanding than the work. The story of his triumph over chronic bronchial illness to become a distinguished Samoan – 'Tusitala', or 'Teller of Tales' – and international best-seller, is certainly that of a man with a genius for life against often fearful odds; but it's unlikely that it would have attracted so much notice without the products of his pen, even if products of the highest calibre are relatively few in proportion to the size of an output heroically voluminous for a man who died three weeks after his forty-fourth birthday. The fashion started by his friend, Sidney Colvin, of regarding the unfinished *Weir of Hermiston* as the best of Stevenson is symptomatic of a perception that none of the finished works quite measures up to the legendary figure of the man. Certainly, the powerful *Weir* fragment is rich in promising material: the dark character of the Lord Justice-Clerk ascending 'the great, bare staircase of his duty', alien to his timorous wife and renegade son; the sensual and moral grandeur of Kirstie Elliott; the treachery of Frank Innes and the strong presence of the Scottish landscape. Stevenson did write to Colvin, 'I expect *The Justice-Clerk* to be my masterpiece'; but, given the completed works, it is niggardly to rest the critical case on a might-have-been.

Nothing was lost on Stevenson even in the professions he tried and rejected. As an apprentice lighthouse engineer in his father's expectation, he accompanied Thomas Stevenson in 1870 to the Isle of Erraid off the Ross of Mull, acquiring a setting for his ballad-like tale of the supernatural, 'The Merry Men', and first-hand knowledge of the island on which David Balfour thinks himself marooned in *Kidnapped*, unaware that he can walk across to Mull at low tide. From his knowledge of law and lawyers he makes credible minor characters such as William Lawson, the Procurator-Fiscal with his incontinent quoting of law Latin in *Deacon Brodie or The Double Life*, the 'shrewd, ruddy, kindly, consequential' Mr Rankeillor in *Kidnapped*, and in *Catriona* Charles Stewart the Writer and the Lord Advocate Prestongrange. He had the true writer's eye for detail and worked so assiduously at style that Joseph Conrad – who never wrote a book as popular as *Treasure Island* or *Kidnapped* – could say, 'When it comes to popularity I stand much nearer the public mind than Stevenson, who was super-literary, a conscious virtuoso of style'. A letter to his friend Mrs Frances Sitwell shows the young Stevenson's sensitivity to style even in the context of affectionate correspondence: 'I hope you don't dislike reading bad style like this as much as I do writing it: it hurts me when neither words nor clauses fall into their places'. He's being hard on himself and missing the point. The problem wasn't style but content. His travel books, *An Inland Voyage* and *Travels with a Donkey*, are essentially collections of stylish essays short on thematic meat, which demonstrate that elegant style alone is insufficient; but he's a great phrase maker. No book of quotations would be complete without a selection from *Virginibus Puerisque* in which he dispenses mischievous *aperçus* in the manner of a renegade dominie. 'Extreme *busyness*, whether at school or college, kirk or market, is a symptom of deficient vitality'; 'Books are good enough in their own way, but they are a mighty bloodless substitute for life'; 'The cruellest lies are often told in silence'; 'There is no duty we so much underrate as the duty of being happy'. The chapter titled 'El Dorado' yields his most famous dictum: 'To travel hopefully is a better thing than to arrive, and the true success is to labour'. Though he often doubted his own prospect of success, he knew very well that becoming a writer required dedicated labour: 'That was a proficiency that tempted me; and I practised to acquire it, as men learn to whittle, in a wager with myself'.

At a period when literature was unsure of its own function in a world being redefined by industrialisation, Darwin and the colonial enterprise the most reliable way into publication for a new writer was the essay. This suited Stevenson, for although his career is one of unremitting dedication to writing, he is almost as shortwinded artistically as he was physically. He had bursts of enthusiasm for drama, for playing the flageolet, and for Pacific politics, which helped him to shift his focus from Scotland's imagined past to contemporary affairs in the south seas. He excels in the epigrammatic pronouncement, the short poem and the short story or novella. Billy Bones, Blind Pew, the 'Admiral Benbow', Long John Silver and Ben Gunn dreaming of cheese will always come alive for readers who care nothing for the style of *Treasure Island*. The house of Shaws, Ebenezer Balfour and Alan Breck Stewart deserve to live beyond the pages of *Kidnapped*; but among Stevenson's full-length novels only *Kidnapped* sustains its energy and art on the same level as 'Thrawn Janet', 'Markeim', 'The Suicide Club' in *New Arabian Nights*, *The Strange Case of Dr Jekyll and Mr Hyde*, *The Beach of Falesá*, and *The Ebb-Tide* which is the best of his collaborations with his step-son, Lloyd Osbourne. If not quite a miniaturist, his true strength is the compactness of moral fable, and he wrote nothing more perfect than 'The House of Eld', posthumously published in the collection of *Fables*. The story is a biblically cadenced parable of Scottish religious sado-masochism and personal guilt which implicitly acknowledges the violence done to Stevenson's parents by his renunciation of the church. When Jack kills the wizard responsible for shackling children at birth, he kills in turn the apparitions of his uncle, his father and his mother. He is in the right, for as his uncle and father fall to the ground, 'a little bloodless white thing fled from the room', a consummately expressive image of evil that holds its own in the imagination with Ridley Scott and James Cameron's gruesome special effects in their *Alien* films. But when Jack goes home he finds 'the uncle smitten on the head, and his father pierced through the heart, and his mother cloven through the midst. And he sat in the lone house and wept beside the bodies'. The shackles that have fallen from the right ankles of his countrymen have become fastened to the left. So even when the cause is just, guilt is inevitable, the past inescapable, and who is to say which shackle is preferable?

The story is an example of the dualism that preoccupied Stevenson. It is hardly surprising that Henry James, connoisseur of ambiguity, should have been so drawn to the work of his Scottish friend. The enquiring moralist is evident in the heavy-handed plays he wrote with his friend W. E. Henley and with Fanny Stevenson. One play stands out: *Deacon Brodie or The Double Life* portrays the psychological subtleties of the divided self, and is a clear precursor of *The Strange Case of Dr Jekyll and Mr Hyde*. Deacon of the Incorporation of Edinburgh Wrights by day and housebreaker by night, Brodie revels in his doubleness as he prepares to exit from respectability into his darker, truer self through his bedroom window:

> On with the new coat and into the new life! Down with the Deacon and up with the robber!...If we were as good as we seem, what would the world be?...Shall a man not have half a life of his own?...(*Addressing the bed.*) Lie there, Deacon! sleep and be well tomorrow. As for me, I'm a man once more till morning. (*Gets out of the window.*)

The Sea Cook, or *Treasure Island* as it was renamed at the suggestion of the proprietor of *Young Folks* magazine in which it was which serialised from July 1881 to June 1882, was based not on a moral idea but on a map which Stevenson devised with Lloyd Osbourne. Like all great books for the young the novel infuses the appeal to youth with adult vision. Lloyd Osbourne says that Stevenson spoke of his belief that children should be helped to face reality:

> A child should early gain some perception of what the world really is like – its baseness, its treacheries, its thinly veneered brutalities; he should learn to judge people, and discount human frailty and weakness, and be in some degree prepared and armed for taking his part later in life. I have no patience with this fairy-tale training that makes ignorance a virtue.

A tale of initiation, the search for hidden treasure shows Jim Hawkins the impurities of a world where romantic expectation is constantly menaced by the likes of Blind Pew, Long John Silver and Israel Hands. The villainous Silver's seductiveness is the toughest part of Jim's education. Stevenson airs the moral issue in 'A Fable: The Persons of the Tale' in a dialogue worthy of John Fowles or Dennis Potter. Two of his puppets, Silver and Captain Smollett discuss the story in which they find themselves. Smollett is bewildered, Silver cocky:

> What I know is this: if there is sich a thing as a Author, I'm his favourite chara'ter. He does me fathoms better'n he does you – fathoms, he does. And he likes doing me. He keeps me on deck mostly all the time, crutch and all; and he leaves you measling in the hold, where nobody can't see you, nor wants to, and you may lay to that! If there is a Author, by thunder, but he's on my side, and you may lay to it!

In reply, Captain Smollett admits his own unattractiveness – 'I'm not a very popular man at home' – but insists: 'I know the Author's on the side of good; he tells me so, it runs out of his pen as he writes'. The worthy Captain is right, of course; the author is on the side of good but, like most of us, he enjoys a clever rogue. Despite the perverse appeal of the satanic James Durie in *The Master of Ballantrae*, Stevenson is not of the Devil's party; but, like Burns and Hogg, he's fascinated by the bad guys.

Alan Breck Stewart is to David Balfour as Long John Silver to Jim Hawkins. Stevenson's most polished novel on Scottish themes, *Kidnapped* is set against the background of the failure of the 1745 Jacobite rebellion when 'the men of the clans were broken at Culloden, and the good cause went down'. Crossing the Isle of Mull David sees the humiliations of the Highlanders, most visible in their dress. He is dropped into history like Scott's Edward Waverley, Quentin Durward and Frank Osbaldistone. Like Waverley, he discovers his country as he finds himself. Cheated of his inheritance by his lethal uncle, he is refined by experience into the young man who reclaims it at the end of the novel. Experience is the tangle of clan hatred, conflicting loyalties and personal danger centred on the Appin murder of Colin

Campbell of Glenure, the 'Red Fox', after the forfeiture of Stewart and Cameron land to the Campbells. Superficially a romance, the book is historically accurate and psychologically realistic. Jacobite glamour is undercut by tipsy toasts and maudlin Gaelic songs in the house of Hector Maclean and by hot-headed egotism in Alan Breck, Robin Oig (son of Rob Roy Macgregor) and Cluny Macpherson. From Cluny David receives unromantic information about Prince Charlie:

> ...I gathered the Prince was a gracious, spirited boy, like the son of a race of polite kings, but not so wise as Solomon. I gathered, too, that while he was in the Cage [Cluny's lair], he was often drunk; so the fault that has since, by all accounts, made such a wreck of him, had even then begun to show itself.

The 'good cause' had its decadence; but if Alan Breck's vanity can make him quarrelsome or cold-blooded as he surveys the corpses of his attackers in 'The Siege of the Round-House', he is also 'a bonny fighter', a 'doughty friend', and a man of principle, an imaginatively maturer instance of the mixed man than Long John Silver, illuminating a more subtly ambiguous world than *Treasure Island*'s. The orchestration of moral issues in such a precisely realised historical setting makes the romantic adventure of *Kidnapped* a masterpiece whose deeper implications may be more readily discerned by twenty-first-century readers comfortable with the generic varieties of contemporary fiction.

Apart from the interest of what happens next to David Balfour and the spooky 'Tale of Tod Lapraik', *Catriona*, the sequel to *Kidnapped*, is a disappointment, muddled both in plot and psychology. In the speed and adult tension of its opening pages *The Master of Ballantrae* promises a further advance on *Kidnapped* in the portrayal of peculiarly Scottish moral conflict. Essentially a ballad of intended epic proportions, the novel achieves a thematic grandeur second only to *Dr Jekyll and Mr Hyde*, and the narrative voice of Ephraim Mackellar is one of Stevenson's best inventions; but, despite the psychological interest of Henry Durie's feeding on his vengeance, the power of the moral fable is diminished by the supernatural in the heavily implicit equation of James Durie with the Devil, the clumsy mechanism of the Chevalier de Burke's narrative and the forced, melodramatic ending; but there's nothing clumsy about *The Strange Case of Dr Jekyll and Mr Hyde* which, Henry James suggests, 'would generally be called the most serious of the author's tales':

> It deals with the relation of the baser parts of man to his nobler, of the capacity for evil that exists in the most generous natures; and it expresses these things in a fable which is a wonderfully happy invention. The subject is endlessly interesting, and rich in all sorts of provocation, and Mr Stevenson is to be congratulated on having touched the core of it.

That James's imagination was susceptible to the core of Stevenson's subject – 'man is not truly one, but truly two' – is evident in his own psychological ghost stories, 'The Private Life' and 'The Jolly Corner'. References to double, divided or hidden selves pervade Victorian literature. In *The City of Dreadful Night*, James (B. V.) Thomson says, 'I was twain,/Two selves distinct that cannot join again'. In 'The Buried Life' Matthew Arnold repines that most people, separated from their true selves, hunger for the mystery of the buried, wild self. In lines that could speak for Henry Jekyll he says:

> But often, in the world's most crowded streets,
> But often, in the din of strife,
> There rises an unspeakable desire,
> After the knowledge of our buried life,
> A thirst to spend our fire and restless force
> In tracking out our true, original course;
> A longing to inquire
> Into the mystery of this heart that beats
> So wild, so deep in us — to know
> Whence our lives come and where they go.

In a sequence of poems entitled 'Blank Misgivings of a Creature moving around in Worlds not realised', Arthur Hugh Clough confesses his susceptibility to 'the vilest things beneath the moon' and laments the inaccessibility of 'The buried world below'. Behind Stevenson's story of duality lay Mary Shelley's *Frankenstein; or, the Modern Prometheus* in which Frankenstein's pathetically humanoid *alter ego* inspires loathing, commits murder and declares that Frankenstein will be his last victim, as, in a sense, Jekyll is Hyde's. The deformed cretin child in Charlotte Brontë's *Villette* embodies the deformity of Lucy Snowe's repressed passional self. Out of Calvinist obsession with the conflict of eternal opposites Scottish literature had produced Hogg's *The Private Memoirs and Confessions of a Justified Sinner*, precursor of many variations on the theme of the double self, including Edgar Allan Poe's short story, 'William Wilson' and what Stevenson called his 'fine bogy tale'. In 1890 Oscar Wilde published *The Picture of Dorian Gray* in which Dorian's essential doubleness is split into his tempter, Lord Henry Wotton, and his good angel or conscience, Basil Hallward, the portrait painter whom Dorian murders. Both Stevenson and Wilde make fables out of a culture they perceive as divided against itself: on the surface urbane and civilised, but underneath degraded and bestial. As a young man Stevenson had found relief from the 'draughty parallelograms' of middle-class New Town Edinburgh in the classless candour of human need in the city's bars and brothels. *Dr Jekyll and Mr Hyde* strikes at the hypocrisy of a society in which the outwardly respectable Victorian drank and fornicated discreetly out of the public eye. In *The Time Machine* H. G. Wells projects this dichotomy into a future when the human race has separated into two antithetical species, the decadent, upper-class Eloi and the brutish, subterranean Morlocks who do the dirty work of society. Emma Tennant's *Two Women of London: The Strange Case of Ms Jekyll and Mrs Hyde* adapts Stevenson's story to the social circumstances of Thatcher's Britain when 'rapaciousness and a "loadsamoney" economy have come to represent the highest values in the land'. There is still 'evil' in the case, but child-worn Mrs Hyde's use of the drug 'Ecstasy' transforms her into the attractive Eliza Jekyll, fondled and promoted by a consumerist society.

Like Hogg's novel and Poe's story, Stevenson's novella is about conscience. When Jekyll discovers the drug that allows his personality to be split, thereby liberating his repressed desires, the grasp of his conscience is at first 'insidiously relaxed', then jolted into conflict with the illicit pleasures he enjoys as Mr Hyde. In a letter from Stevenson to J.A. Symonds, he refers to '*Jekyll*' as 'a dreadful thing...that damned old business of the war in the members'. The phrase is echoed in Dr Jekyll's 'consciousness of the perennial war among my members', and again in Stevenson's reference to 'that double law of the members and the will' in the essay, 'Pulvis et Umbra'. If the ambivalence of human character is the principal motif in his work, it is closely followed by the power of evil, which is the subject of 'Thrawn Janet' and 'Markheim'. Written in the vernacular of the Pitlochry district where Stevenson was spending a wet summer, 'Thrawn Janet' tells how a minister's mind is turned by contact with Janet, a witch possessed by the Devil. The story illustrates a valid general truth about the incapacity of fanaticism to cope with an extreme situation for which its rules make no provision, breaking because it cannot bend. Published shortly before *Dr Jekyll and Mr Hyde*, 'Markheim' is a distinctively Scottish elaboration of Poe's theme in 'The Black Cat' and 'The Imp of the Perverse'. While Poe treats perversity as a psychological phenomenon, Stevenson's Presbyterian sensibility associates it with the theological condition of original sin and 'the war between the members' of good and evil. Once an enthusiastic participant in revivalist meetings, his voice 'the loudest in the hymn', Markheim, like Jekyll, recognises the opposites that make up his own moral nature and that of others: 'Evil and good run strong in me, haling me both ways. I do not love the one thing, I love all'. The story achieves the universality of fable because we recognise Markheim in ourselves. He kills, but we hope for his salvation. We also hope for Jekyll's.

While Dr Jekyll is possessed like Markheim by good and evil, austere Mr Utterson is the perfect foil, 'a lover of the sane and customary sides of life'. Yet the lawyer, too, has his duality which he keeps under control, mortifying 'a taste for vintages' by drinking gin, denying himself the pleasures of the theatre, taking his regular, dull walks with Mr Enfield and ending his Sundays with 'a volume of some dry divinity on his reading desk, until the clock in the neighbouring church rang out the hour of twelve, when he would go soberly and gratefully to bed'. Thus duplicity in Dr Jekyll is matched by repression in Mr Utterson and in Mr Enfield who refrains from asking about the mysterious door, telling Mr Utterson, 'I make it a rule of mine: the more it looks like Queer Street, the less I ask'. Mr Utterson approves the rule.

If he betrays symptoms of depressive withdrawal, Markheim and Jekyll exemplify features of *dementia praecox* or schizophrenia as it was known after Eugen Bleuler introduced the word in 1911 to denote forms of mental illness characterised by splitting of the mind. Towards the end of the nineteenth century the German psychiatrist, Emil Kraepelin, distinguished between *dementia praecox* and manic-depression. The split in Jekyll particularly suggests the bi-polar illness of manic-depressive psychosis as well as a classically Freudian conflict between the interdependent super-ego and the id. It also demonstrates the Jungian coexistence of persona (Jekyll) and shadow (Hyde), 'the shadow compensating for the pretensions of the persona, the persona compensating for the antisocial propensities of the shadow'. In terms of the development of the science of psychology, Stevenson's fable is strikingly precocious.

Markheim is possessed by a compulsion to kill, then in defiance of a smoothly manipulative Devil, to confess and give himself up. Jekyll, too, is finally repelled by the evil he has released and confesses to the representatives of morality and respectability. Yet the attraction of the dark side is what lingers in the mind at the end of *Dr Jekyll and Mr Hyde* (as James rather than Henry Durie stays in the mind at the end of *The Master of Ballantrae*), which implies that good is restriction, evil freedom, and that shedding the 'load of genial respectability' to become pure evil is to 'spring headlong into the sea of liberty'. After the racking pangs of his first transformation, Jekyll's sensations as Mr Hyde are 'incredibly sweet': 'I felt younger, lighter, happier in body... I knew myself, at the first breath of this new life, to be more wicked, tenfold more wicked, sold a slave to my original evil; and the thought, in that moment, braced and delighted me like wine'. But this manic, evil side of Jekyll's dual nature is housed in a small, deformed body. His evil side is 'less developed than the good', and good asserts itself in Jekyll's revulsion from his *alter ego*. The book's acutest insight into the psychology of moral consciousness is in the passage which defines the problem of choosing between circumscribed Jekyll and autonomous Hyde:

> To cast in my lot with Jekyll, was to die to those appetites which I had long secretly indulged and had of late begun to pamper. To cast it in with Hyde, was

to die to a thousand interests and aspirations, and to become, at a blow and forever, despised and friendless. The bargain might appear unequal; but there was still another consideration in the scales; for while Jekyll would suffer smartingly in the fires of abstinence, Hyde would be not even conscious of all that he had lost.

In Vladimir Nabokov's phrase Hyde is 'a concentrate of pure evil'; conscience is the preserve and solitary torment of Markheim's descendant, the morally composite Jekyll.

Henry James was struck not so much by 'the profundity of the idea' in *Dr Jekyll and Mr Hyde* as by 'the art of the presentation – the extremely successful form' of Stevenson's 'short, rapid, concentrated story, which is really a masterpiece of concision'. Underlying the enduring appeal and relevance of its theme, the book's strength comes from its narrative method, its use of atmosphere and its evocation of the affective power of evil. 'Backward in sentiment', Mr Utterson, 'to whom the fanciful was the immodest', is skilfully installed as a reliable commentator trusted by both Dr Jekyll and Dr Lanyon, and trustworthy to the point of respecting Dr Lanyon's direction that his letter is not to be opened until Jekyll's death or disappearance. Opposite in character to 'lean, long, dusty, dreary' Mr Utterson is Dr Lanyon, 'a healthy, dapper, red-faced gentleman, with a shock of hair prematurely white, and a boisterous and decided manner'. The impossible truth appears plausible when two such different temperaments converge on it. With Dr Lanyon's letter the relationship between Jekyll and Hyde is revealed from the outside by a qualified observer in preparation for Jekyll's 'Full Statement of the Case' in which the truth is finally clarified from the inside. Dickensian effects of atmosphere and imagery are used with perfectly judged economy. Like the doctor himself, Jekyll's house is composite, respectable at one end with an imposing Victorian front hall and corridors leading to the laboratory where Jekyll becomes Hyde, entering the world by a door 'blistered and distained'. Sound is used dramatically in the silence of the night when Utterson sees Hyde's face after the approach of swift, ominous footsteps and Hyde's satanically serpentine 'hissing intake of the breath'. Fog infects Soho with portentous mystery. The darkened moon and puffs of wind agitating the flame of Utterson and Poole's candle as they prepare to break down the door of Jekyll's cabinet make conspirators of nature and the supernatural. The force of Hyde's evil is conveyed by its impact on others, as summed up by Dr Lanyon:

> I was struck...with the odd, subjective disturbance caused by his neighbourhood. This bore some resemblance to incipient rigour, and was accompanied by a marked sinking of the pulse. At the time, I set it down to some idiosyncratic, personal distaste, and merely wondered at the acuteness of the symptoms; but I have since had reason to believe the cause to lie much deeper in the nature of man, and to turn on some nobler hinge than the principle of hatred.

The 'nobler hinge' is the principle of goodness to which Hyde is chemically and constitutionally inimical, hence his compulsion to murder the emblematic Sir Danvers Carew, 'an aged beautiful gentleman with white hair', whose face seems to breathe 'an innocent and old world kindness of disposition'. The 'troglodytic' Hyde is perceived as 'particularly small and wicked-looking' by the maid who witnesses the killing of Sir Danvers; Poole sees him as a 'masked thing like a monkey', and he inspires Mr Utterson with 'a nausea and distaste of life'. According to Enfield he is like Satan. Utterson's exclamation, 'God forgive us, God Forgive us' at the end of 'Incident at the Window' is equivalent to the sign of the cross made in the presence of evil. In a work so precisely written there can be no doubt about Hyde's theological value when Dr Jekyll calls him 'my devil' and 'that child of Hell', indications of Stevenson's 'absorption of the devil-ridden folklore of Scotland'. (Of James Durie he writes to Sidney Colvin: 'The Master is all I know of the devil'.)

Does Stevenson's fable imply that evil is potentially stronger than good? Hyde is, after all, the death of Jekyll, the embodiment of evil which 'will not die until it has corrupted the good to its own image and brought it down by its side to a common grave'. His realistic descendant is Huish, Stevenson's 'trivial hell-hound' in *The Ebb-Tide*, whose final and fatal prospect of pleasure is to throw vitriol into the eyes of Attwater, the ambiguous Christian pearl-fisher. The final assertion of good implicit in Jekyll's judgement of himself comes from panic that the evil side of his nature is taking over, that his natural, morally composite identity may be lost to him. The message is that we are inescapably forked creatures: the 'war in the members' is 'the doom and burthen of our life' and 'when the attempt is made to cast it off, it but returns upon us with more unfamiliar and more awful pressure'. The Pyrrhic victory of good is the intolerable pressure Jekyll feels in the prospect of losing his capacity for virtue. The book is thus somewhat less optimistic than the view Stevenson takes of virtue in 'Pulvis et Umbra' ('Dust and Shadows') where he finds men and women, however wretched their circumstances:

> ...without hope, without help, without thanks, still obscurely fighting the lost fight of virtue, still clinging, in the brothel or on the scaffold, to some rag of honour, the poor jewel of their souls! They may seek to escape, and yet they cannot; it is not alone their privilege and glory, but their doom; they are condemned to some nobility; all their lives long, the desire of good is at their heels, the implacable hunter.

Here Stevenson's view of the moral life, 'the desire of good' always in pursuit like a hound of heaven, develops Carlyle's optimistic belief in *Chartism* that, whatever the obstacles, 'Every mortal can and shall himself be a true man'. The desire of good in *The Beach of Falesá* — 'the first realistic South Seas story', according to its author — is personified in the love of Uma which converts Wiltshire from an opportunistic trader beholden to the viciously manipulative Case ('if he's not in hell today, there's no such place') into a true man of feeling who relinquishes his dream of owning a pub in favour of loyalty to his wife and half-caste children. It is Attwater, the sophisticated man of idea, who gets the better of the three derelicts in *The Ebb-Tide*. Yet the idea can't make a true man of everyone. At the end of *The Ebb-Tide* Attwater's religion can't save Huish, who has no desire of good, but does salvage what is left of Captain Davis, while representing only 'nonsense' in 'the growing calamity' of Robert Herrick's irresolute life. Incapable of living by the idea, any idea, Herrick accurately judges himself: 'No pride, no capacity, no force'. The diabolical James Durie's cruellest taunting of Ephraim Mackellar is when he says, 'Recognise in each of us a common strain: that we both live for an idea'. As every Presbyterian knows, the Devil, too, has his dream.

Yes, there is much to be had after *Treasure Island* and *Kidnapped*. RLS's life is a tale of travel about the journey of a writer who laboured until he first found style, then content. How apposite that he should characterise himself as both sailor and hunter in 'Requiem', the epitaph inscribed on his tomb in Samoa atop Mount Vaea, high above his Vailima:

> Under the wide and starry sky,
> Dig the grave and let me lie.
> Glad did I live and gladly die,
> And I laid me down with a will.
> This be the verse you grave for me:
> 'Here he lies where he longed to be;
> Home is the sailor, home from sea
> And the hunter home from the hill'.

In his scrutiny of the moral life he is a sagacious guide and his psychological realism makes him convincing. So he carries us with him beyond the 'Admiral Benbow' and the House of Shaws, an inestimable comrade.

RLS's tomb on Mount Vaea (photo by Sheila Park)

18. New York for Beginners

My first night in America looked for a while as if it might be my last night anywhere. After the ash-tray grey of a Scottish summer's day the infinite azure above the cloud ceiling was holiday-brochure luxury, the flight from Prestwick airport to John F. Kennedy smooth and sunny all the way. At JFK a customs officer, for whom mere obesity must have become a dim and wistful memory, spilled everything from my suitcase and asked me why I'd come. I sure had a lot of books and papers.

'I've been hired to teach some Shakespeare at a college in Nashville'.

'Well say, you enjoy that country ham, Perfesser, and that good country music. You have a good time, hear?'

He flapped his hand dismissively at my jumbled belongings splayed across the inspection table and waddled off to his next victim. It was June, very hot. I dripped copiously on the lecture notes prepared for Nashville, re-packed messily and headed out of the airport to find a bus to the city.

On the bus for 'Port Authority' I sat trying to believe I was in America. A tall black man climbed on board. He came down the aisle and jerked his beard at me.

'This bus go to 42nd?'

Panic, what to say. I haven't been here long enough to engage in conversation with a native.

'Sorry, I'm afraid I don't know. I'm a stranger here, first time in New York. Perhaps one of the other passengers...' The bus was filling up.

'U-huh', the black man said, yawning. He sat down beside me, too bored to enquire further even when the driver arrived and the bus began to move. After some minutes he said, 'Whatcha here doin'?'

'I'm going down to a college in Nashville, Tennessee to teach summer-school Shakespeare'.

'U-huh' he said, and fell asleep.

The bus rolled out of the airport. Soon we were passing tall buildings, driving along expressways. I was beginning to see imagery of the America long familiar from films and newscasts.

From a fly-over I looked down at the highway below. A stretch limousine was running parallel to the bus. The woman in the front passenger seat was immaculate in black, perfectly made up, the hem of her skirt at exactly the optimum position on her tanned thigh, provocative but tasteful. The black man leaned into me, checked my line of sight and nodded his beard at the view.

'That's the other half', he said, and went back to sleep.

Soon there was more traffic and buildings were growing taller. On our left we passed a hill covered with headstones. The black man leaned into me again, nodded his beard at the constellation of graves on the hillside.

'That's also the other half', he said.

At the Port Authority we filed out of the bus to queue for luggage stowed in the hold.

'See ya', my black man said and was gone.

I collected my suitcase and boarded a yellow cab. At the University of Edinburgh I had made friends with an American couple attached to the English Department. When they knew I was going to New York for a few days en route to Tennessee the wife said I must stay with her mother in Manhattan. She'd love to have me. So my destination was 176 West 87th Street, ninth floor. Her mother's name was Dora Ostrow, she told me, but everyone called her Toni, for short.

For a second I thought the apartment door had opened by itself, until I looked down and the tiny lady jumped into my arms.

'Hi, you must be Marshall, I'm Toni. I'm having my Nutriment'.

She was holding a glass of milky liquid. 'Have you eaten?' I hadn't, so after putting her down and dumping my suitcase in the hall, I got her to direct me to a nearby coffee shop. A tasty dish of spaghetti and meat balls later I climbed back up to Toni's and spent the evening hearing about her life, with particular emphasis on her political opinions and strenuous youthful membership of the Communist Party. By this time I felt as though I had walked here from Glasgow, so excused myself and retired. It was still hot, windows open, but despite constant traffic noise with frequent crescendos from fire trucks and police sirens, I was soon asleep.

'Marshall, will you wake up please', the voice said.

'No', I said, 'I can't'.

'Oh, God, Marshall. Wake up please. We have a smell'.

'I don't care'.

'Marshall, I need you to wake up please, for God's sake. To identify the smell'.

Now I was almost awake and caring. A smell? On a ninth floor apartment in Manhattan? On my first night in America? My first night in New York? At three in the morning?

'Okay, Toni. Good morning. Where is the smell?'

'It's right here, Marshall. What is the smell?'

I sniffed testingly. There was something furry in my nostrils, but not furry enough to wake up for.

'It's nothing, Toni. Just something a little furry'.

'Wha-da-ya mean FURRY, Marshall? For God's sake what is the smell?'

'I don't know'.

'Oh, God. I need to call someone'. Toni ran out of the room. I followed her to the kitchen. The smell was stronger there.

'There's more smell here', Toni said, wringing her twig-like hands. I agreed.

'Let's see if it's in the street', I said. We went to the open windows and stuck our heads out over 87th street. The smell was even stronger.

'Yep, Toni', I said, 'I think we can safely say it's in the street'.

'Oh God, Marshall. What is the smell?'

'I think it smells like Brasso'.

'What in the hell is BRASSO, Marshall?'

'It's a liquid cleaner we use in Scotland for cleaning brasses'.

'Oh for Godsakes, Marshall, it's not Brasso'.

'No, probably not'.

'Oh God', said Toni, 'I'm gonna call the Police Department'.

She went to the phone and dialled.

'Hello. Yes. Ostrow. 176 West 87th. We have a smell...Yes, in the apartment. Thank you...Yeah, okay, I'll hold. Oh, God. Hello. Ostrow. 176 West 87th. We have a smell in the apartment. It's outside in the street also...I have no idea...my eyes are BURNING...Thank you. I just wanna know is it poisonous?...Yeah, sorta chemical. Oh, okay. Thank you. Oh, God'.

She hung up.

'Oh God, they don't know what it is'.

'Well', I said, 'that probably means it's not important'; though

I had to admit the smell was very strong in the street, catching at the back of the throat.

'Oh God, Marshall, I can hardly BREATHE. It could be the Chinese. I mean they wouldn't TELL us first, would they? They'd just DO it. Maybe we're gonna DIE tonight'.

'Take it easy, Toni', I said, 'Tell you what, I'll call the Fire Department'.

'Yeah, oh God, yeah, wouldja please, call them'.

She gave me the number. It occurred to me that I might elicit a more attentive and sympathetic response if I was obviously a foreigner of some sort or a newcomer to the city. I decided to present myself as a bewildered, respectful Scottish person.

'Good morrrning, Fire Department', I began, 'please accept my sincere apologies for trrroubling you at this ungodly hour...'

'Sir?' the voice said.

'Ahem. I'm sorry to be botherrring you so early in the morrrning'.

'Yessir'.

'I'm phoning from street number 87 on the West Side of your beautiful city...'

'Sir?'

'I'm calling from West 87th Street'.

'Yessir'.

'There's a mysterrrious aroma over here. It's very pervasive and, och, we were just wonderrring if maybe it could be toxic?'

'Sir?'

'Officer, there's smell in our apartment. It's also in the street'.

'Yessir'.

'Well, Officer, we were wonderrring if we should worry about the smell'.

'Sir?'

'Do you think the smell's dangerous?'

'Dangerous, sir?'

'That's right, Officer. Poisonous. Do you think we're going to die tonight?'

'Sir, we have no casualties at this time'.

'Thank you, Officer'. But I think he'd hung up.

'It's okay, Toni. They don't really know, but nobody's dead yet'.

'Oh God, Marshall. It's the CHINESE. I know it's the Chinese'.

Toni decided we should take chairs to the vestibule where there was another door to the apartment next to hers, but no windows. We could sit there using up air as yet uncontaminated, and wait for the end. After we'd been there for half an hour the next-door neighbour looked out at us.

'What are you doing out here, Toni?' he said. His voice feigned surprise, but you could tell he was being careful not to laugh. Toni was at it again.

'Oh God', said Toni, 'It's the SMELL. Don't you have the smell, for Godsake? It has to be the Chinese'.

'Sure, Toni', the neighbour said. 'Right. The Chinese. I'll bring you both coffee'.

Which he kindly did before returning to his bed, too sleepy to worry about smells and the Yellow Peril.

I drank my coffee.

'Toni, I'm very tired', I said. 'I can't stay awake any longer. If we're going to die tonight I'd like to be comfortable or asleep'.

Toni stayed where she was, hunched up in her upright chair, muttering and wringing her hands.

Later that morning, 4th June 1968, *The New York Times* carried a brief report:

Police Seek Source Of Odor on West Side

Teams of policemen and firemen cruised the upper West Side early this morning in an attempt to determine the source of an acrid, noxious odor that blanketed the area.

By 3 A.M. they had ruled out any gas leak or fire but were unable to say definitely where the smell originated.

Meanwhile residents of the neighborhood bounded by 80th Street and 96th Street off Riverside Drive were calling the police and newspapers to complain of the odor. Some said it caused their eyes to tear and burn,

And there the matter rested until some days later when it was suggested that prevailing winds had blown fumes from a chemical fire in New Jersey across Toni's part of town. So what? After twenty-six Greyhound bus-hours I was far away in Nashville with country ham, country music and Shakespeare.

Ten years later, almost to the day of Toni's airborne toxic incident, research took me back to New York. Toni's next-door neighbour had become a close friend so on this visit I stayed with him and his family. It was another hot June night. Everyone in the household had gone to bed. I was still up, finishing some work for the next day. At about 11 p.m. there was a loud knock on the door and history began to repeat itself. Through the fisheye peep-hole Toni looked even more Lilliputian. I took a deep breath and opened the door.

'Oh, my God, hi Marshall. You're clothed?', she said.

'Hi Toni, how are you? Yes. Pardon?'

'I see you're clothed'.

'Yes, I'm just finishing off a bit of work for tomorrow...'

'Will you go down, please?'

'Pardon?'

'Will you go down, please?'

'Down?'

'Yes, well, my God, as you see, I *can't* go down in my, ah, in my, ah, PEIGNOIR. Jesus'.

'No, of course not, Toni'.

'So will you go down please?'

'Yes, of course I will. Where do you want me to go down to, Toni?'

'My God, DOWNSTAIRS. Will you please go downstairs?'

'Do you mean down to the street, Toni?'

'Yeah, my God the STREET, Marshall, the street, will you go down please? You're clothed and all and I can't, JESUS, wouldja HURRY please?'

'Be glad to, Toni. Exactly why do you want me to go down to the street?'

'My God, I wanna know if we're gonna BURN UP tonight'.

'Burn up, Toni, how might we be going to burn up?'

'Jesus, Marshall THE FIRE, my God, are we gonna burn up in the fire?'

For a crazy moment I thought of calling the Police Department and the Fire Department, reminding them both of the ten-year old smell and asking them if Toni's fire was a close relation.

'Sure, Toni', I said, entering the elevator, 'I'm on my way'.

At street level Toni's building was famous for a restaurant and delicatessen operated by a gentleman calling himself 'Barney Greengrass, The Sturgeon King'. Alfred Hitchcock was a customer. He was said to order ten pounds of 'fatty' sturgeon and have it flown to California to maintain his shape. Irving Berlin used to call in for a plate of sturgeon and a glass of borscht. The story goes that after a concert Heifetz would call Barney on the phone and say, 'Barney, sandwiches', to which Barney would reply, 'Jascha, play for me'. Heifetz would secure his sandwiches by playing to Barney over the phone.

Tonight smoke was billowing from Barney's. There was a fire engine at the kerb and enormous helmeted firemen stood around the entrance, fully accoutred, with axes, torches like clubs and other impedimenta of their profession covering most of their persons. I approached one leaning peacefully on the fire engine.

'Excuse me, sir, is the fire dangerous?'

'Nah. Goddam fry-pan'. He spat on the sidewalk.

'Thank you, sir. Some people in the apartments were getting worried'.

'Nah', he said, 'it's nuthin''.

I knocked on Toni's door which flew open to reveal her still in her peignoir, clearly making no evacuation plans, stoically awaiting her fate and looking like Clytemnestra after the murder of Agamemnon.

'Oh, God', she said.

'It's okay, Toni. It was only a fry-pan'.

'Well, ah, great', she simpered bravely, 'I guess we're not gonna burn up'.

'Not tonight, Toni', I said and added, 'Sorry', because she looked so disappointed.

The Chinese had let her down and now her apocalypse had sunk to the level of a smoking frying pan; but her genius was assured. She had saved up a fire for ten years and delivered it right on time. Thank you, Toni.

19. Holidays with Homicide

'It's murder, Jean', Glasgow's Chief Inspector Taggart would snap at his sickeningly long-suffering wife, 'we're no' going on holiday'.

Bad luck for Jean but good news for us. Not much of a holiday after a hard day at the office to watch a cryptic provincial cop wheel around his mobility-challenged wife in pursuit of recreation. Give us instead the trusty amalgam of fast drams, hard-boiled patter and putrefying corpses. Give us escape from the daily grey, a relaxing TV armchair holiday of corruption, violence and inventive death. And when it's time for our law-abiding summer break of beach or bush what do we pack for entertainment? Thrillers, crime, what they used to call 'bloods'. Whatever the weather, it wouldn't be a holiday without murder most foul.

It takes plenty of writing to supply our holiday requirements. About 25% of all fiction sold in the USA and UK is crime fiction. No wonder Ed McBain, guru of the urban police procedural is, with *The Last Dance* (1999), fifty money-spinning novels on from the first installment of his 87th Precinct chronicle, *Cop Hater*, published in 1956. That's a lot of holidays ago, and a lot of corpses. And Elmore Leonard's Miami, Patricia Cornwell's Richmond, Virginia or James Ellroy's Los Angeles are as far away as McBain's thinly disguised Manhattan from the tweed-and-chintz country-house puzzles Agatha Christie devised for Monsieur Poirot's little gray cells to conjure with. Or Miss Marple's.

What's the appeal? Otto Penzler, sometime owner of New York City's 'Mysterious Bookstore' (around 65,000 whodunits and whydunits permanently on his shelves) used to say that mysteries are adult fairy tales for people who enjoy the elemental battle between good and evil. The detective says, 'The bad guys did something wrong, and I'm going to fix it'. It might not be the way you or I would fix it, but he's the one taking on the challenge in the role of avenger, cleanser of society. Of course hard-boiled '*he*' doesn't have the role to himself any more, not with Cornwell's forensic Kay Scarpetta, Sara Paretsky's feisty Vic Warshawski, Linda Barnes's feminist Carlotta Carlyle, Sue Grafton's methodical Kinsey Millhone, Sandra Scoppetone's lesbian Lauren Laurano and Janet Evanovich's perky Stephanie Plum. Murder is proving a great equaliser; more power to it.

'Adult fairy tale' might have covered the case for Conan Doyle, E.C. Bentley, Josephine Tey or Ngaio Marsh. It might do for the No. 1 Ladies Detective Agency of Alexander McCall Smith's Botswana, featuring the intrepid, kind-hearted, 'traditionally built' Mma Ramotswe ('We are all tempted when it comes to cake'). It doesn't help much with the *roman noir* as practised by Dashiell Hammett, the underrated James M. Cain ('poet of the tabloid murder'), Raymond Chandler, John D. MacDonald and their descendants. The actor Richard Widmark's definition of *film noir* works for the fiction too: 'Shady characters, crooked cops, twisted love and bad luck...a darker side of human nature...the world as it really is'. Or consider high-class hooker Elaine Mardell to private eye, Matt Scudder in Lawrence Block's *In the Midst of Death*:

> Everybody's weird, fundamentally everybody is a snap. Sometimes it's a sexual thing and sometimes it's a different kind of weirdness, but one way or another everybody's nuts. You, me, the whole world.

There's a greater ring of truth here than in disingenuous disclaimers about their interest in crime by British doyennes P.D. James and Ruth Rendell. According to Rendell people read their books 'for the emotions, the interplay of characters, the beautiful pictures James paints of East Anglia. Crime is quite incidental'. This is not endorsed by the James–Rendell corpse count. As D.H. Lawrence warns us, 'Never trust the teller, trust the tale'. Obviously, the crime would not compel without engaging characterisation and convincing settings. We want McBain's sense of the city as well as his metropolitan convention of hoods and hustlers, predatory rapists, con men and blackmailers; we enjoy Linda Barnes's Boston and the septic sprawl of James Ellroy's city of dark angels. We'll even take a pleasant stroll in the East Anglian countryside. But without the crimes we wouldn't take the books on holiday at all. There's nothing incidental about murder, right Jean?

Probably the very literary James and Rendell are reacting against the snooty relegation of all crime fiction to an inferior category, comic books without the pictures, the province of Mickey Spillane and his flint-hearted hero, Mike Hammer, who cruises New York fending off voluptuous broads and blowing hoodlums away with his trusty .45. Spillane insists, 'To me sex and violence are no more than the punctuation marks in a story'. Yeah, maybe, but his stories sure are big on punctuation. This is how Hammer made his début in the dénouement of *I, The Jury* in 1947. Today it reads like parody:

> The roar of the .45 shook the room. Charlotte staggered back a step. Her eyes were a symphony of incredulity, an unbelieving witness to truth. Slowly, she looked down at the ugly swelling in her naked belly where the bullet went in. A thin trickle of blood welled out...Her eyes had pain in them now, the pain preceding death. Pain and unbelief.
> 'How could you?' she gasped.
> I only had a moment before talking to a corpse. 'It was easy', I said.

Pulp to perfection. Spillane stayed there, but Hammett and Chandler, who began writing for the pulps, are now allocated volumes in *The Library of America*, a hallowed company of America's foremost novelists, historians, poets, essayists, philosophers and statesmen.

There's fiction, and then there's crime fiction? The distinction is callow. The Scottish writer, Ian Rankin, believes that crime fiction now leads the way in dealing with social issues. He finds the crime novel the ideal form for saying what he feels about contemporary Scotland:

> In every book I've tried to build up a bit more of this jigsaw of modern Scotland. How did we get here? Where are we going? What should we do to change things? What can't be changed? When it comes to contemporary social issues, it seems that it's the crime novel that's leading the way. Crime writers around the world are pushing the envelope. Take the issue of paedophilia, for example [he deals with this in *Dead Souls*] – I can't imagine a serious, 'literary' novel trying to deal with that problem.

In Shakespeare spoken language is action. It's crucial in crime writing, too. 'They have to be good talkers', Elmore Leonard says of his characters. Like Hammett, Leonard builds his stories out of conversations. Stephanie Plum's character is in her quips. Lawrence Block draws us into his novels by the distinctive voices of his ex-cop, Matt Scudder, and his genial, bookselling burglar, Bernie Rhodenbarr. When it comes to talk, the exemplar is Chandler. Early in his career he put into a story a sentence like, 'He got out of the car and walked across the sun-drenched sidewalk until the shadow of the awning over the entrance fell across his face like the touch of cool water'. The editors took it out. 'Their readers didn't appreciate this sort of thing', Chandler recalled, 'just held up the action. And I set out to prove them wrong'. He did, even if Clive James has a point when he notices that Chandler's metaphors can 'leap off the page so high that they never again settle back into place, thereby adding to the permanent difficulty of remembering what happens to whom where in which novel'. But when the talk's as good as Philip Marlowe's – from five different novels – plot drops into second place. Clive James made the compilation:

> He was a big man but not more than six feet five inches tall and not wider than a beer truck...Even on Central Avenue, not the quietest dressed street in the world, he looked about as inconspicuous as a tarantula on a slice of angel food...'I don't like your manner', Kingsley said in a voice you could have cracked a Brazil nut on. 'That's all right', I said, 'I'm not selling it'...The minutes went by with their fingers to their lips. Then there was a small knocking on wood...It was a blonde. A blonde to make a bishop kick a hole in a stained-glass window...She smelled the way the Taj Mahal looked by moonlight. She gave me a smile I could feel in my hip pocket. 'Cops are just people', she said irrelevantly. 'They start out that way, I've heard'...I poured her a slug that would have made me float over a wall.

Marlowe's acuity of observation is the mark of his moral eminence. Language is his badge of superiority, the charger on which he rides, knightly, into the mean streets, his method for ordering a resolutely iniquitous world, bringing it to heel by wit.

Hammett provides the model crime fiction in *The Maltese Falcon*. The black bird is the least of it. The book's enduring attractions are, first, the image it gives of a world of unstable values and false appearances; second, the ambiguous character of the 'blond satan', Sam Spade; third, the mercenary seductiveness of the *femme fatale*, Brigid O'Shaughnessy. Is Spade corrupt or just corruptible? He knows that Brigid is a liar, but makes love to her with his eyes burning 'yellowly'. He discovers that she has killed his partner, Miles Archer, but concedes that he's 'nuts about her'. The closest he comes to moral grounds for turning her in is an argument about rules and his determination to survive. In all this the reference point is Archer's death in the fog, the core truth that people manipulate and kill for profit.

Which is what they're still doing in the rash of crime fiction from Scandinavia, or 'Scandi-crime' as they call it in London bookshops. The star, so far, is Swedish Stieg Larsson. At the time of his untimely death at 50 from junk food and Marlboro Lights he had written three unpublished novels, marketed as the *Millennium Trilogy*: *The Girl with the Dragon Tattoo*, *The Girl Who Played with Fire* and *The Girl Who Kicked the Hornet's Nest*. From popularity at home to international best sellers to a triptych of acclaimed films, they reflect Larsson's dedicated campaign against neo-Nazis and all forms of Fascism. Never merely gratuitous, the extreme violence of the novels expresses his passionate evaluation of the damage done by corruption in government institutions and corporates. If he stays ahead of the other Nordic writers it will be because his stories are energised by fierce moral integrity and because he has created such an original heroine in the computer genius, laconic young Lisbeth Salander, foil to middle-aged journalist Michael Blomkvist. She recoils from emotional attachments and thinks the worst of everyone. Hardly surprising when you hear about her childhood and the monstrously abusive father she commendably sets on fire, later splitting his head with an axe. The *Millennium* series has sold over a million copies in Britain and some three million in Sweden.

Iceland's Arnaldur Indriðason presents taciturn Detective Erlendur of Reykjavik in *Jar City* — also a movie — *Hypothermia* and *Arctic Chill*, dealing with such themes as spiritualism, new-age belief and anti-Asian racism. Another Swede, Henning

Mankell, gives us morose Inspector Wallander, brought to the small screen in Britain by Kenneth Branagh, attracting over five million viewers. The prolific Mankell spreads his net as far as South Africa in *The White Lioness*, demonstrating his world-wide concern for the well-being of humanity beyond the expected scope of the genre in a story which recalls the forces intent on halting Nelson Mandela's rise to power and frustrating South Africa's escape from apartheid. Judge Birgitta Roslin replaces Inspector Wallander in *The Man from Beijing*. After the police make a mistaken arrest, a red silk ribbon found in a restaurant near the crime scene leads her from a massacre in north Sweden to two maltreated Chinese brothers labouring in the 1860s on America's cross-continental railroad in Nevada. The trail leads to a Chinese entrepreneur intent on vengeance for crimes against his family. Norway's Jo Nesbo — two million sold in Norway and climbing — introduces alcoholic detective Harry Hole, who specialises in woman trouble and bringing to book perpetrators of some of the genre's most gruesome murders. See the hideous device called 'Leopold's Apple' in *The Leopard* and the ghoulish snowmen the villain uses as a signature warning in *The Snowman*. If Nesbo's writing is tighter than Larsson's, you feel an anger in his books comparable to the Swede's. Corruption in high places accounts for much of the impact of *Redbreast*, *The Redeemer* and *Nemesis*. All these writers demand a better world.

Lots of murder, Jean, not fairy tales but metaphors for the cut-throat world as it really is all around us. As James Lee Burke says in *Cadillac Jukebox*: 'You learn soon or you learn late: There are no islands'. What a relief to admit it, a holiday treat away from the rules and doubletalk by which we maintain, more or less, our precarious survival.

20. Praise of a MacCaig

Norman MacCaig hated death. Not his own death in prospect, but the deaths of friends. 'Will you have a heart-starter?' he would ask on meeting, as if the dram would guarantee him your company for a while before you faded like the rest of them. Feeling in himself the death of his friend, Angus MacLeod, he wrote:

> To carry two deaths
> is a burden for any man:
> and it's a heavy knowledge that tells me
> only the death I was born with
> will destroy the other.
> Now I have another death in me: yours.
> Each is the image of the other.

But MacCaig's words have left the living MacLeod behind, along with the poet's sense of loss and connection and all the other heart-starters in *Collected Poems*.

'A threequarter Gael', MacCaig felt at home both in Edinburgh and in the village of Inverkirkaig near Lochinver in Sutherland. His favourite mountain was Suilven. 'I love Suilven', he said, 'because from the West it looks like the top joint of your thumb. But he cons you: there's a ridge and there's a pinky at the far end... so that when you get on to the ridge, suddenly you see miles and miles instead of just what was under you'. His idea of a miracle in 'Above Inverkirkaig' is the coupling of the mountains, Suilven and Cul Mor, to produce 'a litter of tiny Suilvens, each one/the dead spit of his father'. In 'Climbing Suilven' a dizzying shift of scales and perspectives intensifies the poet's sense of physical self:

> Parishes dwindle. But my parish is
> This stone, that tuft, this stone
> And the cramped quarters of my flesh and bone.
> I claw that tall horizon down to this;
> And suddenly
> My shadow jumps huge miles away from me.

This poem is from the volume, *Riding Lights*, in which MacCaig abandoned the New Apocalypse practices of his earlier work, a major step in what he called his 'long haul towards lucidity'. His triumph is to have developed a style which could tackle anything without needing to be obscure. Yet there is a tension in a MacCaig poem that comes from the sense that each word, each line has passed a rigorous test of validity in competition with the appeal to the poet of leaving the subject alone without interference from him. He is laconic almost, but mercifully not quite, to a fault. Impelled to use words, he remains suspicious of them: 'the ones I use', he says, 'often look at me/with a look that whispers, *Liar*' ('Ineducable me'). There are no lies in the non-verbal realm of the thrush, the newt and the gannet, 'A free world, a world without hyprocrisy, without masks' ('Hard Division').

He is often wryly aware of his own act of perception as in the poem 'An ordinary day' in which either he takes 'his mind a walk' or his mind takes him a walk, whichever is the elusive truth of it, and in the earlier 'No consolation' from the volume, *Surroundings*:

> I consoled myself for not being able to describe
> water trickling down a wall or
> a wall being trickled down by water
> by reflecting that I can see
> these two things are not the same thing:
> which is more than a wall can do,
> or water.

Referring to what he can't describe, the poet consoles himself with the thought that, unlike the wall and the water, he is a discriminating consciousness. Of course, what he has done here, with no recourse to the hieratic tone, is define the central mystery of our humanity. We are the only species with the ability to know that 'these two things are not the same thing'. What the imagination can do is elicit strangeness from ordinary reality, heightening perception by making water into a wall, or making the wall trickle like water. Nature or reality is like one's wife. The poet has a promiscuous imagination and can be loyal to his wife by transforming her into somebody else, making her new, and MacCaig's genius specialises in charging the ordinary – landscapes, animals, people – with celebratory newness, revealing a world of 'teeming unpredictables'

('Centre of centres') which he exposes but never appropriates or binds.

Few poets have been so lacking in posture. The 'miraculous declarations' he shows us are always out there to be wondered at for themselves, not to be applauded as evidence of his skill in divulging them. How can he enlanguage the given object, how elicit its essence without fuss? In nature he is our roving reporter. So, straws lie on grass 'like tame lightnings' and 'a hen stares at nothing with one eye/Then picks it up' ('Summer farm'); sprinting plover 'have no acceleration/and no brakes' ('Ringed plover by a water's edge'); a dog flows 'through fences like a piece of black wind' ('Praise of a collie'); he thinks about a loved one 'in as many ways as rain comes' ('No choice'); a toad looks 'like a purse' and crawls 'like a Japanese wrestler' ('Toad'); the lochs of his beloved north-west may be 'just H_2O in a hollow' but they stand 'huge mountains on their watery heads' ('Small lochs'). In darker mood he trembles for the stag who will be 'an old rug rotting in the heather' ('Two focuses'); the hearts of world leaders can't secrete the devil who 'sits crosslegged,/grinning and cracking his finger joints' ('Leaders of men'); American skyscrapers walk around 'with atom bombs slung at their hips' ('Rewards and furies'); and in the circus of life outside the 'Big Top' crowds panic 'towards exits/ that aren't there'. The Duke of Sutherland is a thief who steals the land from the people, driving them from their homes to the shore, where the tide steals it again, and on to Canada ('Two thieves'). In 'A man in Assynt' metaphor gives way to undecorated anger about the depopulation of the Highlands first by the Clearances, later by 'English businessmen and the indifference/of a remote and ignorant government':

> Who owns this landscape?
> The millionaire who bought it or
> the poacher staggering downhill in the early morning
> with a deer on his back?

If MacCaig contemplates his own darkness he objectifies it, hating the word 'confessional'. In 'Go away, Ariel', he finds the grid of himself in *The Tempest* from whose cast Caliban is a more welcome visitor than 'heartless, musical...supersonic Ariel', even if he does blubber about Miranda and go on about his mother:

Phone a bat, Ariel. Leave us
to have a good cry— to stare at each other
with recognition and loathing.

Norman MacCaig at home in Edinburgh

As you would expect, he detested cant. In response to a ponderous question about his work he replied, 'Oh, I think that kind of talk stinks the joint up, as Ellington said when they asked him if he was influenced by Debussy'. The academic is 'the tone-deaf man in the orchestra', the 'frog/who wouldn't a-wooing go' ('An academic'). Socio-psychological cant got no quarter either. He had only contempt for the excuses people make for their evil blunders: '"Wisnae me, came from a broken home" — all that stuff. "I had a black-out" — this is after sawing a woman in quadruplets'. His poem about the abrogation of responsibility is called 'The first of them' the title referring to the snake which has been blamed and hated since Adam and Eve.

Poor snake. He crawls on his belly
dropping amber tears in the dust and whining
I was only obeying orders.

No more need be said about Nuremberg or *Obersturmbann-führer* Eichmann. Equally, no more need be said about the blame game. Religion, too, is cant in a world which mixes adders and butterflies, torture and Schubert. God is 'an absentee landlord' in 'The Kirk', reaching down from 'some Bahamas in the sky' to collect 'the price of suffering with which to pay/a pittance to his estate workers'. (Wickedly, he professed to believe in the Devil but not in God, which made him, he said, 'a Zen Calvinist'.) The effort of balancing beauty and suffering shakes his mind in 'Assisi' and 'Equilibrist':

I had a difficulty in being friendly
to the Lord, who gave us these burdens,
so I returned him to other people
and totter without help
among his careless inventions.
     ('Equilibrist')

The reported totter is internal, never public and rarely aesthetic, in a body of poetry in which language does an inimitable version of its best. Like the MacLeod to whom he built a perdurable monument in the poem, 'Praise of a Man', MacCaig went through a company 'like a knifegrinder', making dull minds 'razory', 'useful'. Alive, he became necessary; dead, he is the sum of the revelatory images he made and an unforgettable voice. In Scotland we have no doubt: he is among our great ones.

21. Lismore

It's a slice of ancient limestone, formed by collisions and slippages of rock some five hundred million years ago. The name means 'Great Garden' but from the air it's a long-nosed green fish about ten miles long and up to a mile and a half wide, swimming south from the Great Glen of Scotland towards the east coast of Mull. The island sits in the middle of a landscape created by the long-extinct volcano whose core now comprises Ben More, the highest peak on Mull. Approaching it by ferry across Loch Linnhe from Oban it's secretive, low-lying and featureless until you're close enough to make out the Iron Age Pictish broch at Tirfuir on a vantage point easy to defend, and whitewashed Kilcheran house, a Roman Catholic Highland seminary in the early nineteenth-century, later a boarding house.

Towards the south end of the island is what's left of Achinduin Castle, built by the MacDougalls in the second half of the thirteenth century, with a commanding view of the Macleans' Duart Castle and the Sound of Mull. For a time it accommodated the Bishops of Lismore. Below Achinduin you can see Bernera Isle, reachable at low tide. Tradition says Columba sometimes preached to a thousand people under the shadow of a yew tree on Bernera. He prophesied that man's pride and greed would hew down the noble tree, but that retribution would overtake the vandals. Their crime would be expiated by water, blood and three fires. In the nineteenth century the proprietor of Lochnell Castle near Oban, probably the Earl of Dundonald, ordered the tree cut down to make a grand staircase for his castle. When the tree was felled a workman was crushed to death and when the timber was taken to Benderloch on the mainland a storm arose and several men on the boat lost their lives. Three fires damaged the castle but the staircase survived.

On a clear day Achinduin has a line of sight to the medieval ruins of Castle Coeffin, another spectacularly positioned MacDougall stronghold on the Morvern side of the island. Built on the site of a Norse fortress, Castle Coeffin has a story to tell:

> Once upon a time there lived a princess whose name was Beothail. She lived at Port Castle or Castle Coeffin

in Lismore. She was a Norwegian princess. Now Princess Beothail had a betrothed who went away to the wars in Norway. Word came that he was killed and Princess Beothail died of a broken heart.

Before she died Princess Beothail said she didn't want to be buried in Lismore; she would never rest until her body was buried in Norway beside her lover. Her Norwegian brother lived in Castle Coeffin and she haunted him until he agreed to send her body to Norway for burial.

Norwegians came to Lismore for her bones. They moved the bones to a well, washed them and took them to Norway. But still the Princess did not rest and they found that her smallest finger bone was missing. [Some versions of the story say it was two joints of her toes.] She continued her haunting until the Norwegians returned once more to Lismore. They went back to the well and found the missing bone, then Princess Beothail rested in peace.

Achinduin

Lismore's best-known story is about the two saints, Columba and Moluag. In AD 562 the two holy men arrived on the west coast of Scotland. They both wanted headquarters for their Christian missions. Each chose Lismore and sought to requisition it by landing there first. Tradition pictures their coracles racing towards the island, oarsmen urged on by the missionaries. As they approach the shore Moluag sees that his rival's boat will win. Picking up an axe, he places his little finger on the gunwale, severs it from his hand and throws it on the shingle ahead.

'My flesh and blood have first possession of the island', he cries, 'and I bless it in the name of the Lord'.

Legend makes Columba a bad loser He curses Moluag.

'May you have the alder for your firewood'.

'The Lord will make the alder burn pleasantly', answers Moluag with saintly equanimity.

Columba attacks again.

'May you have the jagged ridges for your pathway'.

'The Lord will smooth them to the feet', replies Moluag, still beyond provocation.

So Moluag got the island. Columba went north to Iona, becoming the most famous saint in Celtic history. Moluag's pastoral staff survives. The *Bachuil Mòr* (Great Staff) or *Bachuil Buidhe* (Yellow Staff) is a piece of curved blackthorn wood 85 cm long. Entrusted to the guardianship of the Livingstone Barons of Bachuil, the staff may be viewed, by appointment, at Bachuil House.

In the early nineteenth century the population was over 1700. Lismore supplied lime for building and agriculture to the West Highlands and Islands. Evidence of the limestone industry is scattered throughout the island with important centres at Port Ramsay and Sailean. The industry generated employment for quarriers, labourers and for the sailing smacks bringing coal for the kilns from Lanarkshire. Completion of the Callander and Oban Railway made possible the delivery of much cheaper bulk supplies and a death blow was dealt by more economical production of lime in other parts of Scotland and in the north of England. The island's farming economy declined and population dropped through the post-World-War-One depression. Today there are some 180 residents. The number of deserted and ruined dwellings, home only to nettles and thistles, makes for an emptiness which lends a ghostly poignancy to the loveliness of the island. You think of the people who went away and remember, sadly, Oliver Goldsmith's phrase in *The Deserted Village*: 'Allured to brighter worlds'. Yet, what world could be brighter than this?

Happily, the midge population is also small, presumably due to meagre bracken cover and quick absorption of rain through the top-soil into the limestone beneath. It's a bonus to be relatively free from swarming clouds of these gnat-like blood-suckers. In his *Beasts of Scotland* Edwin Morgan imagines them massing for attack in a smirr of summer rain. The loch lies silent and the air is still; there's a smell of supper in the exposed flesh of the unsuspecting holiday-makers. The leader of the midges exhorts her vampire sisterhood:

See the innocents, my sisters,
The clumsy ones, the laughing ones
The rolled-up sleeves and the flapping shorts,
There is even a kilt (god of the midges,
you are good to us!). So gather your forces,
leave your tree-trunks, forsake the rushes,
fly up from the sour brown mosses
to the sweet flesh of face and forearm.
Think of your eggs. What does the egg need?
Blood, and blood. Blood is what the egg needs.

On muggy summer evenings the Attilas and Amazons of Skye and Loch Maree count on an orgy of human blood. Their dispirited Lismore cousins risk an occasional, faint-hearted nip. It's a rare respite in the Highlands and a marketable attribute of the Great Garden.

For us, in Glasgow, Lismore always began with a taxi. Taxis only came for us when we were going to Buchanan Street railway station for the train to Oban and the Lismore ferry. Holiday excitement started with my father's substitution of sports jacket and flannels for the formality of his workaday three-piece suit, and the arrival of the black cab. Settled into our second-class compartment on the train, I was then free to inspect the splendour of the locomotive and coax a 'Good morning' from the driver which made me feel I was helping him along. By Loch Lomond, the Pass of Brander and Loch Awe the ride from Glasgow to Oban was sagging luggage racks, cracked leather window straps, roosters of steam, coal smuts and piercing whistles from the guard when it was time to leave each country station along the way. At Oban waited the gangway to the 'Lochinvar'. Once aboard there was a visit to the clanking, oily mysteries of the engine room, then up on deck to watch the island of Kerrera slip past on the port side and to starboard, poised over the sea on the brink of its crag, Dunollie Castle, another ruined fortress of the MacDougalls. Lismore was less than an hour away across the Lynn of Lorn, a ribbon of dark green backed by the gaunt hills of Morvern.

Our Lismore home was the boarding house at Kilcheran with a view of the sea and the Kilcheran islands, chief among them *Eilean na Cloiche* — Island of the Rock — conspicuous by its 60-foot stack of yellow stone which looked like the Sphinx from one angle and from another the conning tower of a submarine. Closer in to Lismore itself was *Eilean nan Gamban* (Island of the Stirks [year-old calves]) with a tiny stretch of sandy beach tucked incongruously into shoreline rocks draped by sneezing, sun-worshipping seals. My mother would read and go for walks, delighting in vistas of the mountainous mainland and the constantly changing theatre of skyscapes. She made friends with ladies of the island, mostly farmers' wives, and never returned to wartime Glasgow without produce. She made a point of two dozen eggs for pickling. My father and I would fish either Loch Kilcheran where the trout were small and infrequent, or Loch Fiart, below the island's highest point, the Barr Mòr, where they were a little bigger and more inclined to be caught. After a day on Fiart my father and I would walk our catch back to Kilcheran hoping my mother would come to meet us, and singing 'She'll be coming round the mountains when she comes'. Decades later, one cold but brilliantly sunny December, when I took my wife on a pilgrimage to the island, I tried to commemorate all this:

Lismore
For Cláudia

Snug in your sea-circle you don't miss much.
Picts came first to give you eyes to watch
A pair of rival saints, northmen from the Lynn,

A princess to be held in Viking stones,
Then crofters, lairds and tourists for the trout
That lie by reeds in Fiart and Kilcheran,
And all of Scotland from the Barr Mòr.

A formal father was my island friend
In gum boots, oilskin, rod and chocolate.
Your lochs cast off the city man
With creak of rollock, gullcry, fishy magic.
Bass wet with trout, nodding to Cruachan,
We marched the catch to where his love
Was coming round the mountains when she came.

She often came, they went, but you go on,
Green, limestone-ribbed and built to last,
A storied headstone for their arch of love,
A garden still, but not mine as before.
Rooks cawed from elms and lambs implored,
Brown trout still rose along the reeds.
You told me what to do to get them back.

'You saw their love', your limestone said.
Rooks cried, 'Find yours' and lambs cajoled.
I journeyed, tested, failed, and fell
At last, for once, in love to bring to you.
You saw me coming with my girl,
You held the sun above us and approved.
December limestone rang with Spring.

On Sundays, when Presbyterian custom still frowned on
Sabbath fishing, we would all climb the 417 feet of the Barr Mòr,
the island's chief marvel, an easily accessible eminence of emerald
turf ribbed and punctured by folds of limestone. As a vantage point
it has no equal on the Highland coast. When you're up there you
can see almost the whole Great Glen of Scotland. You can imagine
sunlight flashing on the oars of Vikings and relish the panoramic
sweep from Ben Cruachan in the east to the hunched shoulder of
Ben Nevis to the north and, southward, the Isles of the Sea, Scarba
and the Paps of Jura.

The view from Barr Mòr

I am in paradise. Lismore is my 'island that likes to be visited', like the faery island J. M. Barrie invented for his other-worldly heroine in *Mary Rose*. Not that it tempted me to a career as an island ghost, like Barrie's elfin Mary, though it was always a wrench to leave when the holiday was over and we were pulled back to the mainland by my father's job and the new school term. There's a Gaelic song, 'Fàgail Liosmor' ('Leaving Lismore'). Here's a clunky, prosaic English approximation:

> Tears fill my eyes, my utmost joy has gone,
> The ship is trim which will carry me across the sea.
> O, I am leaving you, isle of my heart,
> Solace and peace be upon you, and joy.
>
> Mull of the cold hills, Morvern my joy,
> Sunlit Appin, my beloved Lorn
> And the little green island in the embrace of the sea,
> The isle of my tender allegiance.
>
> Asleep or awake I'll hear in the distance

The young milkmaid singing by the cattle fold
On an early May morning, and the thrush on a branch
Tuning her pipe for music.

I would not wish for silk or satin
Nor jewels nor riches nor a high, fleecy bed.
My lasting abundance the little green shieling
And a sound sleep bedded on the floor.

Farewell to the woods, farewell to the shores,
Farewell to beauty, farewell to gentle amity.
Now that I am leaving you, isle of my heart,
Solace and peace be on you, and joy.

There were many leavings for us, but never a farewell. Lismore was always part of our present. Until he died my father talked of the island, fondly reminiscing about our days on the lochs. When elderly and reliant on a wheelchair, my mother took her mind for her favourite walks. Even dementia couldn't take away her strolls to Fiart or down to Miller's Port, below Kilcheran House, to marvel at the glistening, multi-coloured pebbles in the bay. And though I may never again walk on its ancient earth, the beloved island is to me a constant source of solace, peace and joy.

22. Pop Goes the Culture

Here's a vexing question. What's 'popular' and what's the opposite? Madonna and the Stones versus Bach and Mahler? Stephen King versus Tolstoy? *Avatar* versus *L'Avventura*? In the age of the periphery, the canon, whatever it may have been, is shot. If Elgar is a classic so are The Beatles. The old centres can't and shouldn't hold in the fibre-optic-veined global village at the end of the information super-highway. The market is adjudicator of worth. A stout British empirical tradition is there to support it, notably in Dr Johnson for whom, 'in questions that relate to the heart of man', the ultimate arbiter is 'the common voice of the multitude, uninstructed by precept and unprejudiced by authority'. The multitude now includes Puerto Ricans, Indians and West Indians, Africans, Malaysians, Polynesians and Indonesians, Japanese and Chinese, the European Community, gays, feminists, green-earthers, save-the-whalers, and members of the Volkswagen Club of America, vegetarian section.

Response to a work of art can hi-jack it from canonical privilege, resulting in 'hackneyed' or a new lease of life. Perhaps we should learn from our students. In the early seventies I taught at a university in Memphis, Tennessee. After some weeks of a sophomore survey course on English literature we advanced on Coleridge. To ingratiate the poet with my often somnolent customers I told them, a day or two before we were scheduled to bear down on 'Kubla Khan', that when Coleridge wrote it he was stoned. The hint was sufficient; at least half of my congregation came stoned to the Coleridge class. But not all. When we had read the poem and I invited comment, a paradigmatically fresh-faced, buttoned-down, short-back-and-sides, plainly Republican white youth told the class what he thought Mister Coleridge meant. There was a pause. A large black arm floated upwards and waved. It belonged to a Vietnam veteran in a leather jacket. I acknowledged the wave and asked him to give his opinion of the view expressed by Buttoned-down. 'Like, shit, man', he intoned, coming out of his haze, 'This cat Coleridge, he says, like WOW!' A new lease of life in spades.

New literatures are, happily, exploding as surely as old politics are falling apart, but truly popular works are still kept in their place, which is out of the academy, and good old-fashioned élitism lives on in the intimidating embonpoint of the new critical jargons. Structuralists, Deconstructionists, and post-Deconstructionists circle the arts like a hostile Sky-Lab. Critical discourse sounds Martian. People queued to see London's recent exhibition of invisible art, a *ne plus ultra* of élitism. Cowpokes, Private Eyes, Sky-walkers and Lovers — the western, the detective story, the science-fiction novel and the romance — are kept on the margin, despite scattered attempts to get them their peculiar dues. Yet such writings and related films carry basic questions into the realm of images that raise or lower the devices of narrative to create the multi-media mythologising muzak without which western culture would now be inconceivable, twentieth-century consumerism eviscerated and non-western cultures deprived of goals. Attention paid to them might help us to understand why Ronald Reagan made it to the White House and prepare us for the accession of Arnold Schwarzenegger or Brad Pitt.

Hamlet was a hit in its time and still does pretty good business, so why not consider a more recent hit like *Farewell My Lovely*, Elmore Leonard's *Glitz* or Stieg Larsson's *The Girl with the Dragon Tattoo*? After all, Raymond Chandler's formula, 'When in doubt have a man come through the door with a gun in his hand', is Shakespeare's trick too with Hamlet's father's ghost, Dickens's when Magwitch drops in from Australia on his boy Pip, Henry James's when the governess sees Peter Quint on the tower, Beckett's when the Boy in *Waiting for Godot* enters to tell Vladimir and Estragon that 'Mr Godot...won't come this evening but surely tomorrow'. What are the real differences between Shakespeare, Dickens, James and Beckett and, say, *The Silence of the Lambs*, *Dallas*, *The Shining* and *Alien Resurrection*, apart from the fact that we can be sure neither Vladimir nor Estragon would go to Lieutenant Ripley's length to rid the other of worms?

It might be found that Dashiell Hammett or Patricia Highsmith or Henning Mankell is the equal of Hawthorne or Faulkner or Ian McEwan and better than much of Hemingway; that *The Virginian* and *Shane*, their genre kept alive by over a hundred titles from Louis Dearborn L'Amour — many available bound 'in rugged, simulated leather of sierra brown...with the fine "weighty heft" of a trusty Colt revolver' — and the spaghetti variations of Sergio

Leone, Ennio Morricone and Clint Eastwood, reflect a culture's need for a particular mythology as pressing as its need for Uncle Tom, Huckleberry Finn, Ishmael and Ahab; that behind the space ships and robots the essential software appeal of science-fiction as practised by Isaac Asimov, Robert Silverberg or Philip K. Dick is a serious, if not obsessional, concern for the future of the planet, and that *Gone With the Wind* broke records because Americans of all climes, complexions and degrees had been waiting for its glamorously sanitising reconstruction of a sickening piece of their history. 'The poetry does not matter', Eliot says in 'East Coker', and often, in popular fiction, the prose doesn't. Yet something does. What is it?

As George Steiner says, cheap music, childish images and the vulgate in language can penetrate to the depths of our needs and dreams and assert irrevocable tenure. The 'happening to us' of a work of art, however low-brow, tends to beggar understanding. Steiner admits that 'the opening bars, the hammer-beat *accelerando* of Edith Piaf's "Je ne regrette rien" — the text is infantile, the tune stentorious, and the politics which enlisted the song unattractive', tempt all his nerves, drawing him into 'God knows what infidelities to reason' each time he hears it played or hears it, uncalled for, recurrent inside him. I would swap the whole of Verdi for Sinatra doing 'I've got you under my skin', surely the most pornographic of popular songs. Of course we are all devotees of Milton, Mozart and Proust, but, as Steiner reminds us:

> It is also the bad rhymester, the pedlar of facile images, the organ-grinder whose work is not only ineradicable from our memories, but continues to nourish, to quicken our innermost wants. No man or woman need justify his personal anthology, his canonic welcomes. Love does not argue its necessities.

The ratings, no doubt, have been an issue in any culture since before the Burbages measured audience responses to Shakespeare's plays. Melville, chastened by dismissals of *Moby-Dick* as 'maniacal...intellectual chowder', recognised the significance of the ratings when he said of his vast philosophical poem *Clarel* that it was 'eminently adapted for unpopularity'. Yet part of the paradoxical appeal of the Pop Art movement was the effrontery with which it defied current standards of popular taste in a relation to the public as aggressively independent as Marinetti's 1909 manifesto of Futurist poetry in *Le Figaro* against 'pensive immobility, ecstasy and sleep', but much funnier. Whatever long-bearded pronouncements might be made by artists and critics, there's no gainsaying the fun of Warhol's 'Green Coca Cola Bottles', 'Four Campbell's Soup Cans' and his dayglo Marilyns, Claes Oldenburg's 'Giant Blue Pants', Roy Lichtenstein's 'Whaam' and Tom Wesselmann's 'Great American Nudes' which pun on the clichés of commercial sex, alluding to the soft-porn gloss of much advertising and magazines like *Playboy*. This fun is a pleasurable sense of the often absurd, conformist exuberance of a consumer culture which includes Coca Cola, Pepsi, Budweiser, Campbell's soup, hamburgers and hot dogs, comics, McDonald's, rock music, Country and Western, Michael Jackson, Madonna and *Twin Peaks*. These are components of what has been called the closest approximation there is today to a global *lingua franca*, drawing the urban and urbane classes of most nations into a federated culture zone.

Popular Culture is a complex phenomenon in which social and aesthetic comment often raucously plays with vulgarity. The Pop artists' use of commercial images was ambivalent; 'making it new', they may have been expedient nihilists in relation to established, even modernist, art conventions, but in general their works are, at some level, optimistic. Lichtenstein's meticulous blow-ups of comic-book images express the inordinate power of comics, the comforting inanity of their escapist clichés of love, war and domesticity, and nostalgic pleasure in the histrionics of the strips. In fiction the private eye usually cracks the case, give or take some broken bones, multiple hang-overs and come hithers from dark ladies with figures, in Woody Allen's phrase, 'to cause cardiac arrest in a yak'. Love is assertive in the romances if not always triumphant.

Apocalypses never go out of fashion with the movies. In *The Matrix* the Wachowski brothers took their cues from Plato's cave and Descartes to invent a force even more satanic than communism. Machines have taken control of a ravaged planet, enslaving humans and reducing them to a food source. Human beings doze in uterine pods of goo while a master race of artificially intelligent robots suck their life-giving heat. To keep their victims alive while they graze, the robots wire them to a main-frame of dreams, a virtual human world whose illusions are known as 'The Matrix'. We are rescued from this ungodly neural, interactive simulation by a godly all-American trio: Morpheus, a black God-the-Father; kung-fu virtuoso Trinity, a mother-cum-holy-spirit in PVC bondage gear; and Neo, a clean-cut computer hacker whose name is an anagram for the 'One', so presumably a cybernetic-age Christ. A dystopian fantasy of considerable ingenuity, *The Matrix* is a serviceable parable of our time when, thanks to biotechnology, *homo sapiens* may be evolving into a race at once more and less than human. Unfortunately the film slides from its apocalyptic premise about free will as illusion (unless we fight the malevolent forces controlling us) into a comic-strip, computer and pop-Zen-philosophy-enhanced martial arts extravaganza. Parable surrenders to hokum. The film achieved cult status. Fans explicate it and its two garbled sequels to each other in cyberspace. The films gloss our paranoia, instating the machine as *éminence grise*, appealing to our common experience of what machines can do to us now and speculation about what they might do to us in the future. We have been warned.

Another warning accompanies an American flag on the moon and the legend, 'We came in peace for all mankind'. In *Independence Day* a fifteen mile-wide alien space ship coming from that direction is not reciprocally peace-bound. It will disappoint earthlings who hope it'll bring back Elvis. On earth the US President's ratings are slipping despite his early popularity as a fighter-pilot in the first Gulf War (Bush, *pére*). His fickle electorate now think him inert, an ageing wimp. The monstrous ship is one of a fleet approaching earth. It casts its shadow over Brooklyn Bridge and over gleaming twin towers, then over Capitol and White House. Welcome wagons are greeted with sheets of flame. The 4th of July Independence Day Parade is in trouble. To win back his electorate the President must defeat the aliens (Bush, *fils*). He accordingly flies against them himself; but it's the help who make victory politically correct. A Jewish computer boffin (get that, Israel?) transports a virus into the alien ship's computer in a spacecraft piloted by a patriotic black airman. The Black has already thumped an alien while quipping, 'Welcome to Earth', but his promotion has been blocked because he plans to marry an 'exotic dancer'. He'll be okay now. Everything will be okay. Europe, Russia, the Middle East and Asia are all on side with the USA, United Nations versus the aliens, which outclasses their record on paltry earthly problems in Rwanda, Kosovo, Chechnya, Somalia and the Congo. Now we can add Syria. The sanctity of the 4th of July is intact. America's heroism and genius are accorded multilateral support and applause. American survival and freedom are survival and freedom for all. *Independence Day* is a popular, narcissistic movie for world consumption. Director Roland Emmerich may not be the sharpest knife in the Hollywood drawer and *Time Out Film Guide* calls his film a 'scrappy, spectacular, juvenile remake of *War of the Worlds* and 101 other sci-fi movies'; but, aside from its sentimental ending, much of *Independence Day* might have been directed by Nostradamus with production touches from a gleeful Osama bin Laden, a prophetic fantasy based on themes from 11th September 2001 and the war in Iraq. We might have avoided our rabbits-in-the-headlights look on 9/11 if we'd paid serious attention to this pop projection instead of relying unthinkingly on the West's so-called intelligence services. 'Remember', advises John Le Carré, 'that these are the organisations who brought us the biggest failure in intelligence history'. Notwithstanding the Alien's warning in *The Day the Earth Stood Still* that we must live peacefully or be destroyed as a danger to other planets, science fiction usually sees humankind surviving, with the notable exception of Lars von Trier's terrifying *Melancholia* in which Earth is annihilated by terminal collision with the film's eponymous planet.

Works in all popular genres can be useful. In the cult novel *Dune* Frank Herbert preaches respect for ecology, and in the setting of a decayed, post-atomic Los Angeles in *Do Androids Dream of Electric Sheep* (*Blade Runner* in its movie incarnation) Philip K. Dick makes empathy the key to it all. John le Carré's inestimable Karla trilogy uses the secret services of Britain, America and the USSR to offer conspiracy as metaphor for everyday ways of the world. His prose, always polished, certainly matters and his popularity merits special attention because the complexity of his plots demands such intelligent engagement. His popularity has remained steady since *The Spy who Came in from the Cold* in 1963 and has survived the end of the Cold War — the death, we might have thought, of his subject matter — with his fierce indictment of the pharmaceutical industry's exploitation of the Third World in *The Constant Gardener*. Two screen adaptations of *Tinker, Tailor, Soldier, Spy*, the first novel of the Karla trilogy, have been universally acclaimed. The BBC's serial adaptation with Alec Guinness as the seasoned spymaster, George Smiley, deservedly won golden opinions as a landmark in British television. Director Thomas Alfredson's recent film version with Gary Oldman in the part of Smiley, John Hurt as Control and Colin Firth as the traitor, Bill Haydon, has been widely hailed as 'The perfect film...stylish and sophisticated...a spellbinding espionage thriller'.

Cover, Sceptre edition, 2011

Le Carré's essential message is succinctly expressed at the end of *The Honourable Schoolboy*, volume two of the Karla triptych. Smiley writes to his wayward wife, Ann:

> I chose the secret road because it seemed to lead straightest and furthest toward my country's goal... Today, all I know is that I have learned to interpret the whole of life in terms of conspiracy. That is the sword I have lived by, and as I look round me now I see it is the sword I shall die by as well.

If there was as much buffoonery as satire in the Pop Art movement, it wasn't just a bunch of jokers wisecracking at the objects of everyday life. Even a work by Oldenburg could be useful, for example his enormous, phallic vinyl lipstick placed by Yale undergraduates beside the Beinecke Research Library to signify their contempt for an administration that spent millions of dollars on a fancy library dedicated to research while their contemporaries were still fighting and dying in Vietnam.

Music can make the charts with useful satire. America's fall from the grace of its founding idealisms is Laurie Anderson's theme in 'O Superman'. An electronically processed vocal pulse — the monosyllable 'Ha' — supplies a hypnotic accompaniment to satirical incisions delivered in Anderson's unnervingly robotic voice. Composed in 1981, the piece is still a trenchant text for our times. Replaying the Abraham Lincoln log cabin to White House myth, Clark Kent progresses from the Old World planet Krypton, via telephone box and body stocking, to embody a Nietzschean übermensch myth of New World individualism, moral purity and indestructibility which transcends its comic-book origin; but Anderson sees the myth crash in the ruins of contemporary reality. We don't look up at the sky and exclaim, 'It's a bird, it's a plane, it's Superman!' After 9/11 we look up and say, 'It's a plane all right, and there could be terrorists at the controls'.

Anderson calls American fundamentals in question: Superman, that is the type of the heroic individual, whether Abe Lincoln, George Washington, Clark Kent or Bruce Wayne; 'Judge' and, by implication God as well as democratic justice; Mom and Dad and the family. They are all lapsed or occluded ideals, once as pure as blue-haired, airborne Clark Kent in his chase red trunks, now displaced or obsolesced by automation, electronics, petrochemicals and militarism. Human contact is as spontaneous and intimate as a message on the answerphone — 'Hi. I'm not home right now. But if you want to leave a message, just start talking at the sound of the tone'. Solicitude for human well-being is reduced to the inessential options, 'smoking or non-smoking'. Blind nationalism is enjoined. 'Here come the planes', the disembodied voice tells us, satirising their mission by allusion to a grandiose expression of the United States' Postal Service's devotion to duty: 'Neither snow nor rain nor gloom of night shall stay these couriers from the swift completion of their appointed rounds'. This is the flatulent rhetoric of politicians. Whatever the 'appointed rounds' may be, don't worry: the planes are American, made in America, you can't ask for more. When truth is gone there's always chauvinism and the slide from love to justice to force to 'Mom' encapsulates American decadence from the egalitarian dream of the Declaration of Independence to brutish imperialism with mindless sentimentality as fall-back position. America began as a brand-new culture designed to give; now it's 'the hand that takes'. The sweet, natural sound of birdsong is the final irony in this moribund, automated scheme of things.

Despite some portentous intellectualising of Pop Art, analyses of popular films and the twilight zone between high and lower brows occupied by some Beatles' songs, Sondheim's grittier musicals, novels by Kurt Vonnegut and Ursula Le Guin and the operas of John Adams and Philip Glass, a sturdy if vaguely based complacency about the distinction between serious and popular has persisted. In Britain this complacency survived The Who's 1969 flirtation with opera in *Tommy*, subsequently adapted for Broadway by Pete Townshend to thrill 'audiences of responsible American forty-somethings with its energy and hit-power'. It survived Pink Floyd's bids for the grandiose in their 'concept' albums, but trembled when Nigel Kennedy repackaged himself and Pavarotti filled the stage in Hyde Park, performing in the open air like the supergroups. In America Madonna was disconcertingly appointed vice-president of the Institute of Contemporary Arts. Philip Glass composed his 'Low' Symphony, reworking material from a 1975 rock album by David Bowie and Brian Eno. The English National Opera launched 'New Visions, New Voices', a project open to anyone under 30 who wants to 'do' opera, applicants to the scheme being encouraged to use their own preferred forms of music, whether house music, heavy metal or plain old pop. Ivory towers were crumbling and cultural uniforms shedding their insignia in this jumbling of categories, with the producer in charge of 'New Visions, New Voices', saying that he would be happier 'if people turned up to a first night at the English National Opera in jeans, rather than the furs and diamonds that make my heart sink'. Culture, as it doggedly continued to be even when Malinowski redefined it to mean the material and mental habitat of a people, was pushing out from behind the red ropes of the museum. It began to look as though popular culture might be the only culture and sponsors began to withdraw from art once designated high. In March 1992 British Telecom declined to renew its £250,000 sponsorship of the Royal Shakespeare Company, preferring to back to the tune of £100,000 a tour of Agatha Christie's *Witness for the Prosecution*. As far as British Telecom was concerned, 'the Christie play appeals right across the social spectrum'. It was also less than half the price, an auspice of the bland leading the bland.

Then we heard a musical setting of a prayer inscribed by an eighteen year-old girl on wall 3 of cell no. 3 in the basement of 'Palace', the Gestapo headquarters in Zakopane, Poland:

> No, Mother, do not weep,
> Most chaste Queen of Heaven
> Support me always.
> 'Zdrowas Mario' ['Ave Maria'].

The tragic graffito gave Henryk Górecki the text for the second movement of his Symphony No 3, subtitled the 'Symphony of Sorrowful Songs'. 'Serious' and 'popular' miraculously coincided. Composed in 1976, first performed the following year to a mixed reception, the symphony was recorded twice and gained a small following. In 1992 it was recorded again by the London Sinfonietta conducted by David Zinman with the American soprano Dawn Upshaw. Each of its three movements centres on a text of harrowing sorrow. First there is a fifteenth-century Polish prayer known as the Holy Cross Lament which is the voice of the Mother of God talking to Christ: 'My son, my chosen and beloved/ Share your wounds with your mother'; the third movement sets a folk song of the Opolskiego, the Opole region, in which a mother laments the death of her son, killed during an uprising. The music is marked 'Lento' throughout and, as Sibelius said of his Fourth Symphony, 'there is nothing of the circus' about it. In June 1992 the distributor, Warner Music, announced the sale of 300,000 copies with the work reaching No. 1 in the UK and USA classical music charts and simultaneously achieving No. 6 in the British Pop charts. Since then sales have risen to over a million. So the symphony is both a 'serious' and 'popular' cultural phenomenon in America and Britain. When the disc was first released critics were tentatively favourable. After further reflection they massed to the attack: 'A load of gloomy piffle' (Alexander Waugh in *Evening Standard*); 'There is less to this music than meets the ear' (David Mellor in *The Guardian*); 'Why this really rather dreary symphony has sent all those people into the record shops baffles me' (Michael Kennedy in *The Sunday Telegraph*); 'Henryk Górecki seems a very nice man, and it is because of perverse resentment of its popularity that I do not possess the now famous recording of his third symphony' (Stephen Pettit in *The Times*).

Henryk Górecki

Symphony No. 3

Dawn Upshaw, *soprano*
London Sinfonietta
David Zinman, *conductor*

This last comment is the most revealing. It begins with condescension — 'Henryk Górecki is a very nice man' — and then comes clean: the critic hasn't bought a copy of the recording because he resents the work's popularity. His admission that the resentment is perverse amounts to a substantial critical concession, implying that popularity taints though it shouldn't, that serious music-lovers can't help being snobs, and that they are at fault for putting élitism before art. He offers the proposition that the popularity of a work is, axiomatically, sufficient ground for rejecting it and, above all, admits that this is wrong. But wrong or not, and despite examples like *Uncle Tom's Cabin*, *Doctor Zhivago*, Beethoven's Fifth Symphony and *West Side Story*, these muddled responses to the Górecki symphony imply that the periphery is where the popular permanently belongs.

The success of Górecki's work has been attributed to marketing, an explanation which fails to take account of the kind of object for sale. It has been suggested that people use the symphony as New Age wallpaper or musical Mogadon, but who is easily tranquillised by the intensity of grief the music expresses? Perhaps, then, we must wonder at the popularity of a work which speaks of primary things, of mother and son, love, victimisation and loss, and, finally, the possibility of redemption; which teaches us anew how to weep for Auschwitz, for Bosnia, Somalia and now for Syria and, in doing this, melts cultural boundaries to the spiritual credit of more than a million people. The appeal of this work to people on both sides of the line formerly supposed to divide serious from popular may be one of the best hopes we have had for some time.

If so, it is a hope generated by multi-media processes from a typically complex late twentieth-century situation. Harassed and suppressed as a subversively avant-garde and Catholic composer by Poland's former Communist rulers, Górecki worked on obscurely in his home town of Katowice, watching his back. His mellifluous, accessible symphony was an affront to fashionable serialism, dismissed as religious minimalism. His sudden prominence resulted from multiple coincidence: Poland changed in the context of the Soviet break-up; the new music of Britain's John Tavener and Estonia's Arvo Pärt undermined the authority of post-Boulez laboratory music; the compact disc revolution created a huge new market for quality hi-fi and music recordings; the rise of neo-fascist movements in Germany, Britain, Scandinavia, South Africa and Russia brought Hitler's final solution and the eighteen year-old Gestapo victim of Górecki's second movement into a new, contemporary focus. Górecki became a topical subject for newspapers, magazines, music journals and news and arts programmes on radio and television. Knowing my admiration of the music, a friend in Scotland telephoned me in New Zealand to tell me how exalted she felt after hearing the work performed in Glasgow, played by a Russian orchestra with an Australian soprano. Before the performance an announcement was made to the audience: Mr Górecki had just telephoned from Poland to wish the musicians well. In the old McLuhanesque sense the 'Symphony of Sorrowful Songs' had become village music. As the student in Memphis put it, 'Like, WOW!'

The magnitude of its success makes the Górecki symphony a special case, but gravity of theme occurs unexpectedly in the multifarious world of Pop culture. Before taking office in January 1961 President John F. Kennedy described his programme as 'The New Frontier', the intellectual, physical and moral challenge in contemporary American life which had replaced the old geographical frontiers. When Captain Kirk of the 'Star-ship *Enterprise*' invoked space as 'the final frontier' and reminded viewers of *Star Trek* that his mission was 'to go where no man has gone before' he spoke to a stock American sympathy — and one near enough the surface of popular consciousness to warrant making the reference in every episode. In 1979 Tom Wolfe published *The Right Stuff*, his history of the American space programme. Wolfe finds that the material of which astronauts are made is a combination of stamina, guts, fast synapses and old-fashioned hell-raising. The men of the new frontier, where Russian Sputniks took the place of Indians, were cast in the mould of the pioneers.

A striking popular variation on this optimistic updating of the frontier myth is the sequence of 'Alien' movies. As the wiry he-woman on intractable frontiers in *Alien, Aliens* and *Alien 3*, Sigourney Weaver's Lieutenant Ripley triumphs over the alien organism by a combination of physical stamina, intelligence and technical know-how, a flesh-and-blood Wonder Woman. In *Alien Resurrection* the organism penetrates her and she carries it down to possible death in a lake of molten lead; but the last image is ambiguous. Lieutenant Ripley has died to save the world, but has the alien died with her? Have her trendily unisexual powers been sufficient to save America and the world from the relentlessly lethal organism and the equally relentless determination of 'the Company' to protect and harness it as a biological weapon? 'The business of America is business', Calvin Coolidge said in 1925. Is business all that's left of America? In a time of global recession does anything matter except economics? Is Górecki sullied or invalidated by 'the Company's' promotion of his symphony? Can there be a place for Abe Lincolns and Clark Kents in a world of ruthless corporations and duplicitous banks? Has the hand that takes anything more to give? Will future environments justify the optimism that underlies the energy of so much in popular culture? Did Lieutenant Ripley die in vain?

23. Sibelius: Why 'The Big Man'?

In 1931, HMV's Walter Legge, 'autocrat of the turntable', devised a plan to collect advance subscriptions for record albums of music so far unrecorded. He created different societies of subscribers for different composers, beginning with Hugo Wolf's songs. The Beethoven Sonata Society followed with performances by Artur Schnabel, and before the Second World War the list of dedicated societies included Bach's organ works from Albert Schweitzer, his unaccompanied cello suites played by Pablo Casals, Haydn's quartets, and orchestral works by Delius and Sibelius. The overriding, unfulfilled yearning of my youth wasn't for a cricket bat autographed by Denis Compton or my first Aston Martin but for the six gold-lettered brown albums of the Sibelius Society.

Here were all the symphonies, many still tantalisingly unknown to me, theatre music for *Pelléas et Mélisande* and *The Tempest*, and tone poems I'd never heard, let alone collected on the 78 rpm shellac discs of the time: *En Saga, Night Ride and Sunrise, The Bard.* If I could only possess Volume One I'd know what *Pohjola's Daughter* sounded like, along with the Fifth Symphony; Volume Two would bring me the Third Symphony played by the London Symphony Orchestra under Sibelius-approved maestro, Robert Kajanus, and the Seventh played by the BBC Symphony Orchestra conducted by the legendary Serge Koussevitsky; Volume Three would introduce me to the elusive Sixth Symphony under George Schnéevoigt, even if Sir Thomas Beecham noticed discrepancies of tempi and balance between the score and Schnéevoigt's interpretation. Oh, I lusted after them all, and even wrote to HMV for copies of the free programme notes to go with the records — written, I think, by Walter Legge himself. Alas, such expensive treasures were far beyond my reach. I made do with a gift of the Second Symphony in a powerful, still commanding performance by Eugene Ormandy and the Philadelphia Orchestra on four blue-label Columbia 78s; but for the rest of the seven I had to wait for the pioneering LP set by Anthony Collins with the London Symphony Orchestra, issued by Decca from 1952 to 1955, each individual record in the series being the object of my shameless beseeching at Christmas and when a birthday was imminent. Who could have foretold the riches we can choose from today? Many illustrious performances of yesteryear by Beecham, Stokowski and Barbirolli have been re-issued on CD. There are turbo-charged versions by Leonard Bernstein — as well as a few duds — some magisterial interpretations by Herbert von Karajan with his gleaming Berlin Philharmonic Orchestra, and the finest complete symphonic cycles by Colin Davis, Vladimir Ashkenazy and Osmo Vänskä. In 2007, the fiftieth anniversary of Sibelius's death, the Swedish company, BIS, began to release a 13-volume edition of all his music. Back in the 1930s Sibelius seemed almost a lone champion of the symphony, reasserting nineteenth-century conventions while making them new by the originality of his harmonic language and architectural strength. But how to explain the unique appeal of his music to a youngster? There was stiff competition from several great —many would say greater — composers. Why should this music, above all others, so captivate a schoolboy and, until crabbed age, remain pre-eminent?

Decca LP sleeve

He arrived when I was twelve. By this time, to the detriment of strictly academic endeavour, I was a confirmed music junkie, day-dreaming to a sound-track of Beethoven, Tchaikovsky, Brahms and Rachmaninov. I had never heard even the name of Sibelius until our new music teacher, Eric Adams, played 'The Swan of Tuonela' to a usually restive, inattentive class. Nobody stirred or made a sound, even in the pause while Mr Adams turned the record over. As strings filled the room with dark waters and eternal twilight, the impact was immediate. The *cor anglais* lamentation was mesmeric. There was a shock of recognition: this music told the truth. I was in a kind of delirium. Of course I went hunting for more Sibelius, nervously because I was frightened of the possibility that this might have been a musical fluke, a single instance of exceptional magic. I needn't have worried. The Second Symphony came next, raising the Sibelian voices to a higher power. When I heard it for the first time in a Glasgow performance by the BBC Scottish Orchestra under Ian Whyte I wanted to shout, in the middle of the first movement, 'Yes, that's right. That's what it's like. That's what I mean too'. Sceptical about this 'modern', my father had come to listen with me. He was hooked by the Symphony. We called Sibelius 'The Big Man'. The more we listened to him the bigger he became. The Third Symphony gripped with the throbbing vitality of its first movement, lilting grace of its second movement and the hymn of triumph in the finale. Then the First arrived. Freshly sounding in my mind on a visit to the isle of Lismore, it became permanently associated with sitting, oilskinnned and sou'-westered, on a rock at the north end of the island looking towards Ben Nevis, watching the weather of the north-west rehearse its repertory in the Great Glen of Scotland. The Fourth Symphony knew about everything gaunt and sombre in the world. The Fifth covered the gamut of human emotions. The Sixth cleansed the spirit. The Seventh instilled courage to face ultimate questions.

Even by those who would flinch from a symphony, he's known for the patriotic brass and tender lyricism of *Finlandia*, with its dramatic fanfare motive on a single note; the *cor anglais* song of *The Swan of Tuonela*; the spectral dance of *Valse Triste* and the tuneful buoyancies of the *Karelia Suite*. He composed chamber music and songs, a violin concerto to stand with those of Beethoven, Brahms, Mendelssohn and Tchaikovsky and incidental music for the stage; but what makes his *oeuvre* massively vertebrate are his orchestral tone poems and the seven symphonies which established him in the tradition of great symphonic thinkers. He also composed money-spinning miniatures, many of which might best be forgotten, along with the bulk of his piano music. Twenty-six years separate his First and Seventh Symphonies. Then he laboured to produce an Eighth. He may have completed it, but if he did, self-criticism made him burn the score. What agony that must have been, or what relief? He composed his last, greatest symphonic poem, *Tapiola*, wrote his most imaginative theatre music for Shakespeare's *The Tempest*, then fell silent. When he died on 20th September 1957 it felt like a personal bereavement. The silence had lasted thirty years, yet the thought that now it could never be broken, that there really could never be more Sibelius was all but unbearable.

Something unusual was happening in the school playground. The senior boy approaching me was an aristocrat in the student hierarchy, entitled to a resplendent gold-braided blazer proclaiming him a member of the First-fifteen rugby team. An alien from another planet.

'I've been told you like Sibelius', he said.

'Yes, I do, very much. In fact he's my favourite composer', I said, wondering how on earth this sporty type could have heard anything about my musical preferences, an unlikely topic for the locker room.

'Well, last night on the radio I heard his Violin Concerto. It's super', he said, flushing with enthusiasm, 'Great. Really beautiful. Tremendous. Do you like it?' He paused, looked behind him to make sure he wasn't caught, a First-fifteener, talking to Specky, the oddball who spent games-day afternoons listening to classical music in the gramophone room.

'My favourite violin concerto'.

'I was just wondering', he said with diffidence I wouldn't have expected from a braided First-fifteen man, 'I'd really like to hear more of his music. Do you think you could recommend some other things he's written?'

Happily I could, with pleasure, and did. The Concerto has achieved a degree of popularity that would have surprised Sibelius as much as this denizen of the rugby pitch surprised me and is now included in most concert violinists' repertoire. Of course the violin was Sibelius's instrument. 'The violin took me by storm', he said, recalling his first lessons at the age of fourteen, 'and for the next ten years it was my dearest wish to become a great virtuoso'. According to his long-suffering wife, Aino, he became 'quite literally dizzy' while composing the Concerto:

> He's awake night after night, plays wonderful things, and can't tear himself away from the marvellous music he plays — there are so many ideas that one can't believe it is true, all of them so rich in possibilities for development, so full of life.

Like Mendelssohn's Violin Concerto the work begins without introductory flourish, giving the impression that the music has been playing before we have begun to hear it. There's no violin concerto in which the violin sounds so much like a human cry, but suddenly the soloist is a bird climbing the air, then winging down into a full-throated response from the orchestra. This is close to Sibelius's heartbeat and the core of the Concerto. A good work for a novice Sibelian to start with.

'But *why* do you like his music so much?' persisted First-fifteen. He had done some serious listening by now and was trying to make sense of his own responses.

Maybe it's something to do with being Scottish, I suggested, something to do with earth. In his memoir, *My Record of Music,* Compton Mackenzie considers the similar impact of harsh climates on Finns and Scots:

> Until a Scottish composer of equal genius arises I shall continue to feel that the spirit of Scotland has been more richly expressed by Sibelius than by anybody. It would be absurd to draw a parallel between the relation of Finland to Russia and the relation of Scotland to England, but it is not too far-fetched to claim that the struggle against natural disadvantages of climate and soil has moulded the Finnish character along the same lines as the Scottish. Therefore, when the differences of racial origin have been taken into account, a marked spiritual affinity seems to emerge.

Which took us a little further than Aino's 'wonderful things', 'marvellous music' and 'so many ideas that one can't believe it's true', but not much.

In my conversation with Tim Dodd in *Music for Life* I'd recalled a memorable evening of musical talk. In the autumn of a year in the late nineteen-fifties the Polish conductor, Paul Kletzki, directed noble performances by the Scottish National Orchestra in Glasgow of Mussorgsky's *Pictures at an Exhibition* and Sibelius's Second Symphony. After such an outstanding concert all seats were taken for a 'Friends of the Orchestra' evening with the charismatic conductor. After Maestro Kletzki had given a sparkling talk about his life in music there were questions about his background in Poland, Germany, Italy, Russia and Switzerland, how he fled the Nazis, how he gave up composing for conducting, how as a conductor he approached an unfamiliar orchestra for his first rehearsal with players new to him. It was a rare evening of stimulating talk, but there was trouble ahead. A petal-complexioned, fur-coated lady in the autumn of middle age rose, coughed self-deprecatingly and assaulted the Maestro with The Dreadful Question.

'Mr Kletzki, that was a really lovely concert you gave us on Saturday, but would you please tell us who is your own *favourite* composer?'

A deathly hush signalled universal embarrassment. No problem for the Maestro. He smiled at his simpering interlocutor.

'Madam, I cannot tell you', he said. 'You see, all the Great Composers, when they die, they go Upstairs. So if I tell you who is my own favourite composer, when I die and go Upstairs, all the Other Composers will catch me and ————!'

The index finger he drew wordlessly across his throat was the Other Composers' vengeful blade.

Game, set and match to Maestro Kletzki; but if I were ever asked The Dreadful Question I'd take my chances with the Other Composers. 'Sibelius', I'd answer; yet now First-fifteen was asking the follow-up question, 'Why?' and I wasn't doing much better than, 'Because that's just the way of it'. The beginning of his sway over my feelings is unforgettable: I can re-live the day and the look of the schoolroom, even the weather when Mr Adams set us on a course of music appreciation with 'The Swan of Tuonela'. Since then his supremacy over all other music, over literature and all the arts, is unshakeable and it's possible, even for someone who is not a professional musician, to say something about what happens in his music. But the *why* of it all remains elusive.

I hoped I might be enlightened by Sir Colin Davis when I interviewed him at his London home on 10th October 1997. He had recorded all the symphonies with the Boston Symphony Orchestra in the 1970s and just completed a second cycle with the London Symphony Orchestra. Surely he would have something helpful to say about the Sibelian mystery.

> *MW*: Why do you think you have this affinity with Sibelius?
>
> *Davis*: I don't know. Who can know the answer to such a question? Why do *you* have the affinity? What does he mean to you?
>
> *MW*: That's the mystery I'm trying to understand. Maybe it's the stage I was at in life when I heard him first. I was a boy hungry for music and he went in deep because I got him early. Maybe it's a northern feeling, a Finn speaking to a Scot. Maybe it's the palette. What is the palette? Maybe it's the vigorous, even joyous acceptance of tragedy.
>
> *Davis*: The palette is low — lots of low flutes and pedal point. Of *course* it's tragic...The [Seventh] Symphony is about death. He confronts it...It's all in the way he puts the pieces together — like life — making it cohere. Then, like life, it's over. And there's lots of space. Sibelius needs space. He's a wild, emotional man.

I thought it was a bit mean of Sir Colin to throw my question back at me — I'd come thirteen thousand miles from New Zealand to his posh house in Highbury Terrace, London N5 for an hour of his time — but what can we take from this? Let's think about Sibelius's method of ordering his musical material and ponder Sir Colin's characterisation of him as wild and emotional.

The finale of the Second Symphony gives a model narrative of 'the way he puts the pieces together'. (I tried out my amateur perception of the way on Sir Colin). He finds a theme, in this case the theme he will use for the conclusion of the Symphony, then departs from it. It's as if he feels he has to prove the sufficiency of the theme by assessing other potentialities. You always get more than one quote for a job. This procedure is not the same as the classical sonata progression of statement, development and recapitulation, which can rely on the built-in security of the well-known form. It's a riskier sequence of discovery, test and return. So at the beginning of the finale his theme is announced by the woodwind over swirling strings and a soft drum roll, but as the music rises over a *pizzicato* figure it fragments and climbs away from the theme. There follows a richly orchestrated melodic episode, which proposes but fails to sustain a new trajectory; after another change of direction a song-like passage collapses. Then a trumpet returns to the initial theme. Options have been tested; the theme has been contextualised and approved. Foregoing episodes which may have seemed wrong turnings now cohere from the vantage point of the recovered theme and what follows. (Sir Colin agreed. 'That's right. He has to take it apart and put the pieces together again. That's the story. And there's *always* a story'.) Similarly, in the middle movement of the Third Symphony flutes introduce a charming dance-like theme which he lets go, digressing into other, derivative ideas before returning to one of his most beguiling tunes. The pattern is less obvious in the Fourth Symphony, but it's a salient feature of the Fifth. The middle movement of the final version of 1919, *Andante mosso, quasi allegretto*, develops an unassuming, smiling little phrase first heard in *pizzicato* on violas and cellos. This grows into the folk-like theme that carries the movement until hints of disturbance in string *tremolandos* — perhaps the intrusion of troubled times beyond the seclusion of Sibelius's home at Ainola — and menace in the brass disconcert but can't break the prevailing mood of amiability or thwart the music's return to the security of the theme. The character of the music is similar to the corresponding movement of the Third Symphony and just as winsome.

What about wildness? Severity may have been fundamental to his symphonic aesthetic, but he is certainly on record as enjoying a binge. If Sir Colin Davis is right to think of him as a wild man, his music harnesses wildness as energy. Take the beginning of the First Symphony. After an introductory drum roll and a dark clarinet melody that would be at home in Tuonela, a sudden power surge of strings arrests attention. Energy is even more imperative in the tensions and brass declamations of the second movement of the Second Symphony. In the *scherzo* of the Second a plaintive oboe melody is offset by a quicksilver *moto perpetuo*. The melancholy oboe lingers in the mind, but a mounting climax acts as a bridge towards energetic probings that broaden into the epic affirmation of the Symphony's conclusion. With the muttering of deep-throated cellos and double-bases in unison at the start of the Third Symphony we are immediately in the midst of things and climbing fast. This symphony is Sibelius at his most succinct, but if that's severity it's energy too, packed and radiant. After the pastoral lull of the second movement the dynamism of the opening *allegro* returns in the stately, jubilant music of the finale and the work builds swiftly towards what Sir Donald Tovey calls its 'one and all-sufficing climax', demonstrating that for Sibelius form is energy, adrenalin controlled and directed.

Emotional energy animates the Fourth Symphony, paradoxically Sibelius's most personal symphony and his deepest repudiation of prolix romanticism before the Seventh. Inspired by the mountain forests and Lake Pielinen at Koli in the northern Karelia — if you go there you can *see* the music — the Fourth is, in Herbert von Karajan's opinion, 'one of the few symphonies... that end in disaster'. Hugh MacDiarmid called it 'Sibelius's gaunt El-Greco-emaciated ecstatic Fourth'. While composing the Symphony he was also working on a setting of Edgar Allan Poe's poem, 'The Raven'. The setting was abandoned but the portentous gloom of Poe's 'midnight dreary' and the balefully ominous influence of his 'ghastly grim and ancient' ebony bird may underlie the darknesses of the Symphony:

> 'Ghastly grim and ancient Raven wandering from the
> Nightly shore —
> Tell me what thy lordly name is on the Night's
> Plutonian shore!'
> Quoth the Raven, 'Nevermore'.

Reviewing a performance under Beecham at the Queen's Hall in London in December 1937 Walter Legge wrote that the Symphony 'is the limit even he has reached in sparseness...The few who left the hall at the end...must have been surprised to see that there is still active life on this planet'. More reserves of energy had to be found for the Fifth Symphony. 'Struggling with God', he exclaims in his diary while working on the final revision. He must also have been struggling to come to terms with a world dominated by the First World War and the Bolshevik revolution at a time when Finland finally achieved independence from Russia only to be rent by civil war between the Marxist Reds and the democratic Whites. Listening to the original 1915 score of the Fifth we can appreciate his almost intolerable wrestle with the original material to shape it into the final version's comparative severity of form.

So much, then, for the ordering of his material and his energy; but there's a third characteristic: courage. If each new and profoundly different symphony demanded energy and a fresh approach to form, finding a way to express his evolving perception of the human condition also required courage. He called his symphonies 'confessions of faith', and his faith was changing. After the emotional heat of the hammer-blows that make the conclusion of the Fifth Symphony the most original, certainly the most ambiguous of symphonic endings, came the 'pure, cold spring water' of the Sixth Symphony — Sir Colin hears 'frightening things in the dappled woods' — followed by the climactic masteries of the Seventh Symphony and *Tapiola*. It took great courage to make the last of his symphonies and his final tone poem. They seem to be complementary parts of a whole, perhaps even question and answer. The Seventh Symphony starts with a summons on the timpani before a rising scale on strings sends the music forward. As if to signal affinity with the Symphony, *Tapiola* begins with a similar call to attention, before an icy gust sweeps us into the forest's deep freeze. Years before the Seventh was finished he described its projected character: 'The VII Symphony. Joy of life and vitality, with *appassionato* passages'. The Symphony's progression of seamless organic transformations rises to another 'all-sufficing' climax. The axis of the work is the imperious solo trombone theme that emerges in full at the first major climax about eleven minutes into the score and, most movingly, at the closing peroration. The music's questing energies are brought to order in a conclusion even more breathtaking than the astonishing end of the Fifth Symphony. There are moments of repose, plenty of vitality and achingly intense intimations of joy, but doesn't the music culminate in the majesty of a profoundly vexed sensibility heroically confronting the unknowable, the possibility of a void? What guts the man had to end on such a question, raw, nakedly doubting and beseeching, a challenge to God. What courage was called for as he stood on the precipice of the Symphony's strings-rich C major, daring to look out from the edge of the abyss towards *Tapiola*'s colossal emptiness and quintessential cold.

Sibelius's greatest music is neither of place nor occasion but of nature and the human spirit. He knows about exaltation, perplexity, aspiration and resignation. He is both distinctive and transparent, an Aeolian harp sounding universal propositions that make a myth not of gods and heroes but of the soul itself. It was the part of the myth called Symphony No. 5 that made me aware of the singular, essential difference between my relationship to his music and the music of others. I am gratefully moved and hope I'm enlarged by the *Eroica*, the *Pathétique* Symphony, Mahler's Fourth, Vaughan Williams's Fifth and Shostakovich's Eighth. Demanding to be heard and heard again, they are all familiars whose unimaginable disappearance would leave me inconsolable. When they happen, when they come to life in the concert hall, in a recording or in my mind, they live at a distance from me as a painting lives on its gallery wall at a distance from the observer. Attentive, open-pored responsiveness is what narrows the gap between the work of art and the observer or listener; but for me, for whatever reason, with Sibelius there's no gap. I first felt this, without being able to express it, when Mr Adams played 'The Swan of Tuonela' in the school music room; with the enchantment of the music came a sense of homecoming, of being inside music that knew who I was. So, in the Fifth Symphony, the embryonic horn call at the beginning involves me at once in the musical process. It's as if I'm being played; I am the trumpet and flute that echo and confirm the work's germinal idea and I'm absorbed into the unifying energy with which the music confronts nature's enigmas and grandeurs. My nerves are the flickering strings and my heart's in the desolate bassoon. I'm swung by the bell-like rises and falls. Fanfared by trumpets, I'm urged on by brass over violin arpeggios, and sent racing home. There's no distance at all between me and the music, no gap to mind. When the time comes I won't be merely watching the Big Man as he looks out at whatever void from the summit of the Seventh Symphony; I've no head for heights, but I'll be standing on the edge of the precipice, right there where the music has put me. Long before this supreme Sibelian climax, of course, I have pursued headstrong Kyllikki in *Lemminkäinen and the Maidens of the Island* and ridden into the forest with huntsman Björn to be bewitched by a *Wood Nymph*; I've seen the moon-god's daughter spinning in Northland in *Pohjola's Daughter*, failed to conjure a boat from her spindle and been sent packing. It's late in the day, far too late to own those six historic record albums created by Walter Legge, but I dare say I think I've earned membership of the Sibelius Society.

If Sibelius's vision is finally a tragic one, he knows that this is compatible with human hope, even joy, just as W. B. Yeats, who also learned from swans about the eternal and the transient, wrote of gaiety transfiguring dread in the tragedies of *Hamlet* and *King Lear*. The gaiety is in the art itself, in the gift, as Wordsworth puts it, that empowers the artist to rejoice 'more than other men in the spirit of life that is in him', to meet the human condition head-on, to stand unflinchingly on the high precipice of the Seventh Symphony. Like all great artists he tackles the doubleness of life. 'Life is wonderful', he said, 'even if we are sent here to suffer. In my view he is the richest in spirit who can suffer most'. For Hugh MacDiarmid, we remember, the Fourth Symphony was both emaciated and ecstatic.

I rest my case, First-fifteen. Formal ingenuity in 'the way he puts the pieces together', energy and courage. That's the best I can do with the 'Why?' For now. Thank you for asking.

24. New York: Port Authority

No last elegance
with all the trimmings to remember
at hard tack on your Baltimore clipper.
I KEEP TELLIN' YA FOR CHRISSAKE
IT'S COMIN' FROM THE GARAAAGE
No fine adieux to wharf and gull
before a turbined glide over the pond.
IT'S A NOO DRIVER GODDAMMIT
HE'S READIN' HIS NOTES
This dry dock harbours
only demotic Greyhounds, loping in from Albany,
departing for Detroit. Your beast is late.
IT'LL BE HERE JESUS
You'll eat to fill the time it takes to growl
a way through Harlem.
The counter is a U
with you, your West Side friend
strung round the bend.

The Italian waiter laughs.
'Ha', he says, 'you wanta?'
Your friend knows all the moves.
'We'll have', he says, 'some bacon'.
Mario's day is made.
'Ha, ha', he laughs, 'no bacon'.
'Well, okay', says your friend,
'How about some eggs?'
Mario rocks with triumph.
'Ha, ha', he yells, 'no eggs'.
Elbows shoot from his sides,
Hands dive for joy to his crotch.

Beside your friend sits black Old-Timer,
authorised version, bulb eyes on tubes.
He hangs above a plate of franks,
cuts them in strips with a clasp-knife

the size of the RCA tower. After each cut
he plays the tubes, takes you in.
Mario sings, 'no bacon, no eggs'.
It sounds like the end of Tosca.
'Maybe toast?' – your friend's last shot.
'Toasta, no problem – two? three?'
Old-timer cuts. Your friend
wishes the bus would come.
JESUS GOD IT'S COMIN'
HEAR ME FROM THE GARAAAGE

A thundercloud rolls in beside you,
The biggest black man in the world.
Something inside his cup seems orange.
'Hey, man', he says, 'Too sweet, okay?'
'Hee, hee', goes Mario, 'More-a sugar for you'.
'Jesus, like NO, it's like HONEY, okay?'
'Okay, okay, I give-a you sugar'.
Thundercloud grows twenty feet.
He is Malcolm X, he is Stokely,
He is Jesse Jackson, he is Roots,
He is Saigon and Selma,
Ballistic and silicon,
He is nylon, he is dacron, he is America.
Red sneakers, blue pants, white cheater
and Mississippi dark.
'JESUS MAN NO MAN I WANNA CHANGE IT MAN
IT'S TOO SWEET MAN NO SUGAR JESUS'.

Old-Timer quits cutting, his knife in air
sends Mario an ethnic hint.
There is a moment of perfect stillness
in the Port Authority. Mario hears
the silence, sees the glint, and digs
America. His windmill arms
pump out another orange.
'Ees-a no problem. Have a nice day'.
It sounds like, 'Have a nasty'.
Thundercloud rolls away. Old-Timer cuts.

A girl assistant in a white coat
Is Mario's rainbow.
Jackknifing into his laugh he screams
'Hey, you look-a like *laundry*!'

PITTSFIELD...LENOX...GATE 9
The bus is here, Jesus. Your take-away
Greyhound is ready to go.

25. Reading Red Warren: From South Africa to Vermont

The class teacher gave us a day off school and took us to an exhibition of life in South Africa. Black people, white people, coloured people. Gold mines and vineyards. Broad smiles and enormous spaces. Proteas and thorn trees. Elephants, rhinos and springbok; lions, hippos and giraffes. Rondavels and Cape Dutch gables. Golden beaches. The numinous majesty of Table Mountain and everywhere sunshine, everywhere vitality. I was eleven and captivated. One day I would go there.

When I was twenty-four I went. Post-war Glasgow was a dreich city in the fifties and early sixties. After a year of schoolteaching I had itchy feet. I wanted away from mean streets, kitsch Scottish nationalism and girning politicians and longed for sun, colour, effervescence. I'd never forgotten the exhibition which had made such an impression. Eager to experience the vibrancies of a culture remote from Presbyterian Scotland, I accepted the offer of a lectureship in English at Rhodes University, Grahamstown, in South Africa's eastern Cape province. Probably I'd never have gone if I'd done more responsible and thorough research on the country and understood the depravities of a system that oppressed and abused non-white people. When the anguish of apartheid made its impact I remembered Abraham Lincoln's conviction that 'there is a special place in hell for those who remain neutral in a moral crisis' and joined the South African Liberal Party, the only political party which stood for universal franchise.

Two years later I collapsed with encephalitis. My eyes were paralysed to the extent that they couldn't contract and dilate in reaction to degrees of brightness. Headaches were ferocious, my gyroscope was shot and I had double vision. For two months I lived in a darkened room. Any brightness was pain. A chink of light coming in between incompletely drawn curtains was a needle stabbing my eyes. Recovery from double vision took three months. When I got my balance back, and the use of one eye at a time, I returned to university work wearing a patch over the eye I wasn't using. The first book I read for pleasure when both eyes were normal again was a novel, *The Cave*, by Robert Penn Warren. I had greatly admired his best-selling Pulitzer prize-winning novel, *All the King's Men*. Judged 'the definitive novel about American politics' by *The New York Times*, it chronicles the rise and fall of a Southern demagogue based on Louisiana's Governor Huey Long, a populist whose initially good intentions degenerate into corruption and megalomania. The story begins with a car ride and Warren's prose moves like what the ad-men of Detroit used to call 'liquid drive'. There can't be a modern novel with more kinetic energy in its opening:

> MASON CITY.
> To get there you follow Highway 58, going northeast out of the city, and it is a good highway and new. Or was new, that day we went up it. You look up the highway and it is straight for miles, coming at you, with the black line down the centre coming at and at you, black and slick and tarry-shining against the white of the slab, and the heat dazzles up from the white slab so that only the black line is clear, coming at you with the whine of the tires, and if you don't quit staring at that line and don't take a few deep breaths and slap yourself hard on the back of the neck you'll hypnotise yourself and you'll come to just at the moment when the right front wheel hooks over into the black dirt shoulder off the slab, and you'll try to jerk her back on but you can't because the slab is high like a curb, and maybe you'll try to reach to turn off the ignition just as she starts the dive. But you won't make it, of course. Then a nigger chopping cotton a mile away, he'll look up and see the little column of black smoke standing up above the vitriolic, arsenical green of the cotton rows, and up against the violent, metallic, throbbing blue of the sky, and he'll say, 'Lawd, God, hit's a-nudder one done hit!'

The demagogue, Willie Stark, is a follower of the black line, acting, not unlike Melville's Ahab, according to his interpretation of life in terms of corruption. He can't see the white ground on which the black line is imposed. Mesmerised by his own black abstraction, he finally loses control. Towards the end of his story he tries to 'turn off the ignition', but he has already started his dive to destruction.

After reading the novel, I had been gripped by Robert Rossen's screen adaptation of *All the King's Men* with Broderick Crawford perfect as Willie Stark in his evolution from sweating hick messiah to political gangster, John Ireland as his troubled lackey in search of self and Mercedes McCambridge as his pock-marked moll. The film won best-picture Oscar in 1949 and Academy Awards for Crawford and McCambridge. Though less popular, *The Cave* is a compelling novel based on the true story of Floyd Collins who died in Sandy Cave, Kentucky in 1925. When searching for a potential underground tourist attraction he was immobilised when a dislodged boulder trapped his foot. An opportunistic newspaperman from Louisville went underground to interview him and the story gave Warren his crowd of spectators, the exploiting media and hillside funeral service. By making his cave-crawler, Jasper Harrick, the centre of so many people's lives, Warren turns the Collins story into a modern variation on Plato's allegory of the cave. Like Jasper in his literal cave each character is trapped within the figurative cave of his or her own nature, mistaking shadows for reality. Images of darkness and emptiness associate the various metaphysical caves with Jasper's physical one. Exhilarated by the experience of reading the novel with my restored eyesight — emerging from my own cave — and moved by the depicted lives, I read Warren's latest novel, *Flood*, and, impulsively, wrote him a letter.

21ˢᵗ July 1964
Mr Robert Penn Warren
c/o Random House Inc.
457 Madison Avenue
New York 22
New York
USA

Dear Mr Penn Warren,

I should like to write you, if I may, a fan letter, pure (if possible) and simple — 'unaccustomed as I am...'

Nearly two years ago I read *All the King's Men*; *The Cave* was the first book I read when I had sufficiently recovered from an encephalitic paralysis of the eyes to be able to use print again; and I've just finished *Flood*, obtained still fairly hot from the Gotham Book Mart. Now I'm casting about rather desperately for the other novels and putting in inter-library loan requests for the rest of your work. I do not know whether this is the sort of thing I should be saying — this being my first effort at a fan letter.

Not being F. R. Leavis — an accident for which I alternately praise and abuse the Powers — but merely a Scot attempting to function as an academic in a most disturbing and unpopular country, it can matter little that I see your novels as an important part of what might be called the Great Tradition, American Style. And I'm afraid my gratitude to you will rank as very pipsqueak, not to say presumptuous; but I have had such pleasure from your books that I am moved, nevertheless, to congratulate and to thank you for them. And the quality of your writing leads me to believe that you will not regard this as a mere impertinence.

Yours very gratefully,
Marshall Walker

In the days that followed I felt acute embarrassment, if not remorse. What a nerve I'd had to write such a letter to this exalted person and what a callow, frail message I'd sent. This was a man of high distinction in fiction, poetry and criticism who walked with other eminences in American literature: John Crowe Ransom, Allen Tate, Cleanth Brooks, Saul Bellow, Katherine Anne Porter, William Styron, all names to conjure with in the nineteen-sixties. Well, maybe my letter would be fortuitously lost in the offices of his publisher, the mighty Random House in New York. Then his answer came.

West Wardsboro, Vermont, July 28, 1964

Dear Mr Walker:
It is delightful to have your letter, not merely because you say you like my novels, but I sense that your kind of liking would be the kind of liking I should value most. I am especially glad that you like FLOOD — or do I misread you? All --- all the NYC reviewers

loathed it with a loathing bottomless --- not just didn't like it --- totally loathed and hated it. I did --- and most stubbornly do --- put it my top bracket. Happily, some others do too.

I don't know that I envy you your present address, for reasons too obvious to mention, but I wish I could visit there. I've had a journalistic chance or two, but can't leave my small children to my wife for a long time, we live in the country, etc. Maybe, too, I couldn't get a visa. I should like to see things first hand. Right now I'm doing a book on Negro leadership in the USA. Have been interviewing most of the important, and some not so important, people.

I trust that your eyes are fine again.

Very sincerely yours,

Robert Penn Warren

PS I am taking the liberty of having my publishers send you a couple of my books of poems, one a narrative sort of thing, and the other lyrics. *Selected Poems* out of print now, forthcoming soon.

What is your part of Scotland?

The poetry books arrived: *Promises: Poems 1954-1956, You, Emperors, and Others: Poems 1957-1960* and *Brother to Dragons: A Tale in Verse and Voices*. Would I like them? How awkward and distressing if I couldn't respond positively to this generosity. No cause for alarm. I gorged on the poems and loved his idiom, which conformed to T.S. Eliot's formula: 'The common word exact without vulgarity,/ The formal word precise but not pedantic,/ The complete consort dancing together'. As Seamus Heaney put it in 1986 on the occasion of Warren's appointment as America's first Poet Laureate, 'There is roughage in his poetry. There is subject matter. There is an encounter with the world'.

We corresponded and I told him about Glasgow and my favourite parts of Scotland in Argyll. He was working on *Who Speaks for the Negro?*, the book on black leadership he'd mentioned in his first letter and asked me about the racial situation South Africa. While researching for *Who Speaks for the Negro?* someone had thrown a brick through his motel window in Mississippi. What was my life as a Liberal like under apartheid? Were Liberals harassed, persecuted? I was finding it increasingly frustrating, even dangerous, with the ninety-day detention law giving the police frightening powers. I had spies in my university classes and had discovered I was on the Special Branch's list of undesirables. My house was under surveillance and colleagues were being summarily imprisoned. I told him something of all this:

...It's a great pity that you are unable to come and look at S.A. armed with your insights into the American situation. When I came here I imagined it would be possible to function as an academic without being drawn into the political vortex. This has proved quite untrue. The headlong dive into insanity has taken a much acuter angle since I arrived in mid-62. People of liberal sympathies are tolerated less and less and there is steadily diminishing scope for an alien like myself to contribute anything towards resisting the increasing parallelism between Germany in the 1930s and South Africa in the 1960s. We liberals endlessly discuss the rights and wrongs of settling in and espousing 'the cause', but even that tends to be a pretty shifty concept and it is becoming nigh impossible to function at all clear-headedly in the job. Nineteen days ago two colleagues were arrested under the ninety-day detention law and clapped in prison with the police refusing to say why or for how long. They were released last night, having been fairly well treated and only indirectly *threatened* torture to report.

The mass of students seems thoroughly indoctrinated or else apathetic beyond repair. While there is, no doubt, some mystic validity in simply being here and anguishing, it doesn't quite answer as a practical plan. But you will already know that this sort of problem is common enough over here...

After three years I returned to Scotland, taking up a lectureship at Glasgow University, eventually registering for a PhD with a proposal to discuss Warren's complete *oeuvre*. More than any writer since Dickens he seemed to me to possess the great gift of appealing to the gut while engaging the head. The more I read him, the more I came to see that the core of his work was the imperative to live by ideas, or dreams, and to make the dreams work in the world while recognising that the odds were always fearful. By now he was signing himself 'Red', the friendship deepened and I visited him at his summer home in Vermont. We recorded a long interview which was published first in the magazine *Scottish International,* with an expanded version appearing in the British *Journal of American Studies.* I worked on the doctorate for fifteen years, then the resultant book, *Robert Penn Warren: A Vision Earned,* published in Edinburgh and New York. A copy was dispatched to his other home in Connecticut with a short letter.

14 Ancaster Drive
Glasgow
G13 1ND
Scotland
UK

18 October 1979

Dear Red,
Herewith my 'British Edition' hot from the sluggard press.

I send it, of course, in trepidation. It is full of errors by the printer but it's my own mistakes — as they will inevitably appear to you — that give me most qualm. How insultingly *slim* the volume — an economic necessity — how gawky the critical effort beside the creative one which attracted it.

I've put a disclaimer in the acknowledgements about my source for any biographical matter. There is very little of this and what there is was found in material before the public. I have felt all along that I should not ask you things and then use them — outside our interview — otherwise we might have had less jolly times together. It would be different, of course, if one were doing a biography.

I hope and pray the book, whatever its warts and gaucheries, convinces you that it was at least written in the right spirit and out of love of the work. It is intended as a salute and as thanksgiving.

Yours ever,
Marshall

There was the inevitable, depressive feeling of anti-climax that follows a long haul of work. Sleepless nights when I felt the inadequacy of my attempt to do justice to the life-long creativity of a great artist and wished I could start over and do it all better. When his letter acknowledging receipt of the book arrived I walked the streets for two hours with the letter unopened in my pocket; but it had to be faced at last. I sat on a wall and slowly opened the airmail flimsy.

2495 Redding Road
Fairfield, Connecticut 06430
November 6, 1979

Dear Marshall,

I'd be a monster of ingratitude if I didn't thank fate (and you) for your book. How can I say in the same breath what kindness and what perceptiveness! It wouldn't make logical or psychological sense, would it? But somehow that's what I like to feel.

But I can say, quite objectively, that you have most scrupulously undertaken to deal with multitudinous details in your larger thesis. And that you have written with great and graceful clarity and persuasiveness. And I can say that you have most definitely delineated what I (as far as a man can know his feelings and ideas, growing by what logic over how many years) hope is my history.

I don't know how to thank you. But I can thank my luck for you.

Again, all thanks to the Lord for my luck. Nothing comes simply. We'd love to see you. All good wishes in all ways.

Red

****

Guthrie, Kentucky is a small defunctive town near the Tennessee border, left high, dry and depressed by the tide of progress. When Robert Penn Warren was born there on 24th April 1905 it thrived as a tobacco market town, providing him with his earliest impressions and the material for *Night Rider*, his first published novel. He left Guthrie in his teens but, with time out as research student at Yale and Oxford, he grew up, studied, taught and wrote in the South until 1942 when he went north to be Professor of English at the University of Minnesota. Soon after his appointment as Professor of Playwriting in the Yale School of Drama in 1951 and marriage to Eleanor Clark the following year he and his wife set up house in Fairfield, Connecticut. In 1963 came the holiday home in West Wardsboro, Vermont but he never lost touch with the troubled, complicated region he came from, remaining a Southerner in sensibility. The eternal return was as much a part of his own life as it is of the lives of many of his characters. Contrary to Thomas Wolfe's dictum, 'You can't go home again', Warren's work persistently tells us that you must, even if, like little Billie Potts, it is only:

> To ask forgiveness and the patrimony of your crime;
> And kneel in the untutored night as to demand
> What gift — oh, father, father — from that dissevering hand?

Robert Penn Warren, Fairfield, Connecticut, 1969

At home 'the father waits for the son' and only from the father can the son receive the gift of self-knowledge. The Dantesque scheme of *At Heaven's Gate* projects a group of characters who violate nature and Jerry Calhoun, in denying his true father and taking a phoney father, commits what is for Warren the arch-sin. In *All the King's Men* Jack Burden adopts a series of false fathers, the most notable being Willie Stark himself. Invariably there is alignment of the true father and the truth of the situation. The perfect father would act as the great reconciler of life's contraries, resolving the tension between idea and fact, the Emersonian and the Hawthornian. Unfortunately the point where fact and idea coincide, the perfect fusion, is not, Warren conjectures, in our world: 'But we constantly want to have it in our world, and we only find it by finding a new father, I guess, beyond us, beyond this world'.

He went home imaginatively in his fiction and actually in the work of gathering his material for *Segregation: The Inner Conflict in the South* and *Who Speaks for the Negro?* If he is thus deeply Southern, the range of his achievement testifies to the scope and commitment of his human sympathies. Each intellectual act, whether formally poem, play or novel, or one of the interviews with black leaders in *Who Speaks for the Negro?* is of the nature of a poem, according to his down-to-earth definition of the poem as 'a way of getting your reality shaped a little better'. There is never in his work the meretricious gloss of the merely fashionable, although a popular audience might look to his novels for 'a good story' full of action, sex, violence and earthy humour. Abstracted from their novels the mere plots of *World Enough and Time*, *The Cave* or *Flood* would have little enough to commend them to the attention of the serious reader though, to be sure, the same might be said about the plots of many other vaunted novelists. Warren is a popular novelist in that his novels have made money and occasionally films (*All the King's Men* and *Band of Angels*).

He began his writing life as a regionalist, but a cautious one. In his essay on Hemingway the emphasis is not so much on regionally experienced reality as on the ideas which that reality may embody:

> A writer may write about his special world merely because he happens to know that world, but he may also write about that special world because it best dramatises for him the issues and questions that are

his fundamental concerns — because, in other words, that special world has a kind of symbolic significance for him.

For a writer who wishes to engage with the ideas expressed in this special world of his own experience the chief hazard lies in the possibility that the abstractions — the issues and questions — may get out of control. Like Hawthorne, Warren is alert to the tyrannising effect on the mind of an idea. There's a clear analogy here between his view of the artist's problem and his view of life, for tragedy in his work frequently results from a failure to achieve a balance that will reconcile abstract ideals with the dust and heat of reality. So his resurrected Jefferson in *Brother to Dragons* is forbidden any optimism not based on observation of human nature and compelled to acknowledge the presence of sin in the world, even in his own blood. Part of nature is the murder in December 1811 of a black slave by the sons of his own sister (the first of the great Mississippi Valley earthquakes points the fact that this human convulsion is part of the natural order) and Jefferson comes to see the event as paradigmatic of an ironic world of natural contraries and tangled motives:

> ...and as History divulged
> Itself, I saw how the episode in the meat-house
> Would bloom in Time, and blooms in all characteristic
> Episodes, and blooms in the lash-bite,
> And blooms in the lost child's cry
> Down in the quarters when the Mother is sold.
> Oh, yes, I've heard it, but I know, too,
> How vanity and blood-lust may link obscenely
> In the excuse of moral ardour, and a cause.

At the end of the poem RPW sums up, chanting the lesson in paradox he has learned on behalf of Jefferson and his readers through this terrible piece of history:

> The recognition of complicity is the beginning of innocence.
> The recognition of necessity is the beginning of freedom.

The recognition of the direction of fulfilment is the
death of the self.
And the death of the self is the beginning of selfhood.
All else is surrogate of hope and destitution of spirit.

As a critic Warren insists on close attention to the functional
relationship between the parts of any work of art, but his
organicism isn't the ivory tower variety which would banish both
author and world, leaving just the words on the page throbbing
away in their inter-inanimations. The role of irony as he prescribes
it is to ensure an inter-inanimation between the pure idea and the
world which we know to be rich in impurities. Why, he asks in his
essay on 'Pure and Impure Poetry', should a love poem include
'self-contradictions, cleverness, irony, realism' which call us back
to the world of prose and imperfection? He tackles the problem by
comparing three love poems: Tennyson's 'Now sleeps the crimson
petal, now the white', Shelley's 'Indian Serenade' and *Romeo and
Juliet*. The first two, he says, aspire to purity of effect and exclude
the sordid and the realistic. *Romeo and Juliet*, on the other hand,
includes the bawdry of Mercutio and the Nurse. In suggesting that
all poets should make their peace with Mercutio, Warren implies
that Mercutio is really lurking in Tennyson's and Shelley's would-
be pure poems all the time simply because Mercutio lurks in the
real world. Better to invite him into the poem than have him lurk.
So when Warren himself writes a love poem, for example the early
'Bearded Oaks', his intention is to assert the permanence of love
precisely in the face of the most inward kinds of opposition — the
decay of passion and the erosions of time:

> I do not love you less that now
> The caged heart makes iron stroke
> Or less that all that light once gave
> The graduate dark should now revoke.

The poet's dream of ideals is a 'destructive element'. Joseph
Conrad's character, Stein in *Lord Jim*, might be addressing the
poet in his workshop as well as you and me in our lives in the
speech Warren finds central to understanding Conrad:

> A man that is born falls into a dream like a man who
> falls into the sea. If he tries to climb out into the air
> as inexperienced people endeavour to do, he drowns
> *nicht war?*...No! I tell you! The way is to the destructive
> element submit yourself, and with the exertions of
> your hands and feet in the water make the deep, deep
> sea keep you up.

The dream will destroy a man who attempts to deny it by living on
the dry land of the naturalistic world in recoil from the risk of full
humanity. As a natural creature a man is not 'born to swim in the
dream, with gills and fins, but if he submits in his own imperfect,
"natural" way he can learn to swim and keep himself up, however
painfully, in the destructive element'. Shakespeare's Mercutio,
Warren's 'caged' heart and 'iron' stroke recognise that our way
of submission to the destructive element of the dream is always
flawed .

His first full length prose work, *John Brown, the Making of a
Martyr*, is a carefully researched and argued study of an historical
figure whose impurities had all too often been purged away by a
culture hot for certainties. In our 1969 interview RPW considered
his preoccupation with John Brown:

> [John Brown] had some kind of constant obsessive
> interest for me. On the one hand he's so heroic, on the
> other hand he's so vile, pathologically vile...Edmund
> Wilson...would say, 'But he's *trivial*, he's merely a
> homicidal maniac — forget him!' Now this is *half* of
> Brown. In a strange way the homicidal maniac lives
> in terms of grand gestures and heroic stances, and is a
> carrier of high values, but is a homicidal maniac. This
> is a strange situation; and the split of feeling around
> Brown makes the split of feeling in a thing like my
> character Stark almost trivial.

We would have to agree that John Brown's impact on history has
been greater than Governor Huey Long's, but there is nothing
trivial about the split in Willie Stark, the character Warren loosely
based on the Kingfish of Louisiana. Artistically, *All the King's*

Men succeeds on Warren's own terms. The characters are all embodiments of ideas: Willie Stark, the man of fact, with Lucy his wife-mother, Sadie Burke and Anne Stanton his carnal and ideal mistresses; Adam Stanton the man of ideals and Jack the narrator whose burden is to learn the meaning of Willy Stark, his rise and fall, and discover the truth about himself. These are not merely cardboard figures with allegorical labels because Warren gives them such life that they are both credible in themselves and as the expression of moral values.

Willie Stark is doubly split. His apparently benevolent despotism brings material improvement to the State and the lives of the workers but is conducted in the interest of his own self-aggrandisement and in a spirit of contempt for the people, the hicks: 'Man is conceived in sin and born in corruption and he passeth from the stink of the didie to the stench of the shroud'. This is the only fact that matters to Willie; but he remains, in Warren's sense 'pure', monovalent, and is, paradoxically, split because his one naturalistic fact becomes itself an abstraction that fails to account for the dream, the element of virtue, which is also an object of fact in a complex world. Virtue, however, lies in wait for Willie because, as the choric RPW puts it in *Brother to Dragons*:

> ...despite all naturalistic considerations,
> Or in the end because of naturalistic considerations,
> We must believe in virtue. There is no
> Escape. No inland path around that rocky
> And spume-nagged promontory. There is no
> Escape dead-fall on trail, noose on track, bear-trap
> Under the carefully arranged twigs. There is no
> Escape, for virtue is
> More dogged than Pinkerton, more scientific than the
> FBI,
> And that is why you wake sweating toward dawn.

At the end, sensing his own incompleteness, there's no escape for Willie. He succumbs to a fatal yearning for virtue and is killed by Adam Stanton, the man of absolute virtue who will not allow his moral preserve — the new hospital — to be infected. Stanton, too, is killed: Beauty and the Beast both drown in the same dream.

236

Until the end of his life, energy unabated, Warren wrote poetry. 'Poetry is where my heart is', he said in 1983. He would not give up writing as long as he drew breath, he told an interviewer, 'I don't know what stopping is'. From his own point of view his productivity in poetry was only natural, as he suggests in 'Minneapolis Story' from *Rumour Verified*:

> Whatever pops into your head, and whitely
> Breaks surface on the dark stream that is you,
> May do to make a poem – for every accident
> Yearns to be more than itself, yearns,
> In the way you dumbly do, to participate
> In the world's blind, groping rage toward meaning.

In 1982 he published his long narrative poem, *Chief Joseph of the Nez Perce*. The history of America's shameful treatment of Indian people was vexing the national conscience. In 1979 Sioux Indians were awarded $17,500,000 compensation for the Black Hills of Dakota, confiscated in 1877, the same year in which Chief Joseph of the Nez Perce ('Nez Percé' = 'Pierced Nose') tribe finally surrendered to General Nelson A. Miles in the Bear Paw Mountains of the Montana Territory. The main part of Warren's verse narrative tells of the events leading up to the War of 1877 and the War itself. Betrayed repeatedly in treaty violations by the United States Government in respect of his tribe's traditional homeland at Wallowa in northeastern Oregon, Joseph seeks to lead his people away from the Government's pressure to settle in Idaho. Pursued relentlessly by US army units, he eludes or defeats them all until the last battle. In the mistaken belief that he has crossed the Canadian border he relaxes security and after a devastating five-day battle in freezing weather, is overcome. In defeat Joseph is given generous terms by Miles, only to have them cruelly violated by Sherman. The tribe is moved to an unhealthy area near Leavenworth where many die. Finally, Joseph and his remaining followers are confined to a reservation in eastern Washington State, where Joseph dies on 21 September 1904, according to medical report 'Of a broken heart'.

The conflict of mighty opposites sets Warren's poem on the level of epic tragedy. There's the morally oscillating but implacable might of white American power pitted against the unambitious dignities and moral stature of a peace-loving Indian tribe which gets in the way of land-grabbing avarice. Warren's epigraphs position his narrative between two opposed, authoritative white voices. First, Thomas Jefferson addresses the Miamis, Powtewataminies and Weeauku:

> Made by the same Great Spirit, and living in the same land with our brothers, the red men, we consider ourselves as the same family; we wish to live with them as one people, and to cherish their interests as our own.

Contrast William Tecumseh Sherman:

> The more we can kill this year, the less will have to be killed in the next war, for the more I see of these Indians, the more convinced I am that they will all have to be killed or be maintained as a species of paupers.

Enter ethnic cleansing. This woeful example of the pernicious gap between humane idea and brutal pragmatism yields one of Warren's finest achievements. The story is told partly by the poet himself and partly in the first person of Joseph, their speeches interspersed by comments from white men whose occasional admiration for the Chief will not deter them from hunting him down and forcibly relocating his tribe. The poet begins with a vivid evocation of 'The real people', the Nimipu, in joyous, vulnerable freedom:

> The Land of the Winding Waters, Wallowa,
> The Land of the Nimipu,
> Land sacred to the band of old Joseph,
> Their land, the land in the far ages given
> By the Chief-in-the-Sky. Their ponies, crossed
> With the strong blood of horses, well-bred, graze
> Richly the green blade. Boys, bareback, ride naked,
> Leap on, shout 'Ai-yah!' Shout 'Ai-yee' –
> In unbridled glory. Eagle wing catches sun.
> Gleams white. Boys plunge into water, gay as

The otter at gambol, with flat hands slap water
Like beaver tails slapping to warn, then dive,
Beaverlike, to depth, toes leaving the shimmer,
Uncoiling upward, of bubbles. On sandbars
Boys stretch, they yawn, and sun dries the skin
To glints gold, red, bronze.

After an initial treaty in 1855 favourable to the Nez Perce, protecting Joseph's beloved Wallowa Valley, an influx of goldrush settlers led to an attempt by Government Commissioners in 1863 to persuade Joseph and his people to accept a new, much smaller reservation centred at Lapwai in Idaho. Joseph refuses to sign the proposed new treaty. He contemplates the nature of gold:

Does a grain of gold, in the dark ground, lie
Like a seed-sprout? What colour of bloom
Will it bear? What cunning has it to make
Men rive raw rock where it hides like a murderous
secret?
What cunning to lie in innocent brightness
Like wet sand in water? In water, what dives
The deepest – deep, deeper than the lead pellet?
For all things live, and live in their nature.
But what is the nature of gold?

Imagining Joseph's voice, Warren is an expert ventriloquist, mastering the Indian idiom – guileless, wondering, alliterative, staccato — and the poem merits recognition as another of his heartfelt responses to the complex fate of being an American.

His perennial appeal is the infection of his inner turmoil, his tireless interrogation of the world. And then there's the message from 'Old-Time Childhood in Kentucky', the wry admission – provisional, of course – that, after all the metaphysical striving, maybe the best answer going is his forthright Grandpa's earned vision of how a life should be lived:

'Grandpa',
I said, 'what do you do, things being like this?' 'All you
can',

He said, looking off through treetops, skyward. 'Love
Your wife, love your get, keep your word, and
If need arises die for what men die for. There aren't
Many choices.
And remember that truth doesn't always live in the
number of voices'.

On 26 February 1986, when Warren was 80, he was designated
his country's first Poet Laureate. He was chosen for 'his feelings for
the promise and the frustration of American life' and for depicting
in his work 'the comic, the violent and the tawdry as well as the
grand and heroic'. Asked how he felt about the appointment,
he said he was happy to have been chosen, but that he wouldn't
have agreed to serve if he 'had been required to compose an ode
on the death of someone's kitten'. Reminded of the traditional
function of the British laureate to write ceremonial verse for state
occasions, he said, 'That belongs to the old system of things. It's
part of the trappings of monarchy – a kind of hired applauder, and
I couldn't have any of that'. The appointment ran until 1988. On 15
September 1989 he died at his home in Vermont, ending a career
almost unprecedented in American letters for its length, versatility
and accomplishment and a life which generated an abundance of
friendship, love and esteem.

26. A Bit More

'Let's face it, it is an exhilarating feeling to be shot at unsuccessfully'.
Werner Herzog

This time it wasn't someone else.

'I'm sorry', the Urologist said quietly across his desk, 'it's the most aggressive type'.

He was a considerate man, the Urologist. After a courteous smile in the foyer of the clinic he opened the door to his office, gestured me to a comfortable chair facing his desk and the bright window, glanced briefly at my case file and told me surgery wouldn't help. His face transmitted professional sympathy, but there was something of the crouch in his posture, forearms on the desk, shoulders hunched over them as though he half expected to have to spring to defend himself from a violent reaction to news of life curtailed.

No risk of that. I wasn't the sort to shoot the messenger and besides I intended to go on liking the Urologist. I knew he was a sensitive, principled man, a medical missionary who charitably took his professional services to the afflicted poor of Sierra Leone.

His speciality was the vesico-vaginal fistulas tormenting two million women among the poor in Africa, Asia, South America. Locations with insufficient access to prenatal care and education and only rudimentary medical infrastructure. Think of the bewildered women trudging in pain, in heat and dust to join the queue outside the under-resourced clinic. Women carrying new babies bundled on their backs, careworn DIY reverse marsupials. Carrying tissue destruction secondary to prolonged pressure of the baby's head during obstructed labour. Carrying tissue laceration during the instrumental delivery of Caesarean sections or from accidental injury during hysterectomy. Resulting in discharge of urine into the vaginal vault. Communication between rectum and vagina. Incontinence. Urinary infections. Mess. Profound effect on the patient's emotional well-being. Think of the Urologist, far from his immaculate office and first-world operating theatre, taking his compassionate expertise to these women in the piss and panic and faeces and stench of their misery.

Oh yes, I liked and admired the Urologist. Anyway it's comfortable to like someone with godlike power over you. You couldn't envy him his job. How often had he delivered a message like this to patients who didn't know they were running out of time until they sat down in the same chair? How did he choose the tone of voice for telling them?

'Unfortunately the scan tells us there's metastasis, that's secondaries, in the spine, ribs and pelvis'.

In the street outside uncontaminated people passed in silhouette across the window behind his desk, imperishable people for whom death had not been invented yet, walking with purpose in a world where I was becoming alien. What purpose could I have now? You need future to have purpose. Well, it was simple enough. We're all on death row, after all, as soon as we're born. The end was always coming, but now it was coming sooner. The world was moving on, leaving me behind.

'Can you say anything about life expectancy? I mean, how long do you think I've got?'

'It's hard to say. We often make mistakes when we try to answer this question. Possibly a year. Maybe a bit more'.

Have you ever seen a cancer cell? It's like a peeled brain with prehensile feelers. Perfectly endowed for stardom in a science-fiction horror movie. I'd always thought of cancer as the bodily equivalent of a nuclear bomb waiting to explode inside you, a personal Hiroshima, but somehow, in the pastel formality of the Urologist's office, educated down to size by worldwide ravages of vesico-vaginal fistulas and the suffering women of Sierra Leone, my disease lacked the requisite scale. It was more like scruffy Taliban guerillas penetrating my defensive perimeter. Insurgents were attacking with a cowardly barrage of mortars and grenades. Having lost religion when I was about fifteen my air cover was shot. Only a tactical operations centre remained. That would be my brain. Was that in danger too? Would I go gaga? Wasn't I being told to develop what the military would call a mindset of imminent closure? What could my brain do with a year? What was a bit more?

Do you think cancer cells organise themselves like bees? Maybe there's a Queen Cell. Maybe the drone cells crawl around fetching snippets of bones and organs, tribute to lay at the feelers of Her Disgusting Majesty.

Guilty, suddenly I felt guilty. Trains I'd ridden had stayed on the rails, cars I'd driven had avoided crashing, planes had carried me safely to America, Africa, Australia, Brazil. It was my own body, the one vehicle I was solely responsible for, licensed only to me, which was shamefully out of control. I'd given up the fags years ago and in any case I'd never smoked with my prostate, but I hadn't taken enough care of the engine. It was nobody's fault but my own.

There had been cancer as long as I could remember.

'Uncle John has gone into hospital', my father said, 'I'm afraid it's cancer. It's in the pancreas. They found it too late. It's too far gone'.

That made no sense at all. Uncle John was irrepressible. Everyone agreed he was the most ebullient person imaginable with a gift for infectious merriment, an amalgam of wheeler-dealer and clown. Pernicious cells had no business with the likes of Uncle John.

Then there were haughty Cousin Winifred, dithery Aunt Nellie and my father's gruff golfing partner, chain-smoking Paddy Henderson. Breast, bowel and lung. At school there was popular Donald Murray, most amiable of senior boys, tubby enough to need little padding for the perfection of his waddling strut as Pooh-Bah in *The Mikado*. At eighteen swept in four months from diagnosis to death. A playground in mourning for the Lord High Everything Else.

Aunt Mary copped it at eighty-one after a life of elegant smoking through a filtered holder. Oh, but wasn't she *soignée*. And fun, deliciously vulgar. She bought me all Danny Kaye's records and sang soprano to local acclaim, a stalwart of the church choir. During a break in rehearsal her fellow choristers bragged about their top notes.

'I can get up to high C', says one.

Another songbird ascends to F. '*In altissimo*', she preens.

'I can get up to Pee', says Mary, exhaling a plume of Du Maurier.

Until I visited her in hospital I'd never seen Mary uncorseted. She was lying on her side, her outline beneath the sheets a reposing seal. I hunkered down beside the bed so my face was level with hers.

'Hello, Mary, how's it going?'

'Is that you? Oh, it's kind of you to come. Good to see you. How are you?' Eyes closed, the voice barely audible. I leaned in closer.

'Aye, it's me. I'm fine', sliding my hand into hers under the sheets. 'How are you feeling today?'

'Her breath came in short pants', she said, opening her eyes, 'and as he drew nearer her pants grew shorter and shorter'. Then a Rabelaisian chuckle to break your heart.

Next day she was gone. Nonchalant. Cancer with style.

The day my father was diagnosed with lung cancer I found him sitting in the bay-window of his sitting-room, wearing his Sunday jacket, looking out at autumn.

'I'm so sorry, Dad', I said, hoping he wouldn't mention God.

'I really don't want to die', he said.

God was a problem between us. In early childhood God's presence was confirmed by my father's intimacy with the Lord he thanked in the grace he said at mealtime, a brief conversation which, if one-sided, took amiable divine attention for granted. Bedtime prayers for the well-being of loved ones were a daily assurance that the Lord was listening. The Episcopalian Church broke this short-lived security. At first the Sunday morning services were like big parties. Especially in wartime it was comforting to see so many grown-ups singing and praying together, and it was cosy to sit snug between my parents. My father's Sunday jacket was made of Harris tweed which had a distinctive smell like mixed herbs. He sang with his heart and soul.

'O all ye Works of the Lord, bless ye the Lord: praise him, and magnify him for ever'.

The smell of his jacket seemed to get stronger when he sang. I thought this must be what God smelled like. Then everyone listened to a speech by the man they called the Vicar. It was his party. There was always a bit of the party when he asked us to pray for the sick. I thought this was very kind and prayed fervently for people I'd never seen or heard of before.

'Please, God, make Mr Thomson's bronchitis go away and mend Miss Newton's sore legs'.

The parties stopped being enjoyable when I began to understand the words better. Kneeling between my mother and father I heard their confessions.

'Almighty and most merciful Father', they murmured into clasped hands, 'We have erred and strayed from thy ways like lost sheep. We have followed too much the devices and desires of our own hearts. We have offended against thy holy laws. We have left undone those things which we ought to have done, and we have done those things which we ought not to have done, and there is no health in us'.

This was shattering. I knew my father's health was limited because I'd learned that he was called 'diabetic' and watched him injecting medicine into his thigh; but my mother was visibly fit and strong. Why were they telling God they were sick, lost sheep and miserable offenders? I had been deceived. Then the Vicar told us Mr Thomson died of his bronchitis. No more Sunday parties for me, no confirmation, no God. My father was furious. He had failed in his duty to bring me up as a Christian. My mother was sad. I was wretched.

On one of his last days I was wretched again when his haggard small body jack-knifed in a spasm of pain. Gone the nippy rugby half-back, gone the steady batsman –'Walker slow but sure', the papers used to say of his methodical innings – gone the sou'-westered fisher for trout. There were lochs where he knew every stone. No, no, not yet, please, we need more time, we haven't finished yet. I wanted wailing, pandemonium. Instead, as he came out of the spasm, I heard the Robert Louis Stevenson Vailima prayer he'd learned by heart, getting ready.

'Bless us, if it may be, in all our innocent endeavours. If it may not, give us the strength to encounter that which is to come, that we be brave in peril, constant in tribulation, temperate in wrath, and in all changes of fortune and down to the gates of death loyal and loving to one another'.

'Amen, Dad', I said. 'Amen, amen. Thanks, thanks Dad, thank you', lurching from his bedroom for the last time, my apostasy battered but intact. A staunch member of the stiff-upper-lip generation, it would only distress him to see me in tears.

Now it was my turn for the cells. I had none of Mary's nonchalance and failed to make contact with my father's God. I certainly wasn't confident about being brave in peril or constant in tribulation. Temperance in wrath had never brought much satisfaction; but, thanks to the Urologist, thanks to the drugs he prescribed to give me a bit more, I went back to Africa.

There was an impressive range of drugs from a hefty three-monthly injection into the stomach to the battery of pain-killers that made a pharmacy of the bathroom cabinet and a pill called Tramadol which was mainly for sleep. They said people often dreamed vividly when they took Tramadol. They were right. I spent countless hours in a windowless room, waiting. What was I waiting for? Why didn't they come? Ah, yes, of course, they would bring me the gun. What was the gun for? How could I have forgotten? I had been chosen to shoot Hitler. Another pill delivered first place in the men's tennis singles at the Australian Open. Less of an ego-trip but more fulfilling was digging for survivors alongside crimson-clad Tibetan monks in the rubble of earthquake-stricken Jiegu in western China. From underneath a bed in a collapsed mud-built house we rescued a sixty-eight-year-old woman who said her name was Wujian. The four-year-old girl beside her was too traumatised to speak. Me too, but the role of life-giver was intoxicating. I thought the Urologist might be quite pleased with me. In this busy nightlife I was aloof from predatory cells, immune to internal Taliban, sometimes even helping others to live. I was becoming hooked on this Tramadol.

Decades ago Africa had gone in deep and left scars. Glasgow was a dreich city in the fifties and early sixties. I wanted away from falling and rising damp, ossified class antagonisms and post-war austerities. I wanted new landscapes, sun, colour, effervescence. Eager to experience the vibrancies of a multi-ethnic culture remote from the dourness of Presbyterian Scotland and naively unaware of the similarities between South African racism and the anti-Semitic psychosis of Nazi Germany, I went to work as lecturer in English at Rhodes University in the Eastern Cape Province city of Grahamstown.

When the anguish of *apartheid* made its impact I remembered Abraham Lincoln's conviction that 'there is a special place in hell for those who remain neutral in a moral crisis'. My father's letters usually ended with an imperative: 'KOOP'. That stood for 'Keep Out Of Politics'. Renegade again, instead of turning a blind eye or leaving the country there and then I joined the South African Liberal Party, inspired by the pre-eminent membership of Alan Paton who knew so well how the beloved country cried.

Living and working in South Africa for three years in the early 1960s was a crash course in the perversities of racial segregation. *Apartheid* was another sort of cancer. Not that I contributed much to the struggle. My only weapons were novels, plays and poems. In the South African context literature became a moral science of subversion. Knowing there was often a Special Branch spy in the class and the police were watching your house made you even more determined to apply everything to the political situation. There was the town for whites and there was the 'location' where a single cold-water tap might be shared by a dozen or more families and twenty children died every month from *kwashiorkor*, the crippling disease caused by malnutrition. The teacher at the location's Primary School for African children invited me to present the end-of-year prizes. The school was a concrete box with a tin roof, some forty children, one teacher, rickety desks, next to no teaching materials and perfect discipline. I gave the cheap prize books to the children, shaking hands with each diffident winner, coaxing hesitant smiles. Then the teacher asked the class to stand. They would now sing the anthem of black South Africa, 'Nkosi Sikhelel iAfrica': 'God Save Africa, May her horn rise high up; Hear Thou our prayers, And bless us'. The singing began tentatively, then swelled. I stood to attention as the children's voices filled the classroom and attacked my heart. Part of me has been standing to attention for the people of South Africa ever since that morning in 1963.

All the same I flunked South Africa. Without knocking the graduate student entered my office, finger to lips, and went to my bookcase. He slid the books out shelf by shelf, checking for bugs. Then behind the pictures. He came round to my side of the desk to bend and look and feel underneath.

'Sorry', he said, 'but you know how it is. They're everywhere'.

He sat, across the desk from me, breathed heavily, mopped sweat from his face.

'We know you're on the right side', he said, 'I've come to ask if you'll help us'.

'How?'

I might receive a phone call. Perhaps I'd be told to meet someone, accept a package, take it home, no questions asked. Later there could be another phone call instructing me to deliver the package somewhere. There might be explosions. Would I be willing to follow such instructions? We both knew the system was evil, had to be cut down.

'Please'.

'Give me until tomorrow'.

No sleep that night. Knowing I'd decline the gambit I dreaded meeting my student in the morning to expose my lack of moral fibre. But there was no meeting. The Special Branch had raided Liliesleaf farm in the northern Johannesburg suburb of Rivonia, headquarters of *Umkhonto we Sizwe*, 'The Spear of the Nation', military arm of the African National Congress. Nelson Mandela and his comrades were in custody, expecting the death sentence. My student had fled to Swaziland.

I knew I didn't possess the nerve or guts to be the kind of political activist required by the intensifying struggle. So I left, useless, self-esteem at zero and returned to Scotland's kitsch nationalism and girning politicians.

With the defeat of *apartheid* and the privilege of living to witness Mandela's spectacular achievement after twenty-seven years of detention, anyone could see that the Rainbow Nation still had a long way to go with endemic crime, sub-standard housing in the townships and a thousand deaths from AIDS every day. But the new crisis in the region was the ruin of Zimbabwe dictated by the liberator-turned-madman, Robert Mugabe. Standing to attention wasn't good enough. If the Urologist just stood to attention all those blighted women in Sierra Leone would be doomed to live and die in the agony of their vesico-vaginal fistulas. To hell with cancer. That was no excuse. It was time for action, time to make up for my ineffectuality in South Africa forty years ago.

If the West is serious about making a difference in Africa it must ensure that aid reaches the people it's intended for. This would be my mission. The twin miseries of crop failure and economic collapse had left Zimbabwe's villages without food. Millions were barely surviving on wild fruit. Children were dying out in the bush but foreign doctors had to keep quiet or else they'd be kicked out by the government. The crisis was exacerbated by Mugabe's suspension of humanitarian aid before his one-man presidential runoff. He was depriving opposition districts of medicine and food, using hunger as a political tool to force people to vote for him. People were grubbing for scraps in rubbish dumps, shoulder-to-shoulder with baboons. Nearly five million people needed aid and there was cholera in the cities.

Meticulous planning was required. I rang a friend in Johannesburg. He agreed to organise a fleet of trucks loaded with food handouts, vaccines and medical sundries. The trucks would be driven by sympathetic Africans. Each driver would be given American dollars to bribe the guards at the border crossing. When my friend called to tell me the trucks were ready I flew to Johannesburg.

The trucks set off in convoy. I followed in a discreetly dented Volkswagen. After a rest stop at Messina, five hundred and thirty kilometres north of Johannesburg, there were eighteen kilometres more to the Alfred Beit Bridge across the Limpopo River. The dollars did their work and there was no trouble at the Beitbridge border post. Our destination was Wedza, a small town in the province of Mashonaland East, about a hundred kilometres from Harare. Villagers in the area had been reduced to eating their own dogs and cow dung. Our contact was a young mother, Phumuzile Moyo. We knew her two-year-old son, Godknows, was sick from malnutrition. Her extended family and friends in Wedza and the surrounding countryside would tell people where to come to find us and receive the hand-outs. Doctors working in the area would be advised about the medicines we were bringing.

On the outskirts of Wedza we steered the trucks into a circle, relishing the irony that we were making a *laager* like a defensive ring of Afrikaner ox-wagons, and waited for sundown, the time we'd set for people to come. Phumuzile came first. Godknows flopped in his mother's arms like a six-months-old baby of the Holocaust, wrists and ankles like twigs, dark hollows under his solemn eyes, sores on his face. The drivers began to unload and the people came, silently, barefoot. Ten, fifty, then too many to count.

We distributed the food hand-outs. Phumuzile spooned careful small mouthfuls of mealie-meal between the chapped lips of her son. Under his big eyes the hollows were already fading, the eyes brightening. Three doctors arrived, one English, one Swedish, another Dutch and transferred our medical supplies to their station wagons. We told the people we'd return soon. Smiling and nodding their thanks, they clasped their hand-outs.

'Amandla!', we said, 'Power!' because that's what we said in South Africa. 'Amandla, Amandla!', we said as they melted into the darkness.

The operation had gone without a hitch. As we began the drive back to Harare I savoured the prospect of telling the Urologist all about it.

Approaching Harare I checked the automatic pistol I'd brought with me for security and decided to go for a bit more. I'd cap the mission by shooting Robert Mugabe, or perhaps I'd force him to eat the poison fruit which had killed a family of four in Matabeleland.

No chance. That would have to wait for another night. You only get so much from fifty milligrams of Tramadol.

27. Swift's Gentle Yahoo and the Arts in Our Time

Dr Trench. A tragic life: Bolingbroke, Harley, Ormonde, all those great Ministers that were his friends, banished and broken.

John Corbet. I do not think you can explain him in that way – his tragedy had deeper foundations. His ideal order was the Roman Senate, his ideal men Brutus and Cato. Such an order and such men had seemed possible once more, but the movement passed and he foresaw the ruin to come, Democracy, Rousseau, the French Revolution; that is why he hated the common run of men, – 'I hate lawyers, I hate doctors', he said, 'though I love Dr So-and-So and Judge So-and-So' – that is why he wrote *Gulliver*, that is why he wore out his brain, that is why he felt *saeva indignatio*, that is why he sleeps under the greatest epitaph in history. You remember how it goes? It is almost finer in English than in Latin: 'He has gone where fierce indignation can lacerate his heart no more'.
(W.B. Yeats, *The Words Upon the Window-Pane*)

With Swiftian astringency the young Béla Bartók levelled his *saeva indignatio*, his 'fierce indignation', at religion and declared his own secular Trinity: 'It is perfectly understandable that the weaker man derives *inexpressible comfort* from being able to pray to a Powerful Being...But at the same time it is his inexpressible weakness...if I ever crossed myself, it would signify "In the name of Nature, Art and Science"'. If this recalls Matthew Arnold's prophecy of a mounting reliance on poetry inversely proportionate to the decline in religion, don't Arnold and Bartók – tough-minded moral and cultural avant-gardists in their times – stand today revealed as romantic dreamers? Israel versus Palestine; Afghanistan, Iraq, Syria and Zimbabwe; al-Qaeda; nuclear waste, and the development of unemployment as a new norm in industrialised countries. What next? Are we failed Houyhnhnms or just a bunch of Yahoos? We may allow Bartók his putative worship of art and nature, but his exaltation of science looks like a classic case of the ascetic naïf. And what good have poetry, music and the fine arts done in Damascus?

It was surely the American, Henry Adams, who got it right for our time as well as his own. In *Mont Saint Michel and Chartres* Adams's enquiry into historical causality takes him to twelfth-century France. He is all for an omnipresent Powerful Being. The architecture of Chartres Cathedral and the Abbey of Mont-Saint-Michel seems to him an expression of ideological unity achieved in response to 'the purity, the beauty, the grace, and the infinite loftiness of Mary's nature, among the things of earth, and above the clamor of kings'. Adoration of the Queen of Heaven impelled medieval sensibility into a unifying ideal which held life and art in a lucid social harmony of love, energy, and benevolence. Adams's Mariolatry is suspect to say the least. Clerical monopoly of power did not generate the Utopia he chooses to imagine, but the symbol of the Virgin remains valid as the expression of an ideal. By comparison with the structured, purposeful lives of the century 1150-1250, modern people merely exist, prey to blind forces and chance events. The Virgin has been replaced by the dynamo, a symbol of mechanistic force which drives people into a worship fatal to their own well-being.

In 1900 Adams visited the Paris Exhibition. Describing his reactions in the third person in *The Education of Henry Adams*, he records that to him:

> ...the dynamo became a symbol of infinity. As he grew accustomed to the great gallery of machines, he began to feel the forty-foot dynamos as a moral force, much as the early Christians felt the Cross...one began to pray to it; inherited instinct taught the natural expression of man before silent and infinite force...he could see only an absolute fiat in electricity as in faith.

For Adams, then, Bartók's hopeful trinity of Nature, Art, and Science, had been reduced to a single, malign term – Science – and the mass of life was black. The discoveries of Pierre and Marie Curie showed that physical matter contains its own potential for disintegration, and Radium 'denied its God'. By reducing matter to molecules that collide with each other at intervals varying up to 17,750,000 times per second, the kinetic theory of gas established Adams's belief that nature is full of violence but without system:

> The kinetic theory of gas is an assertion of ultimate chaos. In plain words, Chaos was the law of nature; Order was the dream of man.

In his attempt to impose order on the flux of his existence, man seems to Adams like a spider snaring the forces of nature that 'dance like flies before the net' of its web. The image reappears in T.S. Eliot's 'Gerontion', originally intended as a prelude to *The Waste Land*, modernism's most resonant literary image of a world in disorder. Eliot considers the possibility that the spider might 'suspend its operations', thus consigning the poem's shadowy characters to disintegration in space:

> De Bailhache, Fresca, Mrs Cammel, whirled
> Beyond the circuit of the shuddering Bear
> In fractured atoms.

Now science's commercial *alter ego*, technological pragmatism, has elevated the silicon chip to the bad eminence of Henry Adams's dynamo. We get chips with everything and charm, with a nudge from James Joyce, has absconded to the domain of the quarks. We occupy a world of bureaucracy, management and alienation, which is no longer the hip thing it was even in the nineteen-eighties, but symptom of a time in which, to co-opt Tennyson, 'the individual withers and the world is more and more'. It is a world which slides by on grease, a savage servility, like the automobiles in Robert Lowell's poem 'For the Union Dead'. In schools and universities career-orientation or contribution to the Gross National Product are the criteria of worthiness for a subject, a faculty, a course. This utilitarian brutality is not new. We know from *The Idea of a University Defined and Illustrated* that Cardinal Newman realised he was up against it in the lectures he gave in 1852 as Rector-Elect of the new Catholic University in Ireland; but, despite the best efforts of the Victorians, it was the twentieth century that made it the totem before which we now fall down. In *Schindler's Ark* Thomas Keneally describes German SS preparations for the liquidation of the Jewish ghetto at Cracow. Inhabitants of the section designated Ghetto B were issued with identification cards marked W for army employees, Z for employees of the civil authorities, or R for workers in essential industries. Graft apart, workers in essential industries tended to last longest. How Swift's indignation would have run with this.

The apotheosising of product is a crucial phase in the movement towards a society in which a concern with truth or matters of value is at best aberrant, often contemptible, or, more insidiously, just another marketable trend, grist to the politician's mill. As George Steiner puts it, 'The methodical devaluation of speech in political propaganda and in the Esperanto of the mass-market is too powerful to be readily defined. At decisive points, ours is today a civilisation "after the word"'. To fill the space where God once was with an economic fiat is an abrogation of humanity and its languages, a reckless attempt to climb out of the 'destructive element' Joseph Conrad talks about in *Lord Jim* instead of learning to swim in it. The caprice of God may have been disconcerting, but the fickleness of economics is chaos come again into the life that would be led in terms of what Newman calls real values. We may be right to give economics the credit for getting Communism on the run across Eastern Europe, but how could we condone the insertion of commercials between each movement of Beethoven's Ninth Symphony when television networks across the world screened Leonard Bernstein's Christmas Day 1989 performance from East Berlin's Schauspielhaus to celebrate the dismantling of the Berlin Wall? The juxtaposition of breakfast cereal, washing powder, cat meat and Schiller's 'Ode to Joy' – the joy of freedom in this case – was worthy of Alexander Pope at his most satirical. A culture so pachydermal that its most potent public medium accords equal value to *Freiheit* and cat food needs more of the arts, and the arts need to be militant.

Pressed by the utilitarian insistences of our time, now under the pall of global economic recession and barely conceivable nuclear possibilities, what point can there be in the triumph of a Fidelio, the musings of Proust, the jollities of Dutch genre painting, the anguish of Lear, the socialist effervescences of Jorge

Amado, the symmetries of Bach, or T.S. Eliot's aspiration towards the point where the fire and the rose are one? Doomed, like John Irving's Garp in his effort to protect his family from the world, the artist must take on the image of Verdi's tormented Rigoletto, the archetypal misfit, '*Solo, difforme, povero*'. The persistence of Rigolettos testifies to an unregenerate element of the Yahoo in our make-up, but give the printed circuit a few more years and it may have us all Houyhnhnms, forbiddingly rational creatures without need of the flab of art.

Swift, as Kipling reminds us, was 'scourged through life between the dread of insanity and the wrath of his own soul warring with a brutal age'. Out of this agony, Kipling says – and beyond the academy it's true still – there remains one little book:

> ...his dreadful testament against his fellow-kind, which today serves as a pleasant tale for the young under the title of *Gulliver's Travels*. That, and a faint recollection of some baby-talk in some love-letters, is as much as the world has chosen to retain of Jonathan Swift, Master of Irony. Think of it! It is like turning-down the glare of a volcano to light a child to bed!

This is a puzzling feature of the book: it is, at once, bright with fantasy and a volcano. But how dreadful is the testament? Its appeal is easily distinguishable: pygmies and giants; flying islands and talking horses. The detailed inventiveness; the carefully worked-out scales in Brobdingnag and Lilliput; the comedy of the Lilliputians crawling and leaping under sticks, walking tightropes, their theological debates over the end at which eggs should be cracked; Gulliver's heroism in Brobdingnag with flies and wasps and monkeys and bowls of cream; the Laputans with their Flappers and their meals of rhomboids, equilateral triangles, cycloids and parallelograms. There is some merriment in Book IV too, but not so much, for this last book casts a long shadow backwards over the whole work.

Much of the interest in the first two books resides quite simply in the descriptive narrative and in Swift's delight in exploring the differences in scale. Book I, of course, is a satire principally of England, where the Lilliputians' stature turns all their concerns into affectations. In Book II it is principally Gulliver himself and what, with minute arrogance, he stands for, which are being satirised. But a strain scarcely heard in Lilliput becomes in Brobdingnag a fascinated revulsion as the human body is seen though Gulliver's microscopic eye. The nurse's breast becomes a tumid horror; the naked Maids of Honour, who make him the toy of their concupiscence, fill him with nausea. And he is himself at best a *relplum scalcath*, at worst a *splacknuck*. Book III has some knockabout fun with the Royal Society in which Swift pays off some old scores against his Dublin tutor, Narcissus Marsh. Of the whole ragbag of satirical objects in Book III it is, however, Gulliver's encounter with the Struldbruggs which has the most telling effect on him and on us. In the prospect of immortality Gulliver sees extravagant opportunities for increase in wealth, knowledge and benevolence. But he forgets the work of time and he forgets the body of flesh. Now we remember the flayed woman of *A Tale of a Tub*. Here is the Swiftian carcase again, senseless and unsavoury, rank Yahoo flesh. Beckett country isn't far away.

In Swift's polarising of human attributes in Book IV of *Gulliver's Travels* the Yahoos are usually taken to be the hirsute, nodal point of the excremental vision. The book has been attacked often enough, notably by grumpy F.R. Leavis who seemed to find in the Yahoos all the life-enhancing virtues of D.H. Lawrence's hot young men: 'Swift did his best for the Houyhnhnms, and they may have all the reason, but the Yahoos have all the life...The clean skin of the Houyhnhnms, in short, is stretched over a void'. But Swift is employing a kind of allegory, not writing a novel. It is supererogatory to complain that because Spenser's Red Cross Knight doesn't suffer from gastronenteritis he is a skin stretched over a void. Is it in any useful sense valid to say that 'the Yahoos have all the life', especially when this life amounts to fighting, getting drunk, suffering disease, killing cats, and throwing excrement? It is true that the Yahoos make the deepest emotional impact on us. They appall us as they appalled Gulliver. The Houyhnhnms do live an even, somewhat off-puttingly uncomplicated life. Primarily a satiric construct, the purity of their appeal heightens our revulsion to the Yahoos. Simple satiric inversion has taken place. Give even a horse reason and it can do better than humans.

The most important aspect of Swift's strategy is that the Houyhnhnms are deliberately distanced through the very fact that they are horses. We can't identify with these rational creatures. In Book I of *Gulliver's Travels* we can identify with Gulliver himself and laugh at the trivial malice of the Lilliputians. In Book II we can slip over to the side of the King of Brobdingnag and scorn Gulliver, provisionally, as a member of 'the most pernicious race of little odious vermin that nature ever suffered to crawl upon the surface of the earth'. But here we are trapped. The Houyhnhnms' way of life may be all right if you happen to be a horse, but we are penned in the dirt and indecorum of the Yahoo sty with Gulliver himself. And where can we go from there? Swift's printed-circuit horses may rein us in but we cannot be of them, nor should we wish to be. 'The company of horses', warns America's Hugh Henry Brackenridge, 'is by no means favourable to good taste and genius...and as men naturally consimilate with their company, so it is observable that your jockeys are a class of people not greatly removed from the sagacity of a good horse'.

Everything in Swift's work is sunk in delusion – everything but love, and kindness. In Book I there is Gulliver's own genial nature, in II that of the giant-hearted girl Glumdalclitch, and in IV the cool solicitude of his Master and the love of his friend, the Sorrel Nag who bids him farewell as he leaves, expelled from Houyhnhnmland to meet again the grossness of his own human kind. It's this last farewell from these rational creatures that we need to keep with us: 'Take care of thyself, gentle Yahoo'. So behind Swift's *saeva indignatio* lies this gentleness, not madness; not misanthropy but love, and a triumph, after all, for that sweet unreason that lies at the human core like ambergris in a blasted whale. Swift did his best to make his vision of humankind as disgusting as possible – the human creature as a thing degenerate, without hope of grace – but he couldn't quite bring it off. There was evidence of something else, something residual that even his pessimism could not refine out of existence.

For William Faulkner this residuum was still worth calling 'a spirit', that element in our make-up which tempers the Yahoo in us and would keep us from doing ourselves in:

> I decline to accept the end of man. It is easy enough to say that man is immortal simply because he will endure: that when the last ding-dong of doom has clanged and faded from the last worthless rock

hanging tideless in the last red and dying evening, that even then there will still be one more sound: that of his puny inexhaustible voice, still talking. I refuse to accept this. I believe that man will not merely endure: he will prevail. He is immortal, not because he alone among creatures has an inexhaustible voice, but because he has a soul, a spirit capable of compassion and sacrifice and endurance.

With the 'end of the American century', meltdown in the Middle East, Iran's nuclear equivocations and bankers' bonuses, Faulkner's rhetoric may seem too purple, too stoical, the ding-dong of doom all too plausible, and the words 'soul' and 'spirit' anachronisms of an Arcadian time when the arts justified themselves. Even today, it's hard to avoid using such vocabulary; but a safer word is consciousness – neutral, inoffensive, secular. Consciousness is something we all possess and the last thing we relinquish at death. We cling to consciousness with a tenacity that gives it pride of place over kinship, money, or sex. In Auschwitz, Thomas Keneally tells us, Clara Sternberg, a woman in her early forties, her mind blown by the living nightmare, sought to kill herself by self-immolation on the electric fence that surrounded her camp. Meeting an old acquaintance, Clara asked her 'Where's the electric fence?' Keneally comments:

> In her disarrayed mind, it was a reasonable question to ask, and Clara had no doubt that the friend, if she had any sisterly feeling, would point the exact way to the wires. The answer the woman gave Clara was just as crazed, but it was one that had a fixed point of view, a balance, a perversely sane core.
>
> 'Don't kill yourself on the fence, Clara,' the woman urged her. 'If you do that, you'll never know what happened to you'.

Clara returned to her barracks. As Keneally says, 'It has always been the most powerful of answers to give to the intending suicide. Kill yourself and you'll never find out how the plot ends'.

Human consciousness demands more than the mere facts of the plot. If we were Houyhnhnms we might settle for a Gradgrindian diet of numbers, measurements, food according to our metabolic needs, useful work. But Swift knows his species better than to dream of the order mourned by Henry Adams. We are Yahoos with a pittance of reason, glandular, intransigently messy creatures. 'The lunatic, the lover, and the poet are of imagination all compact', and which of us has not loved? So by Shakespeare's way of it, we are all partly mad, partly poetic. We will retain, 'They fell in love and married' against all clinical pressure to factory-finish the experience into the deep freeze of psychological jargon: 'Their libidinal impulses being reciprocal, they activated their individual erotic drives and integrated them within the same frame of reference'. (The parody is Lionel Trilling's). This might meet the case in the novels of Harold Robbins or *Fifty Shades of Grey*; it won't do for Romeo and Juliet, or for Elizabeth Bennet and Darcy, or for Anna Karenina and Vronsky. Knowing the chemistry of water doesn't prepare us for a sensory perception of the Falls of Iguaçu. We want the sounding cataracts of the romantic poet to help us express our feelings. A geological history from rocks of the Lower Precambrian to those of the Cenozoic era will only partly account for our apprehension in the Grand Canyon of a spectacle so awe-inspiring that we want organ glissandi or chunks of Strauss's *Alpensinfonie* to help us say what we think we have seen and felt. Consciousness, in such cases, calls for art.

The arts are news of life, not merely exercises in aesthetics, but we must understand the aesthetics if we wish to receive the news. There is something crucial to be learned from the satisfaction obtained from the balanced patterns of art. This is best understood if we think of human beings as trying to resolve the split between Houyhnhnm and Yahoo, as striving towards wholeness or such integration as Swift's friend, Pope, intends when he places humankind 'on this isthmus of a middle state' at the end of *An Essay on Man*. The ultimate significance of great works may lie in the fact that they are paradigms of integration, examples provided by genius of that 'wholeness, harmony and radiance' which James Joyce, after Aquinas, saw as the elements of true art. If so, we need not trouble ourselves with superficial questions about the relevance of art.

When Gustav Mahler came to compose *Das Lied von Der Erde* ('The Song of the Earth') he found himself '*vis-à-vis de rien*', facing death. In the last movement of the work, '*Der Abschied*'

('The Farewell'), Mahler added some words of his own to the text he took from Hans Bethge's *The Chinese Flute*:

> Die liebe Erde allüberall
> Blüht auf im Lenz und grünt aufs neu!
> Allüberall und ewig blauen licht die Fernen!
> Ewig...ewig...

> *The dear earth everywhere*
> *Blossoms in spring and grows green again!*
> *Everywhere and eternally the distance shines bright*
> *and blue!*
> *Eternally...eternally...*

Mahler's method of facing death required the certain consolation that when he took his farewell of the world, the earth would continue in its endlessly renewing cycles. Had he written *The Song of the Earth* today he could not have relied on such consolation: it hasn't been available since Hiroshima. Yahoo excrement has turned lethal. This is the deadly distinction of our time, therefore an essential part of the context in which we must finally contemplate the function of the arts.

In his long poem *Mirabell: Books of Numbers* the American poet, James Merrill, holds seances with an Ouija board which bring him visitations and messages. His chief informant is agitated by 'increasing human smog' in which is revealed only the 'CONCERTED USE OF ATOMIC/WEAPONRY NOW FALLING INTO HANDS OF ANIMAL SOULS'. Moving the cup among the letters of the Ouija board, the conjured spirits spell out their injunction: 'FIND US BETTER PHRASES FOR THESE HISTORIES WE POUR FORTH/HOPING AGAINST HOPE THAT MAN WILL LOVE HIS MIND AND LANGUAGE'. Bearing witness to the rewards as well as the perils of consciousness, the arts teach love of mind and language. Thus they offer their potent motivations towards the maintenance of peace in a blood-stained world. 'Take care of thyself, gentle Yahoo', was the Sorrel Nag's farewell to Gulliver. Yahoos all, we need the arts to nourish the gentleness Swift could find in us and to help us take care of ourselves in our time.

28. The Kailyard and the Kraal

Perhaps we shouldn't have been surprised when the British Foreign Office rejected a Russian student's application to study in Scotland on the grounds that she might not understand the language. Perhaps they thought she'd be taking instruction from one of Glasgow's patois merchants like Tom Leonard or James Kelman, or from a character in Irvine Welsh's *Trainspotting*, or from Edwin Morgan's Loch Ness monster. The Foreign Office made it clear to the student, testily if not quite grammatically, that they found her choice of Scotland downright perverse: 'You cannot satisfactorily explain why you have chosen to attend an English course in Scotland rather than your other options of Oxford or Cambridge, where you should face less difficulty understanding a regional accent'. The inference being that no regional accents are allowed at the two top British (aka English) universities. The Foreign Office was speaking from the Centre; Scotland was the periphery, a kailyard beyond the pale. Braveheart and Alex Salmond gathered their brows. Edward II thought again, smirked and jauped in his tomb. The Foreign Office, taken to task, blamed the British embassy in Moscow.

The auld prejudice, cultural apartheid – no internationalising here. Lewis Grassic Gibbon's Chris Guthrie wouldn't have been surprised: 'everybody knew that the English were awful mean and couldn't speak right'. The Ambassador to Moscow could have done a turn as an Afrikaner Nationalist, dropping in at the kraal to impose his *taal* on the barbarous tongue of Xhosa or Zulu; and, by the way, if you're a Scot stepping out from the kailyard, 'Please adjust your language before leaving'. It was always more than just a matter of being understood. An accent from North Britain identified you as belonging, in Henry Thomas Buckle's opinion, to 'a badly fed, badly housed, and not over cleanly people'. Not the right sort of company for a nice Russian lassie. Far be it for the Ambassador to Moscow to expose her to the Scot: not only unintelligible, but also tight-fisted, brutish, maudlin, canny, repressed, volatile, alcoholic, dourly religious, a muddled barbarian worth exhibiting as one of the world's ethnic sideshows set to music by the pibrochs James Kennaway describes as 'damp, penetrating and sad like a mist'.

But a sensational internationalist riposte was coming and the kailyard was about to rock to the twentieth century's most globalising cultural Esperanto. We heard they were all shook up in the village of Lonmay near Aberdeen. In his book, *The Presley Prophecy,* Allan Morrison said he'd traced the King's ancestry back more than 250 years, using local records and the files of the Church of the Latter Day Saints. On August 27th 1713, eight generations before Elvis's birth in 1935, his ancestor, Andrew Presley, married Elspeth Leg in Lonmay. Their son, also called Andrew, became a blacksmith and was the first Presley to leave Scotland, emigrating to America in 1745. After innumerable begats, behold Elvis. So the King is ours as we've really known since Andy Stewart transposed Donald's jaunty abrogation of trousers to Graceland fifty years ago. After that *The Bogie Man* and Batman in Scotland were bound to come. There is no more provocative nudge in recent literature than Alfred's comment to the Caped Crusader at the end of *Batman: Scottish Connection*: '*You* may have seen Scotland from angles no one else *ever* has, sir...but I enjoyed it immensely'.

So, what *are* the angles? Perhaps they are defined by the extremes of devolution and globalisation, buzz words of the last three decades and still with us. England's letting go of Empire was a kind of staggered, grumpy devolution. Tony Blair's Westminster made it possible for Scotland to devolve into a partial reversal of the Union which inaugurated the United Kingdom. Most Scottish nobles supported the Act of Union made law on 1st May 1707, but in the tower of St Giles's Church in Edinburgh a sardonic carilloner struck his bells into a wedding tune with an ironic title: 'Why Should I Be So Sad on My Wedding Day?' Auspices of divorce already. Scotland kept its own legal and educational systems and its lacklustre church but finally lost the nationhood which had nearly died at Flodden and become increasingly tenuous since the union of the crowns. In Smollett's *Humphry Clinker* the prickly Scotsman, Lismahago, is at his most factious when Matthew Bramble congratulates him on the 'flourishing state of his country' as a consequence of Union. Lismahago will have none of it. The Scots have been dispossessed and demoralised:

> They lost the independency of their state, the greatest
> prop of national spirit; they lost their parliament, and

their courts of justice were subjected to the revision and supremacy of an English tribunal.

'We're bought and sold for English gold', snaps Burns, castigating the Scottish commissioners as 'a parcel of rogues in a nation!' but for many the Act of Union was to Scotland as the birth of Christ to Christendom or Lenin's arrival at the Finland Station to world Communism. Before Union all was primitive, feudal and superstitious, Scotland 'the rudest of all the European nations'. To 'those horrified Englishmen who visited it', says Hugh Trevor-Roper, 'Scotland was a mere desert, inhabited (if at all) by barbarous people whose whole way of life was at worst nasty, at best unintelligible. Returning travellers wrote of it as they might write of a visit to Arabia: those long treeless wastes, the squalid towns in the plains; the savage, unvisited tribes in the hills; the turbulent tribal chieftains; the rabble-rousing mullahs with their mysterious religious organisation'. Union transformed Scottish society. After Union all was auroral promise and progress with eighteenth-century Enlightenment bringing civilisation to a clodhopper society of irredeemable poverty and extreme backwardness, notably in politics and agriculture and, notoriously, religion.

Union meant money. Sir Walter Scott's Bailie Nicol Jarvie in *Rob Roy* defends the Union in terms of its economic advantage to Glasgow:

> Now, since St. Mungo caught herrings in the Clyde, what was ever like to gar us [cause us to] flourish like the sugar and tobacco trade? Will onybody tell me that, and grumble at a treaty that opened us a road west-awa' [westward] yonder?

The globalised prosperity of eighteenth-century Glasgow sugar, tobacco and cotton merchants made them exemplary illustrations of England's success in colonising Scotland by economics and pulling us into its swelling imperial refrain, though the novelist Alan Sharp has another angle:

> The Scots...made a very interesting deal with the English. A sane deal. It had a lot of problems to it but the alternative was to have these bastards come up here and kick your arse every 25 years.

However our merchants may have benefited, Union relegated Scotland to the shallow end of the hierarchy pool in terms of the class system that structured English, now British, social practices. Scots made money, or not, said their grim prayers, tholed the Clearances or lit out for Canada. Whoever, possibly wherever, they were, they were programmed to touch the forelock or curtsy – resignedly, derisively, or subserviently – facing Westminster, now their constitutional Mecca. Only some resisted the programming as vigorously as Lord Macdonald's tenants of the Braes on Skye fought the Scottish landowning aristocracy's abuse of its power.

James Anthony Froude, friend and biographer of Carlyle, travelled to South Africa in the 1870s to gather information and represent the views of the Secretary for the Colonies, Lord Carnarvon. Froude was an advocate for reconciliation between the Dutch states and the British colonies and for justice for the native peoples. Five years after his return he gave a lecture in Edinburgh in which he talked about the British authority's imprisonment of the Zulu chief, Cetewayo, for refusing to disband his army. Froude told his Edinburgh audience:

> A friend of mine lately visited Cetewayo in his prison at Cape Town, and asked him if he did not regret having disobeyed [the command]. Cetewayo replied that had he known all that would happen he would have given the same reply. A brave man might know that he would be beaten, but he would still fight, rather than submit like a coward. His people all felt as he did.
> I think you in Scotland ought to have some sympathy with Cetewayo and his Zulus.

Perhaps Froude was thinking of Cetewayo as Wallace, as we might think of both Wallace and Mandela. The imperial purposes of the kingdom were not served by respect for either the kraal or for the kailyard, so the urbanised kailyard became the Fourth World of east-end Glasgow's excluded and disadvantaged and the urbanised kraal became Sophiatown and Soweto. We'd used up our Wallace and Mandela would be otherwise engaged, but we did still have a spirit which slowly gathered momentum and brought us, at last, our own parliament, our own First Minister and our own laureate

First Poet. Eventually Cetewayo's people would achieve a similar success against much greater odds. What was this spirit?

There's no denying Scotland's collaboration in its own occlusion or the contributions made by opportunistic Scots to the building of empire. We affirmed our own, our native land – especially on Burns Nicht and Hogmanay – and trekked south; we capitulated to the BBC, Oxbridge and Standard English. What are our feelings today when we read *The Glasgow Herald* for Wednesday 9th May 1945, printed a few hours after the official cessation of hostilities with Germany? It reports VE celebrations in Moscow, salutes war efforts by the USA, Canada, New Zealand and South Africa, briefly mentions involvement by the C-in-C Scottish Command in surrender proceedings in Norway and allocates a short column to Scottish DFCs. Sixty thousand people cheer Mr Churchill giving the victory sign from the balcony of the Ministry of Health building in Whitehall. The King's 'Broadcast to Nation and Empire' begins with God, Empire and London:

> Today we give thanks to God for a great deliverance. Speaking from our Empire's oldest capital city, war-battered but never for one moment daunted or dismayed – speaking from London, I ask you to join with me in that act of thanksgiving.

About a sixth of page 4 announces that there will be a 'Scottish Festival of Thanksgiving' in Edinburgh's Usher Hall, and describes 'Glasgow's Crowded Scenes of Revelry' during which:

> A sailor of the Royal Netherlands Navy burlesqued Hitler from the top of the Duke of Wellington statue in Exchange Square. An admiring crowd applauded his buffoonery. It was equally responsive when the Dutchman, changing his mood from gay to serious, made a short speech in broken English, and thanked 'the Scots for the brave part they had played in the liberation of his country'.

That's the best recognition we get. Equal space on the page is taken by an advertisement by Lewis's department store for 'Feminine

Fantasies': 'an exceptionally lovely collection of Model Millinery, designed for June Weddings – Summer Garden Fetes – and all those important occasions on which you must look your best'. The hats are alps in emerald, tan or 'nigger' fur felt with swathes of ice blue or Sherwood green ostrich feathers and 'appliqued leaves in geranium red suede'. Just the headgear for a Gorbals girl wanting to look her best for the returning, war-weary man in her life. After Mr Churchill's official broadcast message the end of the war in Europe is sounded by the buglers of the Scots Guards. The rest is all London and Buckingham Palace.

Can this be a newspaper from Scotland's biggest city – even, as they used to call it, in their language, the second city of Empire, the Engine Room of the Commonwealth? Is this what you hope to read at the end of a war from which your husband, your father, your wife, your son or daughter or your lover may or may not come home to Tobermory, Leith or Peebles? Reading this, on the morning of 9th May 1945 wouldn't you have felt stung? Might you have asked, like Michael Moore, 'Dude, Where is My Country?' As The Proclaimers scolded us in 1988, on a national scale we were a split personality. We fought, when they asked us, we boasted then we cowered. We were 'Cap in Hand' and baffled God. We slept with the enemy. As Capercaille puts it, 'Our country was wearing the Emperor' s clothes'. Frederic Lindsay reminds us:

> In the building of the empire which replaced the one muddled away with the American War of Independence, the Scots had played a disproportionate share. A quick conversion to the Anglican Church got them into the Indian Civil Service; they were missionaries in Africa and the traders who followed them; they instigated war with China in defence of the opium trade and sent the profits home to Dumfriesshire.

Given the long incubation of parliamentary Union, the decisiveness of the Act and its long-term colonial effects it's reasonable to be surprised that assimilation didn't reduce Scotland to a barely distinguishable province of the London-dominated confederation. The paradox of Scotland since 1707 is that it never lost its distinctiveness; despite what the poet Sydney Goodsir

Smith calls 'the Union's faithless peace' it persisted in being a quasi-nation, a country on the cusp. The historian R. L. Mackie's *A Short History of Scotland* ends with the observation that 'after two and a half centuries of political union, and after perhaps ten centuries of southern influence, Scotland still preserves a national identity which may be difficult to define but is none the less real'.

In 'England Your England' George Orwell emphasises the importance of national identity: 'One cannot see the modern world as it is unless one recognises the overwhelming strength of patriotism, national loyalty'. But how did we preserve an identity to be loyal to? Was it because of our languages, or our sense of history? Was it our inexplicable genius for innovation in science, engineering, medicine and whisky galore? ('Your whisky has made you original', wrote Byron to James Hogg.) Was it Burns and Scott, Stevenson and Barrie, Rennie Mackintosh and Harry Lauder? Was it Tammy Troot and the McFlannels, Oor Wullie and Wee MacGreegor, Sean Connery, Taggart and Billy Connolly? Was it our landscapes and climate – forces not to be underestimated: Orwell went to Jura to clear his mind of leftist sanctimony and Tory inertia before writing *1984*. Or was it our religions which bound us in a profound sense that we are incontrovertibly different from the people whose kings, queens and governments had hammered us, seduced us, condescended to us and exploited our land, our labour and our oil? Was it our traditions? But what *are* our traditions?

One theme on which Scottish literary history offers a series of variations is the folk, the lot of common people. Maybe this is a clue to the spirit we're struggling to define. A strong sense of underlying equality is part of the idiom. Expressed as 'the sons of Adam', the idea of a common humanity beyond hierarchical accident or political manoeuvring is mythologically fanciful, but the Scottish expression that we are all 'Jock Tamson's bairns' asserts equality in terms of an imaginable family. The equalising reality of a common end is the basis of Charles Murray's poem, 'A Green Yule':

> Dibble them doon, the laird, the loon,   *Plant/boy*
> King an' the cadgin caird,   *hawking tinker*
> The lady fine beside the queyn,   *girl*
> A' in the same kirkyaird.

The warst, the best, they a' get rest;
Ane 'neath a headstane braw,
Wi' deep-cut text; while ower the next
The wavin' grass is a'.

Mighty o' name, unknown to fame,
Slippit aneth the sod;
Greatest an' least alike face east,
Waitin' the trump o' God.

As one of Jock Tamson's bairns, Mary Brodie tells Walter Leslie in Robert Louis Stevenson and W. E. Henley's play, *Deacon Brodie*, 'It is for every man to concern himself in the common weal', and there's a main vein of humane sympathy that comes up through Sir David Lyndsay's John the Commonweill in *Ane Pleasant Satyre of the Three Estaitis* to the egalitarian strain especially evident towards the end of the eighteenth century even if it doesn't always rise to the measure of what Hugh MacDiarmid calls 'the fearless radical spirit of the true Scotland'. The Presbyterian ideal of the Scottish Reformation was powered by a democratic impulse even if the ideal was sometimes obscured by less attractive items on the political agenda. Scottish writers were precociously in advance of political radicals in works which refrain on the common good and the worth of the individual. The Ulsterman, Francis Hutcheson, a Scot by adoption through his seventeen-year tenure of the chair of moral philosophy at Glasgow University, anticipated by some four decades Jeremy Bentham's equation of moral right with 'the greatest happiness of the greatest number'. The democratic refrain can be heard in David Hume, Adam Smith and Henry Mackenzie and in the poetry of Ramsay, Fergusson and Burns. It can be heard in Robert Louis Stevenson's repudiation of Edinburgh New Town gentility and contempt for the bourgeoisie. It is most forthrightly expressed in political terms by Hugh MacDiarmid who says in his autobiographical memoir *Lucky Poet*:

The working-class policy ought to be to break up the Empire to avert war and enable the workers to triumph in every country and colony. Scottish separation is part of the process of England's Imperial disintegration and is a help towards the ultimate triumph of the workers of the world.

An argument in favour of a democratic or egalitarian line in Scottish literature might seem balked by the massive presence of Sir Walter Scott, or compelled to look in him for the exception that could prove the rule. Scott is, certainly, an ambiguous figure like James Hogg, John Galt, Thomas Carlyle and John Davidson. All were politically conservative men. Scott was a Tory and a Unionist. Hogg allied himself with writers associated with the aggressively Conservative *Blackwood's Magazine*. Galt attacked 'the heresies of liberty and equality'. The arch-dominie Carlyle vilified reformists, feared anarchy as much as Matthew Arnold did, and denounced liberal views of human rights (particularly for Negroes in *Shooting Niagara: and After?*) 'Democracy', he writes in *Chartism*, 'is, by the nature of it, a self-cancelling business; and gives in the long-run a net result of *zero*'. Similarly, John Davidson, that proud, tragic man, denounces socialism in the Epilogue to his play, *Mammon and His Message*: 'Socialism is the decadence of Feudalism; that is to say, it is less than nothing. At its very utmost it is only a bad smell; rejoicing in itself very much at present as bad smells are wont to do'.

But there was another side to each of these ambiguously constituted writers. Scott's aristocratic predilections are offset by his interest in the Scottish oral tradition and by the respect he feels for the independence of ordinary Scottish folk. Hogg's suspicion of reformism is balanced by sympathy for the common people terrorised by sado-masochistic theology. Galt's novels attest his unsentimental love for the small Scottish town, its burghers and peasants. If men could never be equal for the hero-worshipping Carlyle his mistrust of the masses coexists with concern for the plight of the common people. Socialism may be a bad smell to John Davidson but there is no mistaking his humanitarian anger about the life to which his Cockney thirty-bob-a-week clerk is condemned, stoically 'a-scheming how to count ten bob a pound':

> It's a naked child against a hungry wolf;
> It's playing bowls upon a splitting wreck;

It's walking on a string across a gulf
With millstones fore-and-aft about your neck;
But the thing is daily done by many and many a one;
And we fall, face forward, fighting, on the deck.

Even Davidson's Nietzschean *Mammon and his Message* proposes
a world:

Where men are great and conscious of their greatness –
The very meanest intimately sure
That he himself is the whole universe
Become intelligent and capable.

We can move on through Scottish writers noticing Margaret
Oliphant's impatience with pretension in her analyses of
provincial life in both England and Scotland and her illumination
of the inequitous condition of women; James (B. V.) Thomson's
Dantesque (and Eliotesque) vision of the capitalist city as an
alienating dystopia in *The City of Dreadful Night*; George
MacDonald's compassion for the sufferings of the poor, his concern
'for the good of the community' in *Phantastes* and his abhorrence
of the evil city of Bulika's perversions of true community in *Lilith*;
and J. M. Barrie's definition of the oldest Scottish university in
Courage, his Rectorial Address to the students of St Andrews in
1922:

Mighty are the Universities of Scotland, and they will
prevail. But even in your highest exultations never
forget that they are not four, but five. The greatest of
them is the poor, proud homes you come out of, which
said so long ago: 'There shall be education in this
land'. She, not St Andrews, is the oldest University in
Scotland, and all the others are her whelps.

Other symptoms of the democratic strain include the socialism of
Lewis Grassic Gibbon in a 'world rolling fast to a hell of riches';
'the dispensation of the poor' in the mind of Sorley MacLean and
his redefinition of Calvary in terms of 'a foul-smelling backland in
Glasgow' and 'a room in Edinburgh,/a room of poverty and pain';

Bill Bryden's sympathy for a moderate shop-steward in his 'Red Clydeside' play, *Willie Rough* ; the 7:84 Theatre Company's attack on capitalist exploitation of Scotland in John McGrath's *The Cheviot, the Stag and the Black, Black Oil* ; the 'copies of the *Daily Worker*...dove of peace...poster of Paul Robeson' which a pregnant woman thinks she had better hide when a social worker calls to check her suitability for a housing waiting list in Jackie Kay's poem, 'Chapter 3: The Waiting Lists'. A democratic manifesto is implicit in the Scots of Robert Garioch and in Tom Leonard and James Kelman's use of Glasgow *patois* to cut through to the real lives of ordinary people and in doing so to protest, as Gaelic could never quite do, against the bending of a country's mind by 'a police régime of the signifier', to co-opt a phrase of Edward Said's, that is, by the undemocratic authority of a language whose artificial and ossifying 'correctness' derives from the bullying power of a remote parliament and a chimerical throne.

In the poem called 'Good Style' Leonard puns on the title phrase in its Scottish usage for 'vigorously or with flair' and its implication of poetic decorum. Setting out a poem in a phonetic rendering of the language of the people can make it difficult for the outsider. Leonard turns this into a jocoserious gesture of defiance towards imagined objections by supercilious guardians of 'received' or 'standard' English. Ridicule can knock down what anger leaves standing:

> helluva hard tay read theez init
> stull
> if yi canny unnirston thim jiss clear aff then
> gawn
> get tay fuck ootma road
> ahmaz goodiz thi lota yiz so ah um
> ah no whit ahm dayn
> tellnyi
> jiss try enny a yir fly patir wi me
> stick thi bootnyi good style
> so ah wull
>
> *[hell of a hard to read these isn't it*
> *still*
> *if you can't understand them*

just clear off then
go on
get to fuck out of my road
I'm as good as the lot of you so I am
I know what I'm doing
telling you
just try any of your fly patter with me
stick the boot in you good style
so I will]

In case the *patois* has made his point inaccessible to significant readers, Leonard dreams accommodatingly in English:

Scotland has become an independent socialist republic.
At last.

Eh?
You pinch yourself.
Jesus Christ. You've slept in again.

It's okay to wake up now, Tom. Perhaps, with your help, we've found our spirit. Kailyard and kraal – they're on the move.

Globalised into residence on the antipodal edge of the world, you pick up *The New Zealand Herald* on 3rd July 1999 and read this:

Scotland makes royal faces burn

The royal family was subjected to an embarrassing moment during the opening of Scotland's new Parliament, enduring an emotional rendition of a song that mocks royalty.

As the Queen, the Duke of Edinburgh and Prince Charles sat stony-faced in front of the 129-member body, Scottish folk singer Sheena Wellington performed...Robert Burns's socialist anthem, 'A Man's A Man for A' That'.

The song, which marked the highlight of the opening ceremony and was chosen by the organisers instead of Britain's national anthem, 'God Save the Queen', hails the nobility of honest poverty and pokes fun at the titles and trappings of nobility.

One verse goes:

Ye see yon birkie, ca'd a lord,
  Wha struts, and stares, an a' that,
Though hundreds worship at his word,
  He's but a coof for a' that.

Another verse says that 'men of independent minds look and laugh' at the titles of lords, princes and knights.

To members of Britain's nobility, the song was a slap in the face to the royal family.

'By choosing this song and rejecting the national anthem, they are flaunting a sort of separatism in a Parliament which is supposed to preserve the United Kingdom', the Earl of Lauderdale said before the celebration.

In an emotional twist, all 129 new members of the Scottish Parliament loudly joined in for the last verse, which proclaims that a day will come when 'over all the earth' men will become brothers.

Donald Dewar, Scotland's First Minister, added in an ensuing speech: 'At the heart of the song is a very Scottish conviction that honesty and simple dignity are priceless virtues, not imparted by rank or birth or privilege but part of the soul'.

Was this kilted, *Brigadoon* sentimentality or an expression of our true religion, our cultural spirit, the instinctive credo pushing through the liars, murderers and traitors that made what Norman MacCaig called our 'filthy history'? Was this MacDiarmid's 'radical spirit' of the true Scotland, which has burned through English *hauteur*, clan faction, Calvinism and Jacobitism, economic depression, political bickering, complacent paranoia and cultural intimidation to bring us to this quasi-resuscitated nation? Is this now the point from which, remembering Orwell, we may begin anew to construct a national identity to be loyal to? There's a lot of work to be done: the composer James Macmillan read about a Celtic fan slaughtered in a Glasgow street:

As the knives went in I wondered if he called for his mum, his gran, his girlfriend. Did his eyes grow black with terror, despair, resignation? Were his tormentors' faces radiant and engorged with an expression I had seen before, 33 years ago in Cumnock.

Devolved, let us be robust enough to eradicate this lethal squalor from our filthy history and to give and take globalisation. Let's make the village of Lonmay the Graceland of the North. Let's fill our colleges with Russian students. Will we be confident enough to prevent the rise of the kind of xenophobic 'little Scotland' mentality James Macmillan fears?

We've been working on it. Edwin Morgan has proved that an artist can be both resolutely Scottish and internationalist – if not interplanetary – in outlook and appetite. There's not much complacency around when Peter Mullan helps Ken Loach to tell it as it grimly is in *My Name Is Joe*. Maybe we should be grateful that Sergio Leone never made *Once Upon a Time in Glasgow*. Capercaillie's music, rooted in the songs of our earth, moves outward, fusing traditional lilts with pop idioms and, in *Beautiful Wasteland*, North African chant. The Cauld Blast Orchestra recorded what should have been a hit called 'Tango for a Drowning Man'. Bill Forsyth's lyrically anti-urban *Local Hero* internationalises the lone red phone box and proves that a Texas oilman is no match for a Scottish village, but also pokes fun at the greed simmering beneath the Scots pictorial surfaces. Alexander McCall Smith, Professor of medical law at Edinburgh University, gives us crime without gloom via Mma Ramotswe, Botswana's premier (and only) lady detective. In Director Lone Scherfig's film, *Wilbur Wants to Kill Himself*, the multiple tones of Glasgow *angst* are modulated by a Dane. Globalisation may be a dirty word in many people's minds, and with good cause, but globalising energies in the arts are encouraging us to devolve beyond our kailyards towards possession of maturer Scottish selves.

29. Samuel Beckett: 'No lack of void'

'Nothing is funnier than unhappiness', says Nell to Nagg in *Endgame*. Maybe she knew the old joke about a dyslexic, agnostic insomniac who lay awake all night wondering if there was a dog. A risible, pathetic case with the mixture of comic absurdity, verbal slapstick and pain in it that we find in Samuel Beckett. Of course we can explain such a case in terms of psychological disorder, and attempts are sometimes made to explain — even to explain away — Beckett's desperations by reference to the irrepressible boil he suffered on the back of his neck as a young man and the illnesses which prompted him to advise a doctor that 'All life is a disease'. He referred to Ireland as 'the land of my unsuccessful abortion' and called his own books his 'miseries'.

The philosophy of Schopenhauer confirmed his own view that most people live — not unlike Pozzo in Act I of *Waiting for Godot* — by a futile exercise of will in a brutish world of accident and decay. The seventeenth-century Flemish philosopher, Arnold Geulincx, reinforced Schopenhauer by detaching will from act: we can't claim to control even what our minds do, let alone our bodies, those 'ungainly, unlovely, and unintelligent instruments'. We are naked spectators of a psychophysical machine — our combination of mind and body and by extension the universe — which capriciously functions or malfunctions without reference to our wishes. Finding ourselves in a forest, like Beckett's character, Molloy, and aware of our Western cultural traditions we might reasonably expect to hear the celebrated forest murmurs. Nothing of the kind in the world according to Beckett. No Wagnerian forest murmurs, no hunting horn, but from time to time, at intervals, a gong.

It has been suggested that a key to Beckett's work is to be found in an incident that occurred in Paris in 1938 when he was stabbed by a French tramp. The knife perforated one of his lungs and narrowly missed his heart. When he asked the tramp why he had attacked him he was told 'I don't know, sir'. If this example of the random perils of life confirmed Beckett's vision, it did not initiate it. His novel, *Murphy*, published the same year, portrays a destitute Irishman, living in London, who daydreams his time away in a rocking chair until a gas plant explodes and shreds him.

His instructions for disposal of his remains require his ashes to be flushed down the lavatory of Dublin's Abbey Theatre. Instead they're thrown in anger in a pub by the person entrusted with them and, subsequent to their distribution over the pub floor, 'swept away with the sand, the beer, the butts, the glass, the matches, the spits, the vomit'. It has also been suggested that another clue to Beckett's view of life, and in particular to *Waiting for Godot*, is to be found in his experience of the second World War. When Paris was invaded by the Nazis Beckett and his future wife fled to the south of France, hiding by day, sleeping in haystacks and walking at night. This harrowing effort, especially the footsore talk along the way, may be behind the sense of futile wandering implicit in a road that goes nowhere in the play.

In *The Unnamable* — last in the great trilogy of novels that includes *Molloy* and *Malone Dies* — the narrator tries to describe life in terms of subverbal sounds, 'heart-rending cries' and 'inarticulate murmurs'. 'I'll practise', he says, and offers 'chuck chuck, ow, ha, pa...nyum, hoo, plop, psss, nothing but emotion, bing, bang, that's blows, ugh, pooh, what else, oooh, aah, that's love, enough, it's tiring, hee hee...in the end, it's the end, the ending end, it's the silence, a few gurgles on the silence, the real silence'. Inarticulate sounds 'to be improvised, as I groan along' take life to a *reductio ad absurdum* even more dismal than the composite images of *Waiting for Godot* or *Endgame*. Life is atomised to cries and murmurs of relish, excretion, urination, violence and sex, which end in silence. 'Birth and copulation and death' as T. S. Eliot's Sweeney puts it in *Sweeney Agonistes*, 'That's all, that's all, that's all, that's all', to which Doris retorts, 'I'd be bored'. This is the human situation, it seems, on what Pozzo calls 'this bitch of an earth'.

It's a fact of our experience of Beckett — certainly of the experience of many who have read his novels and seen his plays — that boils, anal cysts and the other illnesses his flesh was heir to do not enable us to dispose of his vision as the ravings of a physically afflicted madman. No more does a biographical account of Jonathan Swift's physical and mental symptoms satisfactorily account for his alleged misanthropy or the capacity of his Lilliputians, Brobdignagians and Houyhnhnms to command and vex our imaginations. Both Swift and Beckett present us with visions of extraordinary power and originality in the medium of words artistically deployed. Our business is with the words, the art, and the vision.

Beckett wrote *Waiting for Godot* during the winter of 1948-9 as a diversion from composing his trilogy of novels. The final utterance of the novels — the closing words of *The Unnamable* — repeats the point he makes as the curtain falls at the end of each symmetrical Act of *Waiting for Godot*:

ESTRAGON: Well, shall we go?
VLADIMIR: Yes, let's go.
[*They do not move.*]
(Act I)

VLADIMIR: Well? Shall we go?
ESTRAGON: Yes, let's go.
[*They do not move.*]
(Act II)

Human existence has been shown to be painful and futile. Godot would seem to be nothing but a name for the fact that life, which goes on pointlessly, misinterprets itself as waiting for something. The tramps nevertheless appear unable to quit life by suicide or the place where they're waiting by simply walking away from it. They can't go on, but they go on. So, too, tormented by uncertainty and despair the voice of *The Unnamable* ends:

> I don't know, perhaps it's a dream, all a dream, that would surprise me, I'll wake, in the silence, and never sleep again, it will be I, or dream, dream again, dream of a silence, a dream silence, full of murmurs, I don't know, that's all words, never wake, all words, there's nothing else, you must go on, that's all I know, they're going to stop, I know that well, I can feel it, they're going to abandon me, it will be the silence, for a moment, a good few moments, or it will be mine, the lasting one, that didn't last, that still lasts, it will be I, you must go on, I can't go on, you must go on, I'll go on, you must say words, as long as there are any, until

they find me, until they say me, strange pain, strange sin, you must go on, perhaps it's done already, perhaps they have said me already, perhaps they have carried me to the threshold of my story, before the door that opens on my story, that would surprise me, if it opens, it will be I, it will be the silence, where I am, I don't know, I'll never know, in the silence you don't know, you must go on, I can't go on, I'll go on.

Whatever the pain and the futility, consciousness cannot help but 'go on', just as the two tramps cannot leave either life or the waiting place by the enigmatic tree. Words keep the Unnamable going; Vladimir and Estragon decide 'Don't let's do anything. It's safer'. True nihilism is impossible, even in a hopeless situation where 'Nothing happens, nobody comes, nobody goes, it's awful!' This points to Beckett's recurrent theme, the subject he proposed to the art historian, Georges Duthuit, as the proper business of the contemporary writer:

> The expression that there is nothing to express, nothing with which to express, nothing from which to express, no power to express, no desire to express, together with the obligation to express.

After *Waiting for Godot* and the novel trilogy, Beckett wrote *Endgame*, *Krapp's Last Tape* and *Happy Days*. Thereafter he produced fewer, shorter and bleaker works. The three characters buried in funeral urns in *Play* talk not to each other but to themselves or to the light which shines on their faces, representing anguished consciousness. After the final blackout the entire play is exactly repeated. The point seems to be that an eternity of hell consists not of some dire, continuous apprehension of the universe but of an endless preoccupation with earthly trivia. In *Come and Go* the act of dramatic compression is taken even further. Three women obscured by full-length coats and hats that hide their faces sit facing us on an invisible bench. Each in turn departs and while she is away the remaining pair whisper to each other about some disaster about to befall her. Like *Waiting for Godot* the play is symmetrical in its design and mathematically precise in its permutations, presenting a chilling image of the individual's entrapment in an inescapable doom she can't see. Despite the darkening of his own vision, Beckett never quite lapsed into the ultimate despair of artistic silence, though he came close in *Breath* which lasts for 30 seconds, employs no actors, no dialogue, and specifies 'faint light on a stage littered with miscellaneous rubbish'. In *Not I* a pinpoint of light picks out the Mouth whose monologue proceeds in broken phrases for the fifteen minutes of the play. A dim figure called the Auditor says nothing but raises his or her arms 'in a gesture of silent compassion'. Beckett's last work, *Stirrings Still*, a prose piece of nearly 2,000 words was published in March 1989 in a limited edition of 200 copies. A few months later he entered the real silence: he died on 22 December 1989. The world was told four days later, after his funeral.

Who or what is the Godot for whom Vladimir and Estragon are waiting? Geulincx's philosophy proposes a Deity. Alan Schneider, director of the first American production of the play, reports:

> I plied [Beckett] with all my studiously-arrived-at questions...and he tried to answer as directly and honestly as he could. The first one was 'Who or what does Godot mean?' and the answer was immediately forthcoming: 'If I knew, I would have said so in the play'.

There has been much conjecture about the name Godot. Beckett told his first producer, Roger Blin, that it was suggested to him by '*godillots*' and '*godasses*', respectively French colloquial and military slang words for boots. Waiting for God, perhaps, comes to the same level of significance as waiting for boots — boots that fit, we might add, and don't smell. It has also been noticed that there is a character called Godeau in a play by Balzac. The play is Balzac's *Le Faiseur* ('The Fixer') more commonly known as *Mercadet*. Mercadet is a speculator who blames his financial embarrassment on his former partner Godeau who, years ago, vanished with their jointly owned capital: '*Je porte le poids du crime de Godeau!*' ('I bear the burden of the crime of Godeau!'). Mercadet repeatedly encourages his creditors to believe that Godeau will reappear with the embezzled funds. A false Godeau turns up and is exposed, to

Mercadet's further discomfiture, but at the end of the play the real Godeau is announced: he has returned from India with a fortune. The play ends with Mercadet saying, '*Allons voir Godeau!*' The parallels would seem to be too striking for coincidence, although Beckett insisted that he did not read Balzac's play. In both plays the arrival of Godeau/Godot is the event that will save the situation. Yet whether Godot signifies a supernatural agency or represents an influential human being, his nature is commonly felt to be of minor importance. The play seems not to be about Godot but about waiting.

Nevertheless, there is something disingenuous about Beckett's answer to Alan Schneider's question. If the play is essentially about human life as a rite of passage across what Vladimir Nabokov calls 'the crack of light between two eternities of darkness', Beckett's version of the rite being a brief, anguished suspension between birth and death, it would be ridiculous to deny the association of the title-word 'Godot' with the word 'God' or to suppose that because Beckett chose to write in French he lost his awareness of the resonance of English words. It's much more likely that he has presented us with a deliberate conundrum. The full title of the play unavoidably engages with the post-Nietzschean problem of the death of God. The play retains its contemporaneity: six decades after it first astounded audiences world-wide, we can see, in happy-clappy fundamentalist evangelism and cult cultures as well as the established churches, that people are still trying to hold on to God, or looking for a substitute. The success of such films as Steven Spielberg's *Close Encounters of the Third Kind* and *E.T.* depends on an atavistic yearning for something godlike from beyond the stars, a longing powerful enough to dispose of any requirement that the supreme being need be anything much to look at. God as a bug-eyed caterpillar who can make a bicycle fly will do fine it that's the best offer going. In any case, a cute God sorts better with the commercial and psychological disposition of the times than the doubtful beneficence of a heavenly Father with, as they say these days, a 'raft' of prohibitions. Outside the realms of Hollywood celebrity, sporting fanaticisms or politics, however, God seems to be dead all right, harried to vanishing point by Shelley and his friend Thomas Jefferson Hogg in *The Necessity of Atheism*, zapped from behind by Darwin and Huxley, vaporised by Freud, savaged by Marx and Lenin, rumbled by relativity, bound and gagged by logical positivism, and deep-sixed not only by Nietzsche but repeatedly by economics or, as God would have put it, Mammon. Neither the fundamentalist frenzies of American holy-rolling nor the mumbo-jumbo of a tarnished Vatican nor the militancies of anti-Rushdie Islam hold out much prospect of an agreeable second coming. It would be a rough beast indeed, as we might think and Yeats imagined, that would slouch towards Bethlehem to be born of our *zeitgeist*.

Yet the sense of loss persists. However austere he was in his time, however prohibitive, however psychologically damaging and divisive, he is still included in many toasts to absent friends. In the process of being westernised Salman Rushdie lost his Muslim faith. 'When I was young I was religious in quite an unthinking way', he says. 'Now I'm not, but I am conscious of a space where God was'. 'Where does our yearning come from', wondered the distinguished German choreographer, Pina Bausch, and yearning is an implicit fuse of feeling in Becket's 'miseries', binding together his spiritual desperadoes, compelled to 'go on' when they can't. 'The stars', says Robert Penn Warren, 'are only a backdrop for/ the human condition', but his stargazing brings an admission which, a little wryly, reneges against so naturalistic an astronomy:

> The stars
> Love me. I love them. I wish they
> Loved God, too. I truly wish that.

The controversial American scientist Edward Fredkin has proposed a theory that the universe is formed by bits of information, that atoms, electrons and quarks consist of binary units of information like those in a computer. The question remains: what sort of information? While disclaiming religious belief, Fredkin emerges from his computer analogy tentatively admitting, 'it seems likely to me that this particular universe we have is as consequence of something I would call intelligence'. We await developments, sceptically if hoping for the best, while acknowledging the continuing relevance of Beckett's most famous play.

Furthermore, the attributes of Beckett's Godot clearly suggest a familiar stereotype of God, and therefore particularise the general condition of waiting (and the condition of dependence implicit in waiting) into the specific theme of waiting for some sort of religious illumination or waiting for God. The French essayist and thinker Simone Weil's celebrated work *L'Attente de Dieu* was published posthumously in 1949, three years before Beckett wrote his play in French. I emphasise that I'm not suggesting this is the only sort of waiting the play considers, but that it is one sort and that Beckett refers to both the general condition of waiting for meaning and to the specific posture of waiting for God. If we extract the parenthetical verbiage from Lucky's speech in Act One we are left with this:

> Given the existence...of a personal God...with white beard...who...loves us dearly with some exceptions... and suffers...with those who...are plunged in torment...

Vladimir and Estragon, we may say, are plunged in torment, waiting to find out whether this personal God loves them or whether they are among the exceptions. That the idea of Godot includes the idea of God seems obvious: at the end of Act Two the Boy reminds us of Lucky's image of 'a personal God with white beard' when he tells Vladimir that he *thinks* that Godot's beard is white. In other words there may or may not be a personal God like the stereotype of Lucky's 'Given'. Suffering, assailed by signs we wilfully mistake for wonders, we whistle in the dark and wait to see.

While we wait there is nothing to be done. As Estragon says, 'There's no lack of void'. It's a situation of pain and paralysis in which consciousness uses language to try to fill the void and to protect itself from the chaos of panic. The continuous distress of waiting is reinforced by Estragon's beatings, Vladimir's prostate, Lucky's servitude, and the loss of faculty suffered by both Pozzo and Lucky in Act Two. There's desperation in the music-hall routines by which the tramps try to alleviate their anguish. 'This is becoming really insignificant', Vladimir says in Act One, commenting on the play — which guarantees a laugh — as well as life itself. In Act Two the two tramps believe themselves surrounded by enemies, possibly those who give Estragon his regular nightly beatings. Vladimir urges Estragon to run for cover:

[*He takes ESTRAGON by the arm and drags him towards the front. Gesture towards front*]. There! Not a soul in sight! Off you go. Quick! [*He pushes ESTRAGON towards auditorium. ESTRAGON recoils in horror.*] You won't. [*He contemplates auditorium.*] Well, I can understand that.

When Vladimir contemplates the auditorium he looks at us. As we watch the play we become identified with the enemy, with the inimical features of life in a comic moment that recalls Jean Paul Sartre's famous apothegm, 'Hell is other people'. An aspect of Beckett's hell is its instability, the treacherous flux of time itself which undermines the recognition and identities of other people. The Boy who acts as Godot's messenger fails to recognise Didi and Gogo from day to day. When Pozzo and Lucky first appear neither Vladimir nor Estragon seems to recognise them, and Estragon even thinks Pozzo is Godot. After they have gone Vladimir remarks that they have changed since their last appearance; Estragon says he didn't know them:

VLADIMIR:	Yes you do know them.
ESTRAGON:	No I don't know them.
VLADIMIR:	We know them, I tell you. You forget everything.
	[*Pause. To himself*]. Unless they're not the same...
ESTRAGON:	Why didn't they recognise us then?
VLADIMIR:	That means nothing. I too pretended not to recognise them. And then nobody ever recognises us.

In this waiting world of physical affliction, hostility, pathetic dependencies, crossed purposes and change the only certainty is that birth and death are divided by a brief interval of misery. In Act Two Pozzo provides the imagery first:

They give birth astride of a grave, the light gleams an instant, then it's night once more.

and, a few lines later, Vladimir develops the idea:

Astride of a grave and a difficult birth. Down in the
hole, lingeringly, the grave-digger puts on the forceps.
We have time to grow old. The air is full of our cries.

Vladimir's adoption of Pozzo's image here draws our attention to
the relations between the four principal characters who are less
characters than they are complementary elements of meaning,
a set of emblematic functions which *in toto* express the human
condition. Vladimir, who stinks from his mouth, appears to
represent the intellect; Estragon, who stinks from his feet seems
more physical. They are paralleled by Lucky whose hat, tirade of
words, and capacity to think represent intellect and Pozzo who
is clearly a brute. Each member of either pair is dependent on
the other — the area of possible affection or one of its twisted
variations — and each pair is dependent on the other for diversion,
assistance, audience or the fulfilment of sado-masochistic appetite.

When Lucky and Pozzo fall down in Act Two and lie in a helpless
heap among their scattered baggage, Vladimir says:

VLADIMIR: We wait. We are bored.
(*He throws up his hand.*) No, don't protest, we are bored
                                   to death, there's no denying
                                   it. Good. A diversion comes
                                   along and what do we do? We
                                   let it go to waste. Come, let's get
                                   to work!
(*He advances towards the heap, stops in his stride.*) In
                                   an instant all will vanish and
                                   we'll be alone once more,
                                   in the midst of nothingness!

The realisation that Pozzo and Lucky's appearance is not being
fully exploited as a diversion, a means of filling the void by giving
the illusion of significant action, in what frustrates Vladimir.
Beckett's characters typically seize on an elaborate routine or
some madly pedantic account of a mechanical or mental operation
to push back the truth of the void by the illusion of significance.
In *Molloy*, for example, the narrator deflects his mind from his
wretched circumstances like this:

I took advantage of being at the seaside to lay in a store of sucking stones. They were pebbles but I call them stones. Yes, on this occasion I laid in a considerable store. I distributed them equally among my four pockets, and sucked them turn and turn about. This raised a problem which I first solved in the following way. I had say sixteen stones, four in each of my four pockets these being the two pockets of my trousers and the two pockets of my greatcoat. Taking a stone from the right pocket of my greatcoat, and putting it in my mouth, I replaced it in the right pocket of my greatcoat by a stone from the right pocket of my trousers, which I replaced by a stone from the left pocket of my trousers, which I replaced by a stone from the left pocket of my greatcoat, which I replaced by the stone which was in my mouth, as soon as I had finished sucking it. Thus there were still four stones in each of my four pockets, but not quite the same stones. And when the desire to suck took hold of me again, I drew again on the right pocket of my greatcoat, certain of not taking the same stone as the last time. And while I sucked it I rearranged the other stones in the way I have just described. And so on. But this solution did not satisfy me fully. For it did not escape me that, by an extraordinary hazard, the four stones circulating thus might always be the same four stones. In which case, far from sucking the sixteen stones turn and turn about, I was really only sucking four, always the same, turn and turn about. But I shuffled them well in my pockets, before I began to suck, and again, while I sucked, before transferring them, in the hope of obtaining a more general circulation of the stones from pocket to pocket. But this was only a makeshift that could not long content a man like me.

The equivalent of Molloy's sucking stones in *Waiting for Godot* is Vladimir and Estragon's talk, their clinging to language. The whole of Beckett's work can be seen as a dialogue between speech and silence, consciousness and blankness. It's all right, just, when nothing happens, what is terrifying is that *Nothing* may happen. The tension between speech and silence is the key to the effective production of a Beckett play (the feature of Beckett's work most obviously emulated by Harold Pinter). 403 stage instructions to *pause* punctuate the single act of *Endgame*. The text of *Not I* is interspersed with dots. Billie Whitelaw, who first played the character of Mouth, says that once, during a rehearsal, Beckett told her that in one place she had paused for two dots instead of three. *Waiting for Godot*, too, is full of pauses and silences that make us aware of Vladimir and Estragon's struggle to keep Nothing at bay with language. Instead of parting, or of Vladimir's killing Estragon, the two resolve to talk, and we should be given their talk in a theatrical style which offers each utterance as an arrow aimed at silence, with a feeling of impending hysteria when the talk seems to be drying up and with a sense that the effort to keep the words going is almost, but never quite, too much:

ESTRAGON:	In the meantime let us try and converse calmly, since we are incapable of keeping silent.
VLADIMIR:	You're right, we're inexhaustible.
ESTRAGON:	It's so we won't think.
VLADIMIR:	We have that excuse.
ESTRAGON:	It's so we won't hear.
VLADIMIR:	We have our reasons.
ESTRAGON:	All the dead voices.
VLADIMIR:	They make a noise like wings.
ESTRAGON:	Like leaves.
VLADIMIR:	Like sand.
ESTRAGON:	Like leaves.
[*Silence.*]	

An inveterate pessimist, Beckett refused to appear to collect his 1969 Nobel Prize in literature, having, we are told, lobbied the Swedish Academy not to give him the award. The Nobel Prize committee thought he had 'transmuted the destitution of modern man into his exaltation'. Presumably the committee intended something to do with the exaltation of spirit art can bring from the most appalling human possibilities, the kind of exaltation we feel at the end of *King Lear*. His heroism must surely exalt us, that courage of imagination and prowess of word which enabled him to explore the human condition in its utmost reaches of anguish and to demonstrate, against the lure of nullity, the persistence of consciousness, stirrings still.

30. Keeping it Crisp

Though attributed to Bernard Shaw, the observation that Britain and America are two countries separated by a common language doesn't appear in his published works. Of course we all know about tomato and 'tom-ate-o', lift and elevator, biscuit and cookie, snag and glitch and all those grating spelling mistakes like 'program' and 'color'. Notwithstanding the merry barbs of Oscar Wilde, in humour the chief difference between Britain and America is America's flair for the sharp, pithy saying, the wisecrack. Mark Twain is the pastmaster with treasures like, 'Soap and education are not as sudden as a massacre, but they are more deadly in the long run'; 'Cauliflower is nothing but cabbage with a college education'; 'A classic is something that everybody wants to have read and nobody wants to read'; 'It is by the goodness of God that we have in our country three unspeakably precious things: freedom of speech, freedom of conscience, and the prudence never to practise either'.

Twain was at his most American when he made his visit to the Holy Land as, in his own phrase, 'An Innocent Abroad'. Arriving at the Sea of Galilee he wished to take the standard tourist's boat trip. Offered a place in the boat for an exorbitant fare, perhaps he thought up his own apothegm, 'Guides cannot master the subtleties of the American joke', before declining the offer with the remark, 'No wonder Jesus walked'. Cheeky and irreverent, but entirely calculated, unlike the inadvertently comic moment supplied by Lady Bird Johnson on the tragic occasion of President Kennedy's assassination in Dallas. 'Oh no!' came Lady Bird's horrified *cri de coeur*, 'Not in Texas!' There's a similar moment in another tragedy. In Macbeth Act II, Scene iii MacDuff has just discovered the murdered King Duncan and rushes on stage with the news:

> O horror, horror, horror! Tongue nor heart
> Cannot conceive nor name thee...
> Our royal master's murdered!

To which Lady Macbeth, ever the fastidious hostess, responds with
> Woe, alas!
> What, in our house?

Poor Lady Macbeth: upwardly mobile she may be but gone for ever her chances of Hostess of the Year or the Good Housekeeping Seal of Approval.

The American humourist, S. J. Perelman, entitles one of his books, *Keep it Crisp*; when they do, Americans are at their funniest and most characteristic. James Thurber veered towards the whimsical, but could be crisp when he liked: 'You wait here and I'll bring the etchings down'; 'Early to rise and early to bed makes a male healthy and wealthy and dead'. There's the black comedian, Dick Gregory, who was once asked if he'd been to Mississippi. 'Mississippi?' he said, 'Yeah, I've been to Mississippi. I spent twenty years there one night'. There's the incomparable Groucho Marx, who always kept it crisp in his crackling machine-gun-fire delivery. For example:

I've worked myself up from nothing to a state of extreme poverty.

A child of five would understand this. Send somebody to fetch a child of five.

I don't have a photograph, but you can have my footprints. They're upstairs in my socks.

I never forget a face, but I'll make an exception in your case.

No, Groucho is not my real name. I'm breaking it in for a friend.

There's the novelist Peter De Vries who develops the wisecrack into a sort of dark motto that might pop out of a satanic Christmas cracker:

Our church is, I believe, the first split-level church in America. It has five rooms and two baths downstairs... There is a small worship area at one end.

It is the final proof of God's omnipotence that he need not exist in order to save us.

I think I can say my childhood was as unhappy as the next braggart's.

And when I can no longer bear to think of the victims of broken homes, I begin to think of the victims of intact ones.

I was thinking that we all learn by experience, but some of us have to go to summer school.

Dorothy Parker even made a wisecrack out of her own epitaph: 'Excuse my dust'. One of her better-known observations on Life and Love is the generalisation:

Men seldom make passes
At girls who wear glasses.

Here she borders on the wondrous art of Ogden Nash. In his poetry – if that's quite the word for it – Nash taps language out of shape and into wisecrack pointed by rhymes that are funnier the more strained they become:

Reflections on Ice-Breaking
Candy
Is dandy
But liquor
Is quicker.

The Turtle
The turtle lives 'twixt plated decks
Which practically conceal its sex
I think it clever of the turtle
In such a fix to be so fertile.

Biological Reflection
A girl whose cheeks are covered with paint
Has an advantage with me over one whose ain't.

Some of Nash's best performances expand the wisecrack till it nearly bursts – as in his sceptical take on literature:

> One thing that literature would be greatly the better for
> Would be a more restricted employment by authors of simile and metaphor.
> Authors of all races, be they Greeks, Romans, Teutons or Celts,
> Can't seem just to say that anything is the thing it is but have to go out of their way to say that it is like something else.
>
> That's the kind of thing that's being done all the time by poets, from Homer to Tennyson;
> They're always comparing ladies to lilies and veal to venison,
> And they always say things like that the snow is a white blanket after a winter storm.
> Oh it is, is it, all right then, you sleep under a six-inch blanket of snow and I'll sleep under a half-inch blanket of unpoetical blanket material and we'll see which one keeps warm,
> And after that maybe you'll begin to comprehend dimly
> What I mean by too much metaphor and simile.

Now all these are clever, genuinely witty instances of the American wisecrack and variations on it. I admire and enjoy these, but I will confess that there is a Goonish British streak in me that goes for sheer silliness. I cherish the image of Clark Kent in the phone box, not slipping into the red trunks and body stocking in preparation for take-off, but ringing the dry cleaner: 'Hello, yes...Kent...K-e-n-t... Right...Blue body stocking with a big S on the chest...Yes, and red swimming trunks, red cape...Oh, okay... Thursday?' Poor Clark, thwarted by a dry cleaner from being the man of steel, the man of tomorrow; maybe tomorrow was only Tuesday. While I venerate Groucho, it's Harpo Marx who has given me one of my favourite images, leaning on a tall building at the beginning of *A Night in Casablanca*. 'Whadda ya think you're doin', holdin' up that building?' snaps the cop. Harpo nods his curls vigorously. The policeman angrily pulls him away and the building collapses. Or there's S. J. Perelman's parody of the meeting between the hard-boiled detective and the perfumed vamp. Perelman's story, 'Farewell, My Lovely Appetiser' is aimed particularly at Raymond Chandler's detective, Philip Marlowe, and the novel, *Farewell, My Lovely*, but it also sends up the tough-guy stereotype familiar from innumerable Hollywood films. An ash-blonde has entered the office of private detective, Mike Noonan, and hidden herself in the wardrobe where he keeps 'a change of bourbon'. When she emerges, with an implausible commission for Mr Noonan he naturally asks what there is in it for him:

> 'Anything you want'. The words were a whisper. I leaned over, poked open her handbag, counted off five grand.
> 'This'll hold me for a while', I said. 'If I need any more, I'll beat my spoon on the high chair'... She trailed past me in a cloud of scent that retailed at ninety rugs the ounce. I caught her wrist, pulled her up to me.
> 'I go for girls named Sigrid with opal eyes', I said.
> 'Where'd you learn my name?'
> 'I haven't been a private snoop for twelve years for nothing, sister'.
> 'It was nine last time'.
> 'It seemed like twelve till you came along'.
> I held the clinch until a faint wisp of smoke curled out of her ears, pushed her through the door. Then I slipped a pint of rye into my stomach and a heater into my kick and went looking for a bookdealer named Lloyd Thursday.

Woody Allen's treatment of the same theme is entitled 'Mr Big'. This is how it begins:

> I was sitting in my office, cleaning the debris out of my thirty-eight and wondering where my next case was coming from. I like being a private eye, and even though once in a while I've had my gums massaged

with an automobile jack, the sweet smell of greenbacks makes it all worth it. Not to mention the dames, which are a minor preoccupation of mine that I rank just ahead of breathing. That's why, when the door to my office swung open and a long-haired blonde named Heather Butkiss came striding in and told me she was a nudie model and needed my help, my salivary glands shifted into third. She wore a short skirt and a tight sweater and her figure described a set of parabolas that could cause cardiac arrest in a yak.

'What can I do for you, sugar?'

'I want you to find someone for me'.

'Missing person? Have you tried the police?'

'Not exactly, Mr Lupowitz'.

'Call me Kaiser, sugar. All right, so what's the scam?'

'God'.

'God?'

'That's right, God. The Creator, the Underlying Principle, the First Cause of Things, the All Encompassing. I want you to find Him for me'.

Of course all this is designed to send up the stereotype, to illuminate and spoof that which is in some sense mechanical. The ordinary, mechanical business of phoning the dry cleaner is brought to comical life by the fact that it's Superman who's calling; the policeman is funny because of his reasonable – in that sense 'mechanical' – supposition that Harpo is lying about holding up the building; and the picture of the detective in his clinch is funny because the scene is a cliché from so many movies – with and without Humphrey Bogart – which Perelman is sending up, showing us how mechanical it all foolishly is by his comic embellishments. Everyone expects the private-eye to engulf the lady, but who could have foreseen the wisp of smoke curling out of her ears or that the missing person in Mr Lupowitz's case would be God?

Now that we have strayed into the realm of spoof narrative with its extended wisecracks and punch lines, it would be churlish to omit the great Stephen Leacock just because he had the audacity to be Canadian. Let's turn to *Nonsense Novels* and meet 'Hannah of the Highlands' in her home setting:

It was a gloriously beautiful Scotch morning. The rain fell softly and quietly, bringing dampness and moisture, and almost a sense of wetness to the soft moss underfoot. Grey mists flew hither and thither, carrying with them an invigorating rawness that had almost a feeling of dampness...And meantime Hannah, the beautiful Highland girl, was singing. The fresh young voice rose high above the rain. Even the birds seemed to pause to listen, and as they listened to the simple words of the Gaelic folk song, fell off the bough with a thud on the grass.

When you get formulaic stiffness in language you have a ready-made comic moment. My favourite example is another instance of inadvertent comedy. Accustomed to the lofty independence of the BBC and its scrupulous detachment from business interests to the extent that even household brand names were banned from story lines, it took a while to get used to the ubiquity of the commercial in American broadcasting. A Nashville radio station was bringing us its weather forecast in seductively confiding tones. 'It's been real DRY the last few days', we were reminded. Then, 'Hah!', a throaty gust of our informant's amplified breath, blowing heat and dust back into our living rooms before the punch line, 'But now it's time to get SOAKING WET. The weather brought to you by RUDI'S COUNTRY SAUSAGE'.

Great American comedians have included Shelley Berman and Bob Newhart with their deadpan monologues involving our hearing one side of a conversation often on the telephone. Berman's classic was his 'Department Store' in which an office worker in a city skyscraper attempts on the phone to get help for a woman hanging from the window ledge of another skyscraper across the street. By the time he's been passed from one department to another the woman's 'knuckles are very white'. He's been put through to 'Lingerie', so 'maybe she tried on something and snapped out'. Newhart will always be remembered for celebrating 'a group of men who face death every day in a hundred different ways: America's driving instructors'. In his sketch, 'The Driving Instructor', Mrs Webb is about to take her second lesson with a new instructor. Her last instructor was Mr Adams. 'How fast were you going when Mr Adams jumped from the car?' asks Newhart as the new instructor. 'Seventy-five?... In your driveway... Backing out!' The conversation in 'Introducing Tobacco to Civilisation' is with Sir Walter Raleigh. 'Nutty Walt' has just discovered the uses of tobacco. You can chew it or put it in a pipe or shred it up, put it between your lips, set fire to it and inhale the smoke. Walt is going to have a tough time selling people on sticking burning leaves in their mouths.

If the Irish invented the wisecrack, the Americans polished it. A high point of edgy American humour, Tom Lehrer's brilliantly goofy songs satirised the times and trends of the fifties and sixties and anything else that took his quizzical fancy. Both Irish and American idioms come together in his 'Irish Ballad', a jaunty variation on the story of Lizzie Borden of Fall River, Massachusetts. Having drowned her father in the creek – the water tasted so bad for a week they 'had to make do with gin' – the fair maid systematically dispatches the rest of her family. There's cyanide soup for her mother who dies 'with the spoon in her hand and her face in a hideous grin'; she sets her sister's hair on fire and dances round the funeral pyre playing a violin; she loads one brother with stones before sending him down to Davy Jones and converts her baby brother into an Irish stew to entertain the neighbours. But Massachusetts' Protestant morality gets her in the end. Lehrer's rhymes wind up the story with a wicked *coup de grâce*:

> And when at last the police came by,
>   Sing rickety-tickety-tin,
> And when at last the police came by,
> Her little pranks she did not deny,
> To do so she would have had to lie,
>   And lying, she knew, was a sin.

At the height of the Cold War, when we were even more frightened of nuclear annihilation than we are now of militant Islamic terrorism, Lehrer gave us the astringently cathartic gem, 'We Will All Go Together When We Go':

And we will all go together when we go,
What a comforting fact that is to know.
Universal bereavement,
An inspiring achievement,
Yes, we all will go together when we go.

We will all go together when we go.
All suffused with an incandescent glow.
No-one will have the endurance
To collect on his insurance,
Lloyd's of London will be loaded when they go.

We will all fry together when we fry.
We'll be French fried potatoes by and by.
There will be no more misery
When the world is our rotisserie,
Yes we all will fry together when we fry.

And you can't get crisper than that.

Index

C

Cain, James M. 176
Cameron, James 156
Campbell, Colin Roy of Glenure 159
Campbell, Mary 98
Capercaille 266, 274
Carlyle, Thomas 166, 269
Carmichael, Stokely 221
Carroll, Lewis 134
Casals, Pablo 208
Cauld Blast Orchestra 274
Cetewayo 264-5
Chandler, Raymond 61, 105, 176, 177, 178, 195, 292
Charman, Flight Lieutenant J.W. 81, 82, 85, 94
Christie, Agatha 175, 203
Churchill, Sir Winston 265, 266
Cinquevalli, 130
Clark, Eleanor 230
Clough, Arthur Hugh 160
Coleridge, Samuel Taylor 194
Collins, Anthony 208
Collins, Floyd 225
Columba, Saint 129, 186, 188
Colvin, Sidney 154, 165
Compton, Dennis 208
Connery, Sean 267
Connolly, Billy, 124, 144, 267
Conrad, Joseph 155, 234-5, 254
Cook, Beryl 118
Coolidge, President Calvin 207
Cornwell, Patricia 175
Crawford, Broderick 225
Crichton, Michael 107
Cunningham, Alison 153
Curie, Marie and Pierre 252-3

D

Dante Alghieri 231-2, 270
Darwin, Charles 280
Davidson, John 269-70
Davis, Sir Colin 209, 214, 215, 217
Debussy, Achille Claude 184
Defoe, Daniel 118
Delius, Frederick

Derwent, Lavinia 122
Descartes, René 197
De Vries, Peter 289-90
Dewar, Donald 273
Dick, Philip K. 196, 199
Dickens, Charles 49, 106, 123, 130, 195, 228
Dodd, Tim 213
Doyle, Sir Arthur Conan 61, 106-8, 147, 176
Dryden, John 68, 100
Dumas, Alexander 32
Durrell, Lawrence 52
Duthuit, Georges 278

E

Eastwood, Clint 196
Edward II, King 261
Eichmann, Adolf 185
Elgar, Sir Edward 61, 194
Eliot, George 116
Eliot, T.S. 53-4, 120, 132, 140, 196, 227, 253, 255, 270, 276
Ellington, Duke 184
Ellroy, James 175, 176
Emerson, Ralph Waldo 232
Emmerich, Roland 199
Eno, Brian 202
Evanovich, Janet 175

F

Farnol, Jeffery 61
Faulkner, William 11, 20-31, 195, 257-8
Fergusson, Robert 95, 100-1, 268
Finlay, Ian Hamilton 135
Firth, Colin 200
Fleming, Ian 108
Forsyth, Bill 274
Fowles, John 158
Fredkin, Edward 281
Freud, Sigmund 163, 281
Frost, Robert 132
Froude, James Anthony 264
Furtwängler, Wilhelm 151
Fyffe, Will 123

Music for Life
by
Marshall Walker with Tim Dodd

For over twenty years Marshall Walker and Tim Dodd have been talking to each other about music. Dodd produced Walker's award-winning *Letters to Sibelius* for Radio New Zealand Concert, the programmes reaching listeners in Australia and Scotland as well as New Zealand and forming the basis of Walker's book, *Dear Sibelius: Letter from a Junky*, published by Kennedy and Boyd in 2008. The *Music for Life* conversations that followed were broadcast in December 2009 but the talk went on. This book presents the ongoing conversations in the hope that readers will like to join in.

Topics range from the early days of gramophone recordings and memories of renowned conductors, pianists and violinists to discussions of music by Mozart, Beethoven, Brahms, Tchaikovsky, Sibelius, Mahler, Elgar, Vaughan Williams, Holst, Bax, Villa-Lobos, Copland, Shostakovich, Bartók, Suk, Philip Glass and others. Tribute is paid to the artistry of Paul Robeson, the film scores of Ennio Morricone, the satirical songs of Tom Lehrer and the part played by South African popular music in the movement against apartheid. There is a detailed list of recommended recordings.

'Music is connected not just to itself or to sound, but to the central threads of our lives, as Walker and Dodd's conversations remind us. Factual when appropriate, at other times refreshingly speculative, Walker is not afraid of the fantastical or the ornamental where apposite in recounting his story, relating how music has worked for him throughout an eventful life. Best of all, he inspires us to go back to the music again and to listen with renewed intensity'. *From the Preface by Martin Lodge*

'From Mozart to Villa-Lobos and South African pop, Dodd brings out Walker's gift for illumination; best of all, these conversations have you searching out new-found fare as well as hearing familiar and forgotten music again'. *William Dart*

Dear Sibelius: Letter from a Junky
by Marshall Walker

When a schoolboy in Glasgow, Marshall Walker became addicted to the music of Sibelius. In 1996 he made a pilgrimage to Finland, visiting places of special significance to the composer, his birthplace in Hämeenlinna, the villa 'Ainola' where he lived for over 50 years, the forests and lakes near Koli in the Karelia. Back home in New Zealand Walker began to write Sibelius a thank-you letter for a lifetime's companionship. Walker tells Sibelius how his music helped him overcome childhood ordeals in Scotland. He discovers Sibelian connections in his family, tracing the steps of his grandfather from a Sunday stroll in a Glasgow park to the Elliot Junction railway disaster of 1906 and commemorating his uncle's service on the Salonika Front in WWI. The scene shifts to student days at Glasgow University, problems with God, the kindness of the Scottish conductor, Ian Whyte, and the music of Arnold Bax, Sibelius's 'son in music'. In *apartheid* South Africa Sibelius becomes Walker's medicine man. There's a glimpse of the composer fêted in the USA and a connection between his music and the American writer, Robert Penn Warren. A child falls in love with Sibelius's Third Symphony. From New Zealand Walker sets out on the compulsive pilgrimage which prompts him to try to show how an artist can be a continuous, sustaining presence in a life. There's talk of Sibelius's music throughout the letter – a grateful junky's talk, not a critic's.

'Walker has the rare ability to catch the soul of music through his words... the book is rich in incident and reference and committed in its politics'. *The New Zealand Herald*

'You do not need to be a die-hard Sibelius lover to enjoy Marshall Walker's book, as his self-confessed addiction provides more than enough passion and enthusiasm for the Finnish composer's music'. *Classical Music*

'A testament to how the work of artists and poets, and especially this particular composer, can help you to live'. *PN Review*

'A true writer. Excellent. I must repeat, excellent'. *Lygia Fagundes Telles*

'An open-hearted testimony to the power of music in our lives, a generous, wonderful book, superbly written and life-affirming to a rare degree'. *Waikato Times*

Lightning Source UK Ltd.
Milton Keynes UK
UKOW032257130313

207584UK00005B/40/P